Panentheism

and

Scientific Naturalism

Panentheism

and

Scientific Naturalism

*Rethinking Evil, Morality,
Religious Experience,
Religious Pluralism,
and the
Academic Study of Religion*

DAVID RAY GRIFFIN

Toward Ecological Civilization Series

PROCESS CENTURY PRESS
CLAREMONT, CALIFORNIA

PANENTHEISM AND SCIENTIFIC NATURALISM: Rethinking Evil, Morality, Religious Experience, Religious Pluralism, and the Academic Study of Religion

© 2014 Process Century Press

Process Century Press
An Imprint of the Center for Process Studies
A Program of Claremont School of Theology
1325 N. College Avenue
Claremont, CA 91711

Toward Ecological Civilization Series

This series proposes that the work of Alfred North Whitehead provides the best alternative to the pervasive worldviews that now threaten our civilization with catastrophe. His comprehensive and rigorous philosophy provides the more organic, relational, integrated, nondual, and processive conceptuality needed to support the emergence of an ecological civilization. This volume is the second in the series.

ISBN 978-1-940447-03-2

Printed in the United States of America

Contents

Introduction

The word "panentheism," generally thought to have been coined by Carl Friedrich Christian Krause in the early nineteenth century,[1] refers to the doctrine that our world exists within a divine being—a doctrine often expressed by speaking of God as the "soul of the world."

This doctrine has, in the intervening period, become increasingly widespread. It has become especially popular among philosophers of religion and theologians who seek to bring the religious thought of their communities into harmony with the worldview of the scientific community.[2]

This worldview is now widely called "scientific naturalism," which, in its most fundamental sense, is simply the doctrine that there are no supernatural interruptions of the world's normal causal processes.

NATURALISM$_{NS}$

To emphasize this meaning, I call this doctrine naturalism$_{ns}$ (with "ns" standing for "nonsupernaturalist"). Many philosophers of religion and theologians have decided that scientific naturalism in this sense—which can also be called naturalism in the generic sense—simply must be accepted, because it seems to be true. They also hold, and I agree, that it can be accepted by their religious communities, because it is not incompatible with their deepest religious convictions.

But the term "scientific naturalism" is often equated with a far more restrictive position, which I call naturalism$_{sam}$ (with "sam" standing for "sensationist-atheistic-materialistic"). This position is incompatible with any significantly religious view of reality. This more restrictive position, however, is not entailed by scientific naturalism in the generic sense.

PANENTHEISM VS. PANTHEISM

For many science-oriented religious thinkers, panentheism provides an appealing doctrine, because it allows us to accept scientific naturalism in this fundamental sense without being forced into accept atheism or pantheism. Both atheism and pantheism are problematic because, by denying that there is a Divine Actuality distinct from the world, they undermine any cosmological basis for holding to a distinction between *ought* and *is*—between what ought to be the case in the world, on the one hand, and what finite agents, with their power, have in fact brought about, on the other hand.

Panentheism allows us to hold to this all-important distinction.[3] In contrast with pantheism, which says that God simply is the world, panentheism says that God is the soul of the world and thereby distinct from—more than—the world. This view allows us to think in terms of a divine center of consciousness, purpose, and agency that is seeking to bring the world into line with normative values based on loving concern for all of its creatures.

Panentheism allows us, at the same time, to conceive the relationship between God and the world as an intimate, natural relationship, in which the world's causal patterns are part and parcel of that which exists necessarily, understood as not simply God (as traditional theism says), or simply the world (as atheism says), but God-and-the-world.

Naturalistic Theism

Panentheism is, therefore, a version of a more general doctrine that can be called *naturalistic theism, or theistic naturalism*. In this view, because the existence of the world, with its causal patterns, belongs to the very nature of God, the idea that these causal patterns could be interrupted does not arise. Just as theologians have always said that God could not die or become unloving, because to do so would violate God's own nature, panentheism's view of the God-world relation entails that it would be impossible for God to interrupt the most basic causal patterns of the world, because to do so would be in violation of God's very nature. This, at least, is the implication of the version of panentheism espoused in the present book.

Whiteheadian Process Philosophy

This version is based on the process philosophy developed by Alfred North Whitehead (1861-1947). The name "process philosophy" for this Whitehead-based movement is derived from the title of Whitehead's major work, *Process and Reality*,[4] which he wrote in the late 1920s after coming to Harvard University in Cambridge, Massachusetts, to teach philosophy. Whitehead had been educated at the other Cambridge—in England—where he wrote a dissertation on Maxwell's *Treatise on Electricity and Magnetism* in 1884 and then taught mathematics, including mathematical physics, at Cambridge University until 1910. In some circles, Whitehead is best known for the major work of this period, *Principia Mathematica,* which he co-authored with his former student Bertrand Russell.[5]

In the next period of his life, spent in London, Whitehead increasingly devoted himself to what he called the "philosophy of nature," writing, among other books, an alternative to Einstein's general theory of relativity.[6]

After coming to Harvard in 1924, Whitehead turned to metaphysics, which, as he used the term, differed from the philosophy of nature by including the human subject within the scope of that which is to be explained. The most important task of metaphysical cosmology, he came to believe, is to reconcile our scientific intuitions with our religious, ethical, and aesthetic intuitions—a task that could be achieved only by developing a worldview that is equally satisfactory for the scientific and the religious communities.

Whitehead had been an atheist, or at least an agnostic, during most of his adult life. Shortly after beginning to develop his metaphysical cosmology, however, he came to the view that, if we are to give a fully rational account of the universe—meaning one that is both coherent and adequate to all the relevant facts, including the various dimensions of human experience—it is necessary to posit a nonlocal actuality. Although Whitehead used the term "God" for this actuality, the divine reality to which he referred did not possess omnipotence as traditionally understood. This divine actuality did, however, exert real and even variable influence in the world. It was also influenced by the world. These two features of Whitehead's doctrine of God—real but noncoercive divine power in the world, and responsiveness to the happenings in that world—are at the heart of his panentheism.

nonlocal actuality

WHITEHEADIAN POSTMODERNISM

As my use of the term "postmodern" in this book's first chapter indicates, I consider this Whiteheadian perspective distinctively postmodern. The Whiteheadian position is, however, very different from the kind of position that is now widely associated with "postmodernism," in which any attempt to ground moral and religious practices in metaphysics, especially metaphysical theism, is rejected. But the description of Whitehead's position as distinctively postmodern is not novel. It extends back to the 1960s,[7] with one reference to Whitehead as postmodern even occurring in the 1940s.[8]

Every use of the term "postmodern" in a prescriptive sense has, of course, a particular way of understanding what it is about the distinctively "modern" that is being, or needs to be, overcome. From the Whiteheadian perspective, the fundamental errors of modern thought have been the sensationist doctrine of perception (according to which the mind can perceive things beyond itself only by means of its physical sensory organs) and the mechanistic doctrine of nature (according to which the physical world's most fundamental units are bits of matter that are devoid of experience and operate exclusively in terms of machine-like efficient causation). These two doctrines led to the deistic denial of divine presence in the world and ultimately to the atheistic denial of divinity altogether.

NATURALISM$_{ppp}$ VS. NATURALISM$_{sam}$

This worldview, with its sensationism, atheism, and materialism, can be abbreviated as naturalism$_{sam}$, with "sam" standing for "sensationist-atheist-materialist." This naturalism$_{sam}$ led to the inability of philosophical thought to do justice to many of the presuppositions of human practice. This inability led in turn, especially through the influence of Hume and Kant, to the denial of the possibility of a metaphysical cosmology in which our aesthetic, ethical, and religious intuitions could be integrated with our scientific intuitions in a self-consistent worldview.

Most forms of postmodernism, seeking to make a virtue out of a necessity, heap derision on "metaphysics," suggesting that it should not even be attempted. Whiteheadian postmodernism, by contrast, seeks to overcome the metaphysical errors of early modern thought that led to the conclusion that an integral worldview is impossible.

This attempt led Whitehead to a fundamentally new kind of naturalism, which I call "naturalism$_{ppp}$," with "ppp" standing for "prehensive-panentheist-panexperientialist." The sensationist doctrine of perception is replaced by a prehensive doctrine of perception, in which nonsensory perception is more fundamental than sensory. Atheism is replaced by panentheism. And materialism is replaced by panexperientialism.

[margin note: different notion of perception]

It is important to see that the panentheism of this worldview presupposes both of these other dimensions, namely, panexperientialism and the nonsensory doctrine of perception. Therefore, although this book, as reflected in its title, thematizes panentheism, this term should always be taken as a shorthand way of referring to the complete worldview of which it is a dimension: prehensive-panentheist-panexperientialist naturalism.

OVERCOMING THE CONFLICT BETWEEN SCIENCE AND RELIGION

It is only through this overall worldview, not through a new view of God taken alone, that the perceived conflict between science and religion can be overcome. The naturalism of this view overcomes the perceived conflict insofar as this conflict has been based on the assumption that religion requires supernaturalism and hence a denial of naturalism$_{ns}$. Insofar as this perceived conflict has been based on the equation of "the scientific worldview" with not only naturalism$_{ns}$ but also naturalism$_{sam}$, it is overcome by the replacement of this form of naturalism with naturalism$_{ppp}$.

Some writers, to be sure, seem to suggest that a new solution to the "conflict between science and religion" is a thing of the past, at least insofar as religious thinkers have given up fundamentalist forms of religious faith. But we need only to look at representative statements from the ideological leaders of the scientific community to see that this is not so.

For example, E.O. Wilson, a leading exponent of sociobiology, wrote of "the collision between irresistible scientific materialism and immovable religious faith." Leaving no doubt about which perspective would be demolished by this collision, Wilson said that the scientific worldview has always, in zones of conflict, defeated traditional religion. "The final decisive edge enjoyed by scientific naturalism," said Wilson, "will come from its capacity to explain traditional religion, its chief competitor, as a wholly material phenomenon."[9]

In a similar vein, William Provine, a historian of science, especially of Darwinism, spelled out several points on which Darwinian evolutionary biology, which has been almost universally accepted in the scientific community, conflicts with religious worldviews. "Modern evolutionary biology," Provine said,

> tells us . . . that . . . [t]here are no purposive principles whatsoever in nature. There are no gods and no designing forces. . . . [M]odern science directly implies that there are no inherent moral or ethical laws. . . . [W]e must conclude that when we die, we die and that is the end of us. . . . There is no hope of life everlasting. . . . [F]ree will. . . simply does not exist. . . . The universe cares nothing for us. . . . There is no ultimate meaning for humans.[10]

As Wilson and Provine both saw, modern scientific naturalism conflicts with any significantly religious version of reality, not only with fundamentalist versions of religious faith. Religious thinkers, accordingly, cannot overcome the perceived conflict with science merely by giving up the literalistic form in which religious beliefs have been couched, such as a six-day creation and an incarnation that begins with a virgin birth.

In this book, I bring the overall theme of panentheism and scientific naturalism to bear on four major issues: divine activity, religious experience, morality, and religious pluralism. I show how Whiteheadian panentheism, as part and parcel of a prehensive-panen-theist-panexperientialist form of naturalism, deals with these issues in a way that differs radically from the reductionistic interpretation given to them by modern representatives of naturalism$_{sam}$, such as Wilson and Provine,[11] as well as from the supernaturalistic interpretation provided by traditional theists.

DIVINE ACTIVITY

The first four chapters focus on the issue of divine activity. The first chapter, which serves as an overview, lays out a Whiteheadian version of panentheism, provides several reasons for considering it—as a version of naturalistic theism—to be closer to the truth than either supernaturalism or atheism, and argues that it constitutes a "postmodern revelation."

The second chapter zeroes in on the idea of divine activity as such, showing how it is compatible with scientific naturalism, as long as naturalism is understood only in the generic sense, rather than being taken, as is usually the case, to entail atheism.

Chapter 3 uses Whitehead's panentheistic notion of divine activity to address the question whether the universe is "designed," suggesting that in most senses of that question, the answer is No, but that there are two senses in which the answer is Yes.

Chapter 4 then shows how this panentheistic view of divine activity can overcome the long-standing problem of evil.

RELIGIOUS EXPERIENCE, MORALITY, AND RELIGIOUS PLURALISM

The next four chapters broaden the discussion. Whereas the earlier chapters, by focusing on divine activity, provide an alternative to the atheism of naturalism$_{sam}$, these chapters focus as well on its sensationism and materialism, arguing that, far from being required by science, these doctrines make problems for it as well as for religion and morality.

Chapter 5 shows how naturalism$_{sam}$ has created a presumption against the genuineness of religious experience; argues that in light of the inadequacy of naturalism$_{sam}$ for science, this presumption is baseless; and then shows how Whitehead's naturalism, besides being more adequate for science, allows for genuine religious experience.

Chapter 6 continues this discussion of religious experience by focusing on the way in which naturalism$_{sam}$ has shaped the modern study of religion. This chapter provides the book's most extensive discussion of "naturalism," showing that eight distinguishable meanings are often implicit (in confusing ways) when naturalism is affirmed.

Chapter 7 turns to the way in which the general acceptance of naturalism$_{sam}$ in the academy has crippled modern moral theory, rendering it incapable of doing justice to the presuppositions of our moral experience, especially the objectivity of moral norms. It then points out how the panentheistic version of naturalism overcomes the various difficulties.

Finally, Chapter 8, shows how this panentheistic vision of reality, as a form of naturalistic theism, provides a new basis for religious pluralism, one that does not undermine the distinctive truths and values of the various religious tradition, and also does not lead to a "debilitating relativism" that undermines the universal validity of basic moral norms.

In the Epilogue, I summarize the book's argument and then reflect upon some of the wider implications that the perspective articulated here, if it were to become widely held, might have.

Notes

1. See Günter Meckenstock, "Some Remarks on Pantheism and Panentheism," in Svend Andersen, *Traditional Theism and its Modern Alternatives* (Aarhus: Aarhus University Press, 1994), 117-29, at 121.

2. In his *Panentheism: The Other God of the Philosophers—From Plato to the Present* (Grand Rapids: Baker Academic, 2006), John W. Cooper wrote: "The God of classical theism is often referred to as 'the God of the philosophers.' Today, however, the contemporary theological landscape has shifted in the direction of 'the other god of the philosophers': panentheism. . . . While panentheism is not a new theological system, it has experienced a renaissance, especially among thinkers who study the intersection of science and religion." Alan G. Padgett, professor of systematic theology at Luther Seminary, has said: "Panentheism is a major movement in theology today." Philip Clayton, Professor of Theology at the Claremont School of Theology, has called panentheism "perhaps the most significant movement in twentieth-century theology." The statements by Cooper, Padgett, and Clayton are all blurbs for Cooper's book, which can be found at Amazon.com.

In *Panentheism across the World's Traditions*, ed. Loriliai Biernacki and Philip Clayton (Oxford University Press, 2013), Michael Murphy of the Esalen Institute, having referred to a wide range of thinkers—including Charles Sanders Peirce, Henri Bergson, Teilhard de Chardin, Alfred North Whitehead, Charles Hartshorne, and Sri Aurobindo—said: "I would like to propose that the worldview represented by thinkers such as these constitutes an emerging canon of sorts, which, although it lives today on finite margins of academic, scientific, and religious opinion, is giving rise to a vision that will eventually capture the world's imagination."

3. Critics often fail to understand this distinction, as exemplified in an article entitled "Why I Am Not a Panentheist" by John N. Anderson (*Analogical Thoughts*, January 24, 2012 [online]). Having quoted a philosopher who, having rejected orthodox Christianity, had said, "I

now accept a panentheistic metaphysics in which the universe and human souls are, to put it roughly, in the being of God," Anderson accurately wrote: "On this view, God is neither fully distinct from the universe (as in classical theism) nor identical with the universe (as in pantheism). Instead, the universe exists 'in' or 'within' God." But then Anderson, saying that "panentheism has a fundamental metaphysical flaw," wrote: "Since the universe is *in* God, insofar as there is good in the universe there must be good in God . . . [and] insofar as there is *evil* in the universe there must be *evil* in God. If the universe is a mixture of good and evil (which I take to be an obvious truth) then God must also be a mixture of good and evil, on the supposition that God contains the universe. Whatever pollutes the universe unavoidably pollutes God, on account of the ontological overlap between God and the universe." Although Anderson's criticism might apply to some types of panentheism, it does not apply to process panentheism (and hence not to panentheism as such). For more on this, see Chapter 4, below.

4. Alfred North Whitehead, *Process and Reality: An Essay in Cosmology,* 1929. Corrected edition, ed. David Ray Griffin and Donald W. Sherburne (New York: Free Press, 1978), 1978.

5. Alfred North Whitehead and Bertrand Russell, *Principia Mathematica,* 3 vols. (Cambridge: Cambridge University Press): Vol. 1, 1910; Vol. II, 1912; Vol. III, 1913. Second edition, 1925 (Vol. 1) and 1927 (Vols. 2 and 3).

6. Alfred North Whitehead, *The Principle of Relativity* (Cambridge: Cambridge University Press, 1922).

7. See John B. Cobb, Jr., "From Crisis Theology to the Post-Modern World," *Centennial Review* 8 (Spring 1964), 209-20; Floyd W. Matson, *The Broken Image: Man, Science and Society* (1964; Garden City: Doubleday, 1966), 139, 228; Harold K. Schilling, *The New Consciousness in Science and Religion* (Philadelphia: United Church Press, 1973), 44-47, 244-53; Frederick Ferré, *Shaping the Future:*

Resources for the Post-Modern World (New York: Harper & Row, 1976), 100, 106-07.

8. John Herman Randall, Jr., "The Nature of Naturalism," in *Naturalism and the Human Spirit*, ed. Yervant Krikorian (Morningside Heights: Columbia University Press, 1944), 354-82.

9. Edward O. Wilson, *On Human Nature* (New York: Bantam Books, 1979), 179, 200-01.

10. William Provine, "Progress in Evolution and Meaning in Life," in *Evolutionary Progress*, ed. Matthew H. Nitecki (Chicago & London: University of Chicago Press, 1988), 49-74, at 64-66, 70.

11. Although the other issues mentioned in the quotation from Provine —free will, life after death, and ultimate meaning—are not mentioned in the present book's subtitle, they are discussed in the course of showing that naturalism$_{ppp}$ allows for all the presuppositions crucial to a religious interpretation of the universe.

CHAPTER ONE

Panentheism: A Postmodern Revelation

In this first chapter, I suggest that panentheism is the content of a divine revelation that has been occurring in the cultural life of the West—primarily through religious, moral, scientific, and philosophical experience—roughly over the past two centuries. It is "postmodern" in that it goes beyond, while incorporating the central truths of, the dominant worldviews of the early modern and late modern periods. As indicated in the Introduction, this revelation has recently become widely spread.

The term "panentheism" can be used either generically or more specifically. The *generic* meaning is implicit in the term itself, which means "all in God." Panentheism is thus distinguished from pantheism, on the one hand, and traditional theism, on the other.

On the one hand, by saying that the world is *in* God, thereby saying that God is *more than* the world, panentheism is distinguished from pantheism, which, by saying that "all *is* God," simply identifies God and the world.

On the other hand, by saying that the world is in God, panentheism is distinguished from all forms of traditional theism, according to which our world was created *ex nihilo* in such a way that the very existence of a realm of finite beings is wholly contingent upon a divine decision. Panentheism, by contrast, holds that the existence of the world is integral to the divine existence.

Panentheism is even more fully different from the *classical version* of traditional theism, as articulated by Augustine and Aquinas, according to which God is "impassible," meaning that God is not internally affected by anything that happens in the world.

Therefore, although people have often been led to believe that they must choose from among only three options—traditional theism, pantheism, and atheism—there is a fully distinct fourth alternative, panentheism, which an increasing number of thinkers are finding more satisfactory.

There are various doctrines of "God" that can legitimately be called panentheistic.[1] For the sake of brevity, however, I here simply equate panentheism with *process* panentheism, based on the process philosophies of Alfred North Whitehead and Charles Hartshorne. This doctrine most fully, in my view, embodies the distinctive features of the panentheistic alternative to atheism, pantheism, and traditional theism.[2]

In this chapter's first and second sections, I explain various reasons why the dominant worldviews of the early modern and late modern periods have proven inadequate. The third section lays out process panentheism and then explains why it, by virtue of being a synthesis of the respective truths of these worldviews, overcomes their respective inadequacies.

EARLY MODERNITY'S SUPERNATURALISM

The scientific revolution of the seventeenth century, which is often considered the beginning of modern science, was primarily a worldview revolution.

EXTREME VOLUNTARISM

The new worldview combined the atomism of Democritus, which had been revived by Galileo, with the supernaturalistic theism of Augustine, which had been revived by the fourteenth-century Voluntarists—meaning that they emphasized the divine *will*, saying that things are the way they are because God chose them to be that way. These Voluntarists were called advocates of the *via moderna*: the modern way.

This supernaturalistic theism was then popularized by the Protestant Reformers. According to this version of theism, God created our universe *ex nihilo* (out of nothing) in the literal sense. This supernaturalism can be called *extreme voluntarism*, because the fact that a universe of finite beings even exists is said to be due solely to the divine will. (There can be a more moderate voluntarism.)

For present purposes, the most important dimension of this view is the idea that all the general principles involved in our universe—not only what scientists call the "laws of nature" but also the more general principles that underlie them, such as the principles of causation—are regarded as purely contingent, having been freely established by an act of divine will. The implication of this position is that the divine power is absolute, not restricted in the slightest by any power inherent in the creatures or any causal principles inherent in the nature of things.

Evangelical theologian Millard Erickson, who has affirmed this view, has said that it involves "a definite supernaturalism—God resides outside the world and intervenes periodically within the natural processes through miracles." In this view, the so-called laws of nature can be interrupted, because they are *not really* "natural," in the sense of being inherent in the very nature of things. Rather, having been created by God out of nothing, the natural world, in Erickson's words,

> is under God's control; and while it ordinarily functions in uniform and predictable ways in obedience to the laws he has structured into it, he can and does also act within it in ways which contravene these normal patterns (miracles).[3]

This same understanding was expressed by the 19th-century Calvinist Charles Hodge in response to the question of the relation of God to the laws of nature.

The answer to that question . . . is, First, that He is their author.
. . . Secondly, He is independent of them. He can change,
annihilate, or suspend them at pleasure. He can operate with
or without them. "The "Reign of Law" must not be made to
extend over Him who made the laws.[4]

CREATIO EX NIHILO

Although it had long been assumed that this doctrine of *creatio ex
nihilo* was based on the Bible, recent scholarship has demonstrated,
as I document in Chapter 4, that it was not. Being completely absent
from the Bible, this doctrine was not affirmed by Christian theologians
until the end of the second century, as German theologian Gerhard
May has pointed out.[5] Although those who did begin articulating
this novel doctrine were warned by the Platonic Christian theologian
Hermogenes that it would create an insoluble problem of evil, they
went boldly—and foolishly—forward. The doctrine of creation out of
absolute nothingness soon became the standard Christian doctrine.
In later centuries, it was also widely affirmed by Jewish and Islamic
theologians, so that "traditional theism" within all the Abrahamic
religions has involved this extreme voluntarism.

In Christian theology, the Middle Ages saw the emergence of doctrines of God in which this voluntarism was mitigated, as in Thomism,
with its insistence on the priority of the divine reason to the divine will,
and its doctrine that creatures "participate" in the eternal forms. But
early modernity involved a resurgence of extreme voluntarism overagainst not only Thomist mitigations but also Renaissance naturalisms
of various types—panentheistic as well as atheistic and pantheistic
naturalisms. A central motivation behind this resurgence was, by supporting the supernatural character of Christianity's miracles as divine
testimony to its status as the One True Religion with the "keys to the
kingdom,"[6] to curtail any adoption of religious pluralism.

REASONS AGAINST THE SUPERNATURALISTIC WORLDVIEW

Much of the cultural history of the following centuries has involved multiple reasons to reject this supernaturalistic worldview.

The Problem of Evil: One of these reasons has been the problem of evil, which, given the doctrine of *creatio ex nihilo*, is truly severe, because this doctrine implies that any evil that has occurred—from the rape of a child to the Nazi Holocaust—could have been unilaterally prevented by God. This doctrine also implies that all the structural causes of evil in our world—such as the fact that birth defects, cancer, and nuclear weapons are possible—were freely created by God, even though God, by hypothesis, could have created a world having all the positive values of this one while being free of all these evils.

Hermogenes' prediction came true, as one of the main reasons behind the widespread atheism in modern times is the feeling that "God's only excuse," as a nineteenth-century wag put it, "is that He doesn't exist" (Stendahl). Throughout the Middle Ages and the early modern period, this conclusion was not widely drawn—even though theologians were not able to provide a satisfactory answer to the problem of evil[7]—because it was generally accepted that religious belief rests on authority, to be accepted by faith. Central to the rise of the Enlightenment, however, was the adoption of a "modern commitment"—to support all beliefs on the basis of common experience and reason.[8] Given this new commitment, which implied that religious beliefs are not worthy of acceptance unless they can pass reason's tests of self-consistency and adequacy to the facts, the conflict between the world's evils and Omnipotent Goodness led to widespread atheism. Leibniz's attempt to defend the traditional view that "this is the best of all possible worlds" was widely ridiculed.[9]

rightly so .. [11]

Naturalism: Besides creating an insoluble problem of evil, the supernaturalist version of theism also quickly came into conflict with the naturalistic attitude induced by the scientific mentality. Many of the early scientific giants, such as Marin Mersenne, René Descartes, Robert Boyle, and Isaac Newton, were central figures in the resurgence of supernaturalism, so that it was at first integral to the new "scientific worldview." But science soon became identified with a naturalistic outlook, which ruled out any miraculous interruptions of the laws of nature. Although the term "naturalism" has recently taken on a more restrictive meaning, to be discussed below, I am here referring to naturalism in the generic sense, which I call naturalism$_{ns}$ (with "ns" standing for "nonsupernaturalist"). The supernaturalist idea that there is a divine being who can occasionally interrupt the world's normal causal principles, sometimes called a "God of the gaps," has been increasingly rejected.

Evolutionary Theory: The rise of evolutionary theory provided especially important reasons to reject supernaturalism. The evolutionary perspective ruled out the Genesis-based view that the universe is only a few thousand years old, thereby raising the question of why omnipotence would take so long to create our world. This evolutionary perspective also contradicted the view that our present biological species were created *ex nihilo*. And the Darwinian doctrine of natural selection, whatever its own defects, undermined the argument for supernatural design, by providing an alternative explanation for the amazing ways in which creatures are adapted to their environments.

All these so-called conflicts between evolution and theism, it should be noted, are conflicts not with theism as such but only with the form of theism created by Hermogenes' opponents, who saddled God with a kind of power that would not need to work slowly, through a step-by-step, evil-filled process, to create a world such as ours.

Historical Study of the Bible: In any case, just as natural scientists, such as Darwin, increasingly saw no reason to affirm any gaps in the natural sequences of cause and effect, historians increasingly saw no reason to assume that historical events involved any such gaps. In particular, although supernaturalist assumptions had supported the idea that the Bible reflected infallible revelation and inerrant inspiration, historical-critical study of the Bible found no evidence of supernatural causation in its production. The modern study of the Bible, in other words, can be said to have falsified the hypothesis that the fallibility of the biblical authors was overridden by divine inspiration in such a way that the Bible was, in effect, directly authored by God.

Desire for Peace: The early modern reaffirmation of supernaturalism was used, as mentioned earlier, to undergird the idea that Christianity is the One True Religion. But this idea, especially after the splintering of Protestantism into warring sects, came to be seen as a source of violence. This fact motivated many leading thinkers to reject the theism behind this idea, replacing it with an atheistic conviction, or a different type of theism, which they hoped would promote peace better than (traditional) theism.

Social Critique of Religion: Still another factor behind the rejection of traditional theism was the rise of the social critique of religion, which was formulated most famously (but not systematically) by Marx, who referred to religion as "the opium of the people." This critique portrayed religion as sanctioning the *status quo* by regarding it as divinely ordained and by understanding salvation as an escape from, rather than a transformation of, this world. This critique, by leading to the conviction that belief in God is more harmful than helpful, provided a motive to focus on the objections to, rather than the reasons for, theistic belief.

Critique of Natural Theology: Given the rise of the aforementioned "modern commitment" to support all beliefs on the basis of experience and reason, rather than authority, "natural theology" became vital to rational belief in God. Philosophers such as Hume and Kant, however, realized that reasoning on the basis of common experience alone could not support the existence of a supreme being that had created the world *ex nihilo*. And, because they, like most theologians, simply accepted the equation of "God" with a "being who created the world *ex nihilo*," their critiques were widely taken to have shown the inadequacy of theistic arguments as such.[10]

LATE MODERNITY'S ATHEISM

Through the combined effect of the problem of evil and these other factors, the dominant worldview in intellectual circles moved from theism to deism and then to complete atheism—or in some cases to pantheism, which is similar to atheism in denying that there is a divine actuality distinct from the world.[11]

FROM DUALISM TO MATERIALISM

This shift was, however, simply part of the more general transition from early to late modernity. Early modernity, as mentioned earlier, affirmed Democritean atomism and thereby a purely materialistic, mechanistic view of the basic units of nature, which were understood to be bits of matter wholly devoid of both experience and spontaneity (self-determination). These early modern thinkers did not, however, understand the created world as a whole in materialistic terms. They affirmed, instead, that human beings have minds or souls, which are different in kind from the matter making up their bodies. This dualism between mind and matter, affirmed most famously by Descartes, was considered necessary to protect the beliefs in human freedom and life after death.

Another belief crucial to early modern thinkers was the sensationist doctrine of perception, affirmed most famously by Locke and Hume, according to which we can perceive things beyond ourselves only by means of our physical sensory organs. One motive behind the denial of nonsensory perception was to exclude a naturalistic—which we would today call a *parapsychological*—explanation of Jesus' "mental miracles," in which he demonstrated the ability to know what other people were thinking. Another motive was to rule out what was called "enthusiasm," meaning the direct experience of God, through which some people claimed to have personal revelations that contradicted church doctrine. This denial of a capacity for religious experience was not, however, seen as undermining religion, because the existence of supernatural revelation in the Bible was still presupposed.

As supernaturalism lost its appeal, however, the religious dimensions of early modernity were undermined. Besides the fact that there could be no more talk of supernatural revelation and inerrant inspiration, the decline of supernaturalism also undermined the basis for affirming the human soul. Given the materialistic-mechanistic view of the body, Descartes and other dualists portrayed the mind or soul, with its freedom and consciousness, as absolutely different in kind from the matter composing the body: The mind was conscious, whereas the bodily atoms were devoid of all experience whatsoever; the mind acted freely in terms of purposive, final causation, whereas the bodily atoms acted solely in terms of efficient, even mechanistic, causation.

NATURALISM$_{SAM}$

This dualism raised the question of how two such different things could possibly interact. The only possible answer was that "God does it": God, being omnipotent, had simply ordained that mind and matter, in spite of being completely different, would interact—or at least, as Nicolas Malebranche and other "occasionalists" said, *seem* to interact. Once this kind of answer could no longer be given, however, dualism collapsed into materialism.

All that remained of the early modern scientific worldview was its mechanistic-materialistic view of matter (which had originally been defended partly to show the need for a different-in-kind soul) and its sensationist doctrine of perception (according to which all information about the world beyond ourselves comes through our physical senses). What I have called naturalism$_{ns}$ came to be embodied, thereby, in what I call naturalism$_{sam}$, with "sam" standing for "sensationist-atheist-materialist."

Although naturalism$_{sam}$ has been the dominant worldview of the late modern period, at least since the middle of the 19th century, there has been a growing realization, albeit thus far in limited circles, that this doctrine is problematic in many ways.

THE NEED FOR AN ALTERNATIVE

With regard to the problems created by naturalism$_{sam}$, some of them result from its materialism, the most well known being its mind-body problem. Although its doctrine of "identism," according to which the mind (or soul) is somehow identical with the brain, was adopted to avoid the mind-body problem created by Descartes' dualism, it has, besides not solving this problem, made it impossible to understand freedom and mental causation.

Some of the problems of naturalism$_{sam}$ are rooted primarily in its sensationism. For one thing, the truth of its denial that humans have any capacity for genuine religious experience is thrown into question by its continued failure to come up with an explanation of the origin, persistence, and variety of religion that even remotely approaches adequacy.

Closely related is the fact that sensationism also cannot explain the apparent objectivity—which we cannot in practice help presupposing—of mathematical objects and of logical, cognitive, moral, and aesthetic norms. The atheism of naturalism$_{sam}$, furthermore, makes it unable to explain still more things, including the order of the universe in general and the evolutionary process in particular.

Due to a growing appreciation of these inadequacies, which are discussed in the ensuing chapters, many intellectuals have concluded
that naturalism$_{sam}$ must be abandoned. Many of them, perhaps not
being aware of another alternative, have rejected naturalism altogether
by reaffirming traditional theism. Late modern atheism, especially
as manifested in neo-Darwinism, has thereby stimulated a strong
resurgence of supernaturalism, now in the guise of a fundamentalist reaction against modernity—understood as "Enlightenment
thinking"—altogether.[12]

But a growing number of intellectuals have adopted, or at least
started exploring, panentheism, seeing that it has many advantages,
not least of which is that it can combine theism with naturalism in
the generic sense. In the next section, I discuss process theology's
version of panentheism, pointing out several of its differences from,
and advantages over, both early modern supernaturalism and late
modern atheism.

PROCESS PANENTHEISM

According to process panentheism, God is *essentially* the soul of the
universe: Although God is distinct from the universe, God's relation
to it belongs to the divine essence. This does not mean, however, that
our particular universe—with its quarks, electrons, inverse square law,
and Planck's constant—exists necessarily. Rather, it was divinely created (about 15 billion years ago, according to the presently dominant,
but perhaps inaccurate, view). It was even created out of "no-thing," in
the sense that, prior to its creation, there were no enduring individuals
sustaining a character through time—even no enduring individuals as
simple as photons, quarks, or gluons—which is what we usually mean
in speaking of "things." With Eastern Orthodox theologian Nicholas

Berdyaev, therefore, we can say that our world was created out of *relative* nothingness.[13]

Synthesizing Aristotle and *Creatio ex Nihilo*

From the perspective of this doctrine, the two dominant views in the West, which had long been understood to be in complete opposition to each other, are synthesized. One of these views, associated historically with Aristotle, is that our world is eternal. According to that view, there is no truth whatsoever in the biblical idea that our world was divinely created at some point in the past.

The other dominant view, starkly opposed to the Aristotelean view, is that our world was created out of absolute nothingness, in the sense that, prior to the creation of our world, there were no finite existents whatsoever. In the Christian Middle Ages, this issue was at the center of controversy for many centuries, as it seemed a prime example of a doctrine on which revelation and reason, and hence faith and reason, contradicted each other.[14] And certainly the two views were in utter opposition, so long as the view that the world is eternal meant *our* world (with its planets, stars, and galaxies), and so long as the idea that the world was created out of nothingness meant out of *absolute* nothingness.

However, with the doctrine that our world was created out of *relative* nothingness, we can see that each of these opposing views was witnessing to an important truth. On the one hand, the doctrine of *creatio ex nihilo* witnessed to the truth, massively attested by the evidence for evolution, that *our* world, with its forms of physical, chemical, and biological order, is not eternal, but began coming into existence at some point in the past, out of some sort of chaos. Aristotle was wrong.

On the other hand, the contrary affirmation—that *the* world has always existed—witnessed to the truth that God has never existed all alone.

RULING OUT OMNIPOTENCE

This truth is essential to overcoming traditional theism's problem of evil. If we held that the only actual being that exists eternally and hence necessarily is God, then we would imply that all power *essentially* belongs to God alone, so that God, in creating our world, was not limited by any power inherent in the world. Given this view of divine omnipotence, according to which God literally has *all* the power, God must ultimately be responsible for all the world's evils.

But if we hold that God eternally exists in relation to *a* world, in the sense of a realm of finite stuff of some sort, we can explain our world's evils, while affirming God's perfect goodness, by attributing some inherent power to this stuff. This was the approach taken by Berdyaev: Distinguishing *me on*, or relative nothingness, from *ouk on*, or absolute nothingness, Berdyaev explained why God's power cannot control our activities by saying that our world was created out of "meonic freedom."[15]

In Whitehead's version of this view, this primordial freedom is called "creativity." The relative nothingness out of which our world was created was a chaos of momentary *events*, lasting (in this primitive state of existence) less than a billionth of a second. Each event embodied some iota of creativity, which is the twofold power of an event to exert self-determination on itself and then to exert efficient causation on subsequent events. Each event in this chaos was, therefore, influenced by prior events, and each event influenced future events, so that the creation of our universe was not the beginning of temporal relations and hence of time.[16]

THE BEGINNING OF OUR UNIVERSE

The creation of our universe was, however, the beginning of the particular, contingent form of order that physicists have been progressively discovering and that has made possible the emergence of life in our universe. The creation of this universe involved God's getting this order instantiated in what had previously been a chaotic situation in which no significant values could be realized.

Although this situation was chaotic in comparison with the order that followed, it was not *completely* chaotic in the sense of being wholly devoid of any order. The realm of finite actualities always embodies various necessary (metaphysical) principles, including *causal* principles about how finite actualities are related to each other and to God.

To say that God is *essentially* the soul of the universe means, accordingly, that it belongs to the essence of God to be related not only to *our* universe, now that it exists, but also to *the* universe, in the sense of a realm of finite actualities instantiating these metaphysical principles.

Naturalistic Theism

The most important implication of this point is that it shows process panentheism to be a version of *naturalistic* theism. Besides the fact that the universe—in the sense of *some* multiplicity of finite actualities—exists as necessarily and therefore as naturally as God, the most fundamental causal principles of the universe exist naturally, being inherent in the nature of things, because they exist in the very nature of God, rather than having been created by an arbitrary divine decision. They cannot, therefore, be divinely interrupted, because such an interruption would be a violation of the very nature of God.

These causal principles—including the twofold principle that every finite individual embodies at least some slight power of self-determination and has causal effects on other individuals—cannot be overridden by divine power. Accordingly, although there is divine *influence* in *every* event, there is divine *determination of no* events.

DOUBLE DIVINE DIPOLARITY

Another central feature of process panentheism is its affirmation of divine *dipolarity*. There are, in fact, two senses in which God is dipolar. The dipolarity emphasized by Charles Hartshorne says that, besides having an *abstract essence* that is strictly unchanging, God also has *concrete states* that, contrary to the traditional doctrine of divine immutability, involve change.[17] For God as a concrete individual, time or process is real, so that God constantly has new experiences by virtue of being related to the world, which is constantly changing.

To say that God changes in this sense does not imply, however, that God's character or essence changes. For example, God's (concrete) knowledge changes, because the creatures, with their power of self-determination, constantly do new, unpredictable things. But God always embodies the abstract attribute of omniscience, because God always knows what is knowable at any particular time. Likewise, God's love changes, in that God's love now includes human beings and squirrels who did not exist a century ago, but the fact that God is perfectly loving never changes. According to this first dipolarity, therefore, God has both contingent and necessary aspects, and to affirm change and contingency in God is not to deny divine perfection.[18]

The second dipolarity, which is reflected in Whitehead's distinction between God's "primordial nature" and "consequent nature," emphasizes the fact that God both *influences the world* and is also—contrary to the traditional doctrine of divine impassibility—*influenced by* the *world*. This interaction between God and the world is understood by analogy to the relation of soul and body, which means that, besides thinking of God as the "soul of the world," process theists also refer to the world as the "body of God."

As with any analogy, there are features of the soul-body relation that do not apply to the God-world relation, such as the fact that the

soul emerges out of the body and is thereby dependent on it for its
very existence. The point of the analogy, however, is to emphasize the
intimacy and directness of the relation. My body is the part of the
universe that I directly influence and also the part that directly influences me, being so intimately related to me that I feel its sufferings and
enjoyments as my own. To call the world the body of God is to say that
God directly influences all things, somewhat in the way that we directly
influence our bodies, and also that God has the kind of sympathy with
all creatures that we have for our bodily members.[19]

PANEXPERIENTIALISM AND PREHENSIVE PERCEPTION

The idea that there can be causal interaction between God and the
world has, to be sure, been problematic in the modern period. If most
of the world is composed of insentient, unfeeling bits of matter, how
could God sympathize with it? And if the only mode of perception
that we sentient creatures have is sensory perception, how can we be
influenced by God, who is clearly not an object of sensory perception?

At this point, it must be emphasized that process philosophy, while
affirming naturalism$_{ns}$, breaks with all three aspects of naturalism$_{sam}$.
Besides replacing its atheism with panentheism, it also replaces its
materialism with *panexperientialism*, according to which all individuals
have at least some slight degree of experience and spontaneity.

Process philosophy also replaces sensationism with a *prehensive*
doctrine of perception, which says that sensory perception arises out
of a deeper, more fundamental, nonsensory mode of perception (prehension), which we humans have in common with all other creatures.

These two doctrines explain how the mind can interact with its
brain cells: Although the mind is *numerically distinct* from the brain,
as dualism said, the mind and the brain cells are *not ontologically different in kind*, so that they can interact: The mind feels or prehends its
brain cells, and they feel or prehend it in turn. Besides overcoming the

problems of both dualism and materialism, this doctrine, which can be called *nondualistic interactionism*,[20] also provides an analogy for understanding the interaction of God and the world.

Of course, although this doctrine might solve the mind-body problem and even the God-world problem, we can accept it only if it is believable. But is panexperientialism, according to which all things have experience, credible? We surely cannot be expected to believe that things such as sticks and stones have experience, however simple, and therefore some primitive mode of perception. And this is correct.

The Whiteheadian form of panexperientialism does attribute experience to literally *all things*, but only, as stated above, *all individuals*. Lying behind that statement is a categorical distinction between genuine individuals, on the one hand, and nonindividualized aggregations of individuals, on the other, with sticks and stones being paradigmatic examples of the latter.

COMPOUND INDIVIDUALS

A crucial part of this doctrine is that there are two ways in which low-grade individuals can be combined. They can, on the one hand, be organized in such a way as to form *compound* individuals, as when quarks are organized into electrons and protons, and these electrons and protons are organized into atoms and molecules, and these into organelles, and these into eukaryotic cells, and these into animals. The best clue that something is a genuine individual is that it shows evidence of spontaneity—of making a self-determining response to its environment. They can do this because the low-grade individuals making them up have given rise to a higher-level individual—which in the case of an animal we call the "mind" or "soul"—which gives the thing as a whole a unity of experience, through which it can exercise self-determination.

On the other hand, low-grade individuals can be organized into aggregational societies, in which no higher-level experience emerges, as when molecules form ice cubes. This version of panexperientialism does not, therefore, say that things such as rocks, typewriters, computers, planets, and stars have a unified experience and a degree of freedom. Because of the importance of this distinction, I emphasize that Whitehead's doctrine should be called not simply "panexperientialism," but "panexperientialism with organizational duality."[21]

EXPERIENCE ALL THE WAY DOWN

To be sure, even after it is clarified that experience is attributed only to genuine individuals—not to non-individualized things such as sticks and stones—some people may doubt whether it is credible to say that, with regard to genuine individuals, experience goes all the way down. Few people today would agree with Descartes that human beings alone have experience; most would attribute experience to apes, dogs, and cats, and even mice. However, as philosopher Thomas Nagel has observed: "If one travels too far down the phylogenetic tree, people gradually shed their faith that there is experience there at all."[22]

But how far is "too far"? Writing in the 1960s, philosopher Adolf Grünbaum seemed to think the line below which there is no experience at all occurs at about the level of cockroaches, regarding which Grünbaum was hesitant.[23] In the 1970s and '80s, however, articles in scientific journals began publishing evidence that the lowest form of life, bacteria, were able to make decisions.[24] Today, this view is somewhat commonplace.[25] For example, biologist Lynn Margulis, who received the National Medal of Science, was acclaimed for showing that eukaryotic cells had been compounded out of prokaryotic cells—that is, out of bacteria. Speaking of "consciousness" where Whitehead—who regarded consciousness as a high-level form of experience—would have spoken of "experience," Margulis said that "consciousness is a property of all living cells. . . . Bacteria are conscious. These bacterial beings have been around since the origin of life."[26]

What about going still lower than the most primitive forms of life? Is there evidence that experience goes down even further? Philosopher William Seager has provided evidence for responsiveness to information, and hence a rudimentary mentality, at the quantum level.[27] Likewise, physicists David Bohm and B.J. Hiley said that "even an electron has at least a rudimentary mental pole, as well as a physical pole."[28]

Accordingly, although our prejudices may tell us that at some point, as we go down toward less complex beings, experience completely disappears, science does not support this prejudice. Science evidence instead supports the notion that experience of some sort goes all the way down—a notion that allows us to avoid two unanswerable questions: How could experiencing things emerge out of things that are completely devoid of experience? And where exactly did this amazing development occur? We avoid these insoluble problems by accepting the idea that experience is a feature of being itself—or rather, actuality itself: To be actual is to experience.

Given this perspective, we can see the natural world as constituted by millions of ways in which experiences can be joined together, many of which result in compound individuals. Lynn Margulis wrote: "[D]ifferent bacteria form consortia that . . . associate and undergo metabolic and genetic change such that their tightly integrated communities result in individuality at a more complex level of organization."[29] The "transition from bacterial to eukaryotic genomes," she said, involves a transition to "composite individuality."[30] Discussing green jelly balls, she wrote: "The larger 'individual' green jelly ball is composed of smaller cone-shaped actively contractile 'individuals,'" which "in turn are composite."[31]

In light of the fact that Margulis regarded bacteria as having experience, we can see that she gave support to the

Whitehead-Hartshorne view, according to which the world is entirely composed of experiencing individuals.

NATURALISMppp

Having made this clarification of what is and is not entailed by the doctrine of panexperientialism, the point to be emphasized here is that a panexperientialist doctrine of the world and a prehensive doctrine of perception are part and parcel of process panentheism. Process panentheism is, in other words, an integral feature of a worldview that can be called naturalismppp.

This version of naturalism, like any other, rules out a God of the gaps. But thanks to its panexperientialism and its doctrine of prehensive perception, it allows for ongoing divine influence in the world. Furthermore, even though this theism is naturalistic—meaning that God never acts in some events in a way that is formally different from the way God acts in all events—it can affirm variable divine causation in the world, so that some events can be "acts of God" in a special sense, as explained in the following chapter.

PROCESS THEODICY

The fact that God acts variably in the world does not mean that the world's evil contradicts the goodness of God. Although God has perfect power—understood as the greatest power that any one being could have—this is not coercive power, because the creatures necessarily have their own power (see Chapter 4). On this basis, process theology recovers a doctrine that Whitehead called "one of the greatest intellectual discoveries in the history of religion," namely, Plato's conviction "that the divine element in the world is to be conceived as a persuasive agency and not as a coercive agency."[32]

The second major element in the theodicy of process panentheism, which I have developed at length elsewhere,[33] is the fact that among the metaphysical principles necessarily instantiated in any world that God could create is a set of variables of power and value, which rise proportionately with each other. This point, which implies that even divine power cannot create the good without the risk of the evil, is developed in Chapter 4.

It is sometimes suggested that the literal meaning of "panentheism," according to which *all* things are in God,[34] is problematic because it would mean that there is evil in God. But the way to solve this apparent problem is not to deny that some things are in God, as if only the good events of the world could enter. Divine omniscience means that God knows *all* things, and for God to know something is for it to enter into the divine experience.

The way out of the apparent problem is to ask more precisely in what sense the creatures are "in God." This is one issue for which the dipolarity between the abstract essence and concrete states of God is crucial. As stated earlier, it belongs to the essence of God to be related to *a* world—some world or other. But it does *not* belong to the essence of God to be related to *our particular* world. This world is a free, contingent creation of God. (This doctrine shows that process panentheism embodies a moderate, but not an extreme, voluntarism.) This particular world, with its combination of good and evil, does enter into God, but only into God's concrete states. The world's evils, in other words, are only in the divine *experience*, not in the divine *essence*.

The other dipolarity—that between God as influencing the world and God as being influenced by the world—is also important. It would indeed be erroneous to speak of "evil in God," if this meant that God's causal influence in the world were based on evil intentions. In Whitehead's terminology, this would mean the presence of evil in God's "primordial nature." But this is not what process panentheism entails. God's primordial nature, in terms of which God influences the world, is perfectly good, always aiming at the greatest possible good that can be achieved. It can be called God's "creative love." Insofar as there is evil in God, it is only in God's "consequent nature," which is God responding sympathetically to the world,[35] so that God rejoices with its joys and suffers with its pains and sorrows. This can be called the "responsive love" of God.[36]

In any case, there is evil only in God's experience, not in God's intentions. There is no moral evil in God.[37]

THE POSTMODERN REVELATION

Naturalism$_{ppp}$, with its panentheism, has all the advantages of supernaturalism and of late modern naturalism without their respective problems.

SUPERIORITY TO SUPERNATURALISM AND NATURALISM$_{sam}$

~~Like naturalism$_{sam}$, process panentheism, with its naturalism$_{ppp}$, embodies naturalism$_{ns}$, so that it is not in tension with the basic ontological conviction of modern science. But unlike naturalism$_{sam}$, it can explain how moral, mathematical, and logical principles exist in the nature of things. It can also explain why the world has an order that supports the existence of creatures capable of enjoying high-level forms of value.~~

Unlike supernaturalism, however, process panentheism's naturalism$_{ppp}$ is not embarrassed by the world's evils and the slowness of the process through which the present state of the world was created. And unlike naturalism$_{sam}$, it is not embarrassed by the directionality of evolution.

Unlike naturalism$_{sam}$, moreover, process panentheism can explain why human beings always and everywhere have had religious experience. But unlike supernaturalism, it is not embarrassed by the fact that there is no infallible revelation or inerrant inspiration to give us *the* truth about religious matters.

Still further, panentheism's naturalism$_{ppp}$, unlike naturalism$_{sam}$, can do justice to the reality of human experience and freedom. But unlike dualism, process panentheism does not need to appeal to supernatural causation to explain the relation of the human soul, with its consciousness and freedom, to its body.

Finally, because process panentheism has all the strengths of traditional theism without the latter's insistence on *creatio ex nihilo* and the resulting problem of evil, it provides a far stronger basis for a natural theology, in the sense of arguments for the existence of God, than traditional theism can provide. Whereas virtually all the traditional arguments count in favor of process panentheism, there is *no* evidence against it.[38]

PROCESS PANENTHEISM AS A POSTMODERN REVELATION

The title of this chapter refers to panentheism as a "postmodern revelation." The panentheistic doctrine presented here, being part of naturalism$_{ppp}$, is a *postmodern* doctrine not only by virtue of going beyond the theism of early modernity and the atheism of late modernity, but also by virtue of rejecting the two fundamental pillars of distinctively modern thought: the mechanistic-materialistic doctrine of nature and the sensationist doctrine of perception.

It can be considered a *revelation* for two reasons. On the one hand, many of the features of our experience to which naturalism$_{sam}$ cannot do justice, including our distinctively moral and religious experiences and also our experiences of logic, mathematics, and importance—including the importance of truth itself—result from our direct experience of God, which is to say, God's direct influence on us.

On the other hand, insofar as scientists, philosophers, and theologians have, over the past centuries, come to see supernaturalism to be false, they have done so largely because of their drive to discover truth, which is a divinely-instilled drive. The same can be said about the growing perception, more recently, that naturalism$_{sam}$ is also false. This is the perception that—in combination with the acceptance of naturalism in the generic sense—has led to a naturalistic panentheism.

Reconciling religious and scientific experience

Whitehead's entire approach to reconciling science and religion is based on the assumption that both scientific experience and religious experience contain truths of universal importance, but that scientists and theologians have had tendencies to overstate the truths that they have seen. On the one hand, whereas theists have been correct to speak of divine activity in the world, traditional theists have wildly overstated this truth with their doctrines of omnipotence and *creatio ex nihilo*, which allowed supernatural interruptions of the world's causal nexus.

On the other hand, late modern scientists and philosophers of science have been correct to reject this interruptionism in favor of a naturalistic worldview. They have also been correct to deny mind-body dualism and to affirm that all of our precise observation comes through our physical sensory system. But they have wildly overstated these truths by saying that the rejection of supernatural interruptions means the denial of divine activity in the world altogether; that sensory perception is our *only* means of apprehending anything; and that mind and body are strictly (numerically) identical.

With supernaturalists speaking for "religion" and sam-naturalists speaking for "science," the appearance has been created that we have a clash between science and religion that is irreconcilable.

From Whitehead's perspective, however, this clash is "a sign that there are wider truths . . . within which a reconciliation of a deeper religion and a more subtle science will be found."[39] In order to bring about this reconciliation, Whitehead suggested, both science and religion should be "looking to each other for deeper meanings" and should overcome formulations that, while expressing a measure of truth, have done so in "over-assertive" ways, "thereby implying an exclusion of complementary truths."[40]

These latter statements were actually made with respect to the relation between Buddhism and Christianity, but the approach is the same that Whitehead advocated for science and religion. He, in fact, treated Buddhism, Christianity, and science as three great traditions, with science recently appearing as "a third organized system of thought which in many respects played the part of a theology. . . . Science suggests a cosmology; and whatever suggests a cosmology, suggests a religion."[41]

John Cobb, who has more than anyone else carried through Whitehead's suggestion with regard to Christianity and Buddhism, has also encouraged Christians to appropriate "the universal truth offered by modern science."[42] This universal truth, I suggest, is most fundamentally naturalism$_{ns}$, which, for the reasons given above, can properly be considered a divine revelation. Process panentheism is the attempt to reconcile this revelation with the revelation that has come to us through the Abrahamic and other theistic traditions, aiming thereby for "a deeper religion and a more subtle science."

Notes

1. The first historical study treating panentheism was Charles Hartshorne and William L. Reese, eds., *Philosophers Speak of God* (Chicago: University of Chicago Press, 1953). More recently, see *In Whom We Live, Move, and Have Our Being: Panentheistic Reflections on God's Presence in a Scientific World,* ed. Philip Clayton and Arthur Peacocke (Grand Rapids: Eerdmans Publ. Co., 2004), and John W. Cooper, *Panentheism: The Other God of the Philosophers—From Plato to the Present* (Grand Rapids: Baker Academic, 2006).

2. Many feminists have found process panentheism especially consonant with their religious experience. For example, Carol Christ, having

appreciated the fact that the pantheistic notions of some feminist theologians express a sense of divine immanence, says that her own religious experience suggests that "the Goddess is also a personal presence,
a power . . . who cares about my life and the fate of the world. . . Process
theology's notion of 'pan-*en*-theism' (all is *in* God) provides a way of
understanding God that moves beyond the polarities of immanence
and transcendence, pan-theism (all is God) and theism (God is above
or beyond all)." Carol P. Christ, *Rebirth of the Goddess: Finding Meaning
in Feminist Spirituality* (New York: Addison Wesley, 1997),104-05;
more recently, she wrote *She Who Changes: Re-imagining the Divine
in the World* (Palgrave Macmillan, 2003). For other feminist examples of process panentheism, see Anna Case-Winters, *God's Power:
Traditional Understandings and Contemporary Challenges* (Louisville:
Westminster/John Knox, 1990); Nancy Howell, *A Feminist Cosmology:
Ecology, Solidarity, and Metaphysics* (Amherst: Humanity Books,
2002); Catherine Keller, *From a Broken Web: Separation, Sexism and
Self* (Boston: Beacon Press, 1986), *The Face of the Deep: A Theology of
Becoming* (New York: Routledge, 2003), and *On the Mystery: Discerning
Divinity in Process* (Fortress, 2008); Susan L. Nelson, *Healing the Broken
Heart: Sin, Alienation, and the Gift of Grace* (St. Louis: Chalice, 1977);
Ann Pederson, *Where in the World is God? Variations on a Theme* (St.
Louis: Chalice, 1998) and *God, Creation, and All That Jazz: A Process
of Composition and Improvisation* (St. Louis: Chalice, 2001); Marjorie
Suchocki, *God-Christ-Church: A Practical Guide to Process Theology*,
revised edition (New York: Crossroad, 1989) and *The Fall to Violence:
Original Sin in Relational Theology* (New York: Continuum, 1994).

3. Millard J. Erickson, *Christian Theology* (Grand Rapids: Baker Book
House, 1985), 374, 304, 54.

4. Charles Hodge, *Systematic Theology* (Grand Rapids: Eerdmans,
1982), Vol. I, 607.

5. Gerhard May, *Creatio Ex Nihilo: The Doctrine of "Creation out of
Nothing" in Early Christian Thought*, trans. A.S. Worrall (Edinburgh:
T.&T. Clark, 1994), xiii, 24.

6. David Ray Griffin, "Religion and the Rise of the Modern Scientific Worldview," Chap. 5 of *Religion and Scientific Naturalism: Overcoming the Conflicts* (Albany: State University of New York, 2000). See also my "Whitehead's Philosophy and the Enlightenment," Chap. 2 of Griffin, *Whitehead's Radically Different Postmodern Philosophy: An Argument for Its Contemporary Relevance* (Albany: SUNY Press, 2007).

7. I have argued this case in chapters on Augustine, Thomas Aquinas, Luther, and Calvin, in Griffin, *God, Power, and Evil: A Process Theodicy* (Philadelphia: Westminster Press, 1976); reprint with new preface, Lanham, Md.: University Press of America, 1991; reprint with newer preface, Westminster John Knox (Louisville), 2004).

8. Franklin I. Gamwell, *The Divine Good: Modern Moral Theory and the Necessity of God* (Dallas: Southern Methodist University, 1996), 4-7.

9. I have summarized and criticized Leibniz's theodicy in Griffin, *God, Power, and Evil*, Ch. 11.

10. Although it is widely said that Kant rejected any argument from the world to God, this is only true of "God" understood as a being who created this world *ex nihilo*. What Kant said about the "physico-theological proof" is that the most that "the argument can prove is an *architect* of the world who is always very much hampered by the adaptability of the material in which he works, not a *creator* of the world to whose idea everything is subject" (Immanuel Kant, *The Critique of Pure Reason*, trans. Norman Kemp Smith [New York: Humanities Press, 1950], 522). Kant did not, therefore, reject the idea that the world's order points to the reality of a creator of the sort envisioned by process panentheism—a fact that many interpreters have missed.

11. Although panentheism can rightly be portrayed as a synthesis of, or *via media* between, traditional theism and *pantheism*, I have instead portrayed it as a synthesis of the truths of traditional theism and *atheism*, because atheism is the dominant outlook among intellectuals in the late modern world. Although being a "pantheist" rather than an "atheist" can lead to great differences in attitude, emotion, and even

ethical way of life, the two positions are intellectually the same in many respects. In particular, the fact that both positions deny the existence of a divine reality distinct from the world means that neither position has an ontological basis for distinguishing what *ought* to be the case from what *is* the case—pantheism by saying that everything is holy, atheism by saying that nothing is.

12. In terms of the contrast between "modern" and "postmodern" modes of thought, process philosophy and theology can be best understood as a version of "postmodern modernism." That is, it affirms modernity insofar as it embodies the Enlightenment's formal commitments to reason and morality, namely, the commitment to base our worldview on reason and experience, rather than on authority—which Franklin Gamwell calls "the modern commitment" (*The Divine Good: Modern Moral Theory and the Necessity of God* [Dallas: Southern Methodist University, 1996], 3-4), and the commitment to a universalistic morality. While affirming modernism in this sense, however, process thought rejects many of the substantive presuppositions with which these formal commitments were entangled in 18th-century thought, especially the sensationist doctrine of perception and the mechanistic doctrine of nature, which together led to the denial of divine presence in the world and the inability of theoretical reason to do justice to the presuppositions of practice—and thereby to the modern dualism between theoretical and practical reason.

13. Nicholas Berdyaev, *The Destiny of Man* (New York: Harper & Row, 1960), 22-35; Berdyaev, *Truth and Revelation* (New York: Collier Books, 1962), 124.

14. David C. Lindberg, *The Beginnings of Western Science: The European Scientific Tradition in Philosophical, Religious, and Institutional Context, 600 B.C. to A.D. 1450* (Chicago: University of Chicago Press, 1992), 197-201, 234-43; John Hedley Brooke, *Science and Religion: Some Historical Perspectives* (Cambridge: Cambridge University Press, 1991), 60.

15. Berdyaev, *The Destiny of Man*, 25; *Truth and Revelation*, 124.

16. In "Time in Process Philosophy" (*KronoScope: Journal for the Study of Time* 1/1-2 [2001]: 75-99), I have explained the basis for process philosophy's affirmation that time had no beginning. In "Time and the Fallacy of Misplaced Concreteness" (in David Ray Griffin, ed., *Physics and the Ultimate Significance of Time: Bohm, Prigogine, and Process Philosophy* [Albany: State University of New York Press, 1986], 1-48), I more explicitly explain process philosophy's basis for rejecting the idea that quantum and relativity physics imply a "block universe," according to which what we call past, present, and future exist simultaneously— an idea that, as Frederick Ferré points out in the same volume, would undermine all our moral beliefs.

17. These ideas are most fully developed in Charles Hartshorne, *The Divine Relativity: A Social Conception of God*, 2nd edition (New Haven: Yale University Press, 1964).

18. In the final book by Charles Hartshorne to appear while he was still living, *The Zero Fallacy and Other Essays in Neoclassical Philosophy*, ed. Mohammed Valady (Peru, Ill.: Open Court, 1997), Hartshorne worked out a scheme of sixteen logical possibilities for understanding the relation between God and the world in terms of various polar contraries, such as necessity and contingency. Whereas traditional theism portrayed God as wholly necessary and the world as wholly contingent (N.c) and Spinoza's pantheism portrays them both as wholly necessary (N.n), process philosophy's dipolar panentheism portrays them each as having both necessary and contingent dimensions (NC.cn). Panentheism is as different from pantheism, therefore, as it is from traditional theism.

19. This idea was discussed by Hartshorne in "The Theological Analogies and the Cosmic Organism" (in Hartshorne's *Man's Vision of God and the Logic of Theism* [New York: Harper & Row, 1941]). Hartshorne that this analogy, which emphasizes the radical *superiority* of God to the creatures, needs to be combined with the parent-child analogy, which emphasizes the *personal* nature of the relationship.

20. I have articulated and defended this nondualistic interactionism, overagainst dualism and materialistic identism, in *Unsnarling the World-Knot: Consciousness, Freedom, and the Mind-Body Problem* (Berkeley: University of California Press, 1998; reprint, Eugene: Wipf and Stock, 2008).

21. I include this doctrine in a list of ten core doctrines of process philosophy in the Introduction to my *Reenchantment without Supernaturalism: A Process Philosophy of Religion* (Ithaca, N.Y.: Cornell University Press, 2001).

22. Thomas Nagel, *Mortal Questions* (London: Cambridge University Press, 1979), 168.

23. Adolf Grünbaum, "The Anisotropy of Time," in *The Nature of Time*, ed. Thomas Gold (Ithaca, N.Y.: Cornell University Press, 1967), 149-86, at 152, 179-80.

24. Julius Adler and Wing-Wai Tse, "Decision-making in Bacteria," *Science* 184 (June 21, 1974): 1292-94; A. Goldbeter and D.E. Koshland, Jr., "Simple Molecular Model for Sensing and Adaptation Based on Receptor Modification with Application to Bacterial Chemotaxis," *Journal of Molecular Biology* 161/3 (1989): 395-416.

25. See, e.g., "Bacteria Are More Capable of Complex Decision-Making Than Thought," *ScienceDaily*, January 14, 2010 <http://www.sciencedaily.com/releases/2010/01/100114143310.htm>; "Decisions Made by Communities of Bacteria Trump Game Theory," *ScienceDaily*, October 12, 2010 <http://www.sciencedaily.com/releases/2010/10/101012121439.htm>; "The Genius of Bacteria," *US News Science*, January 25, 2011 <http://www.usnews.com/science/articles/2011/01/25/the-genius-of-bacteria>; Anna Kuchment, "The Smartest Bacteria on Earth," June 2011 <http://www.scientificamerican.com/article.cfm?id=the-smartest-bacteria-on-earth>; Ido Golding, "Decision Making in Living Cells: Lessons from a Simple System," *Annual Review of Biophysics* 40 (June 2011): 63-80; M. Gomelsky, "C-di-GMP-mediated Decisions in the Surface-grown Vibrio

Parahaemolyticus: A Different Kind of Motile-to-Sessile Transition." *Journal of Bacteriology* (December 22, 2011); M. Gomelsky and W.E. Hoff, "Light Helps Bacteria Make Important Lifestyle Decisions," *Trends in Microbiology*, September 19, 2011.

26 Dick Teresi, "Lynn Margulis Says She's Not Controversial, She's Right," *Discover Magazine*, April 2011.

27. William Seager, "Consciousness, Information, and Panpsychism," *Journal of Consciousness Studies* 2/3 (1995): 272–88, at 283.

28. David Bohm and B.J. Hiley, *The Undivided Universe: An Ontological Interpretation of Quantum Theory* (London and New York: Routledge, 1993), 387.

29. Lynn Margulis, "Gaia Is a Tough Bitch," Chap. 7 of John Brockman, *The Third Culture: Beyond the Scientific Revolution* (New York: Simon & Schuster, 1995); also online <http://www.edge.org/documents/ThirdCulture/n-Ch.7.html>.

30. Lynn Margulis, "Serial Endosymbiotic Theory (SET) and Composite Individuality: Transition from Bacterial To Eukaryotic Genomes," *Microbiology Today* 31 (2004): 172-74 <http://www.sgm.ac.uk/pubs/micro_today/pdf/110406.pdf>.

31. Lynn Margulis, *Symbiotic Planet: A New Look at Evolution* (New York: Basic Books, 1998), 10-11.

32. Alfred North Whitehead, *Adventures of Ideas* (1933; New York: Free Press, 1967), 166.

33. Griffin, *God, Power, and Evil; Griffin, Evil Revisited: Responses and Reconsiderations* (Albany: State University of New York Press, 1991).

34. Process panentheism affirms this generic meaning of "panentheism" in two senses. First, all finite events are in God in the sense that, as soon as they have occurred, they are experienced by God, becoming forevermore part of the divine actuality. Second, the world is *spatially*

in God, in that the divine standpoint is co-extensive with the finite realm as a whole. Whitehead made this in response to A.H. Johnson's, question: "Is it possible to indicate God's locus?" Whitehead reportedly said: "in respect to the world, God is everywhere. Yet he is a distinct entity. . . . This is the basis of the distinction between finite and infinite. God and the world have the same locus." A.H. Johnson, "Whitehead as Teacher and Philosopher," *Philosophy and Phenomenological Research* 29 (1969): 351-76, at 372.

35. More precisely, Hartshorne has pointed out, God's responses to the world should be called God's "concrete states," with "consequent nature" referring to that which is common to all these concrete experiences. I have discussed this distinction in my *Reenchantment without Supernaturalism*, 151, 158-63.

36. Divine dipolarity is discussed in terms of this distinction between creative and responsive love in John B. Cobb, Jr., and David Ray Griffin, *Process Theology: An Introductory Exposition* (Philadelphia: Westminster Press, 1976), Chap. 3, "God as Creative-Responsive Love."

37. I have given a critique of John Roth's suggestion that God is partly evil in Stephen T. Davis, ed., *Encountering Evil: Live Options in Theodicy*, 2nd edition (Louisville: Westminster/John Knox, 2001), 93-97.

38. I have argued this case in "Natural Theology Based on Naturalistic Theism," Chap. 5 of *Reenchantment without Supernaturalism*, and more recently in "Process Thought and Natural Theology," in Russell Manning, ed., *Oxford Handbook of Natural Theology* (Oxford: Oxford University Press, 2013).

39. Alfred North Whitehead, *Science and the Modern World* (1925; New York: Free Press 1967), 185.

40. Alfred North Whitehead, *Religion in the Making* (New York: Fordham University Press, 1996 [reprint of 1926 edition]), 145-49.

41. Ibid., 141.

42. John B. Cobb, Jr., *Beyond Dialogue: Toward a Mutual Transformation of Christianity and Buddhism* (Philadelphia: Fortress, 1982), x.

CHAPTER TWO

Divine Activity and Scientific Naturalism

A t the very heart of the perceived conflict between science and
religion—which has existed roughly for the past two centuries—is
the issue of divine activity in the world. On the one hand, the notion
that there is a Divine Power that exerts causal influence in the world
is presupposed by most if not all religions. On the other hand, the
modern scientific worldview, as now usually understood, does not
allow for divine activity.

DIVINE INFLUENCE: PRESUPPOSED BY RELIGIONS

The idea that there is a Divine Power that exerts causal influence in
the world is presupposed by the biblically based religions. The Hebrew
Bible speaks of God as creating the world in a succession of acts, intervening in the histories of the Hebrews and the surrounding nations,
and calling the prophets, with one of the prophets having God say,
"Behold, I do a new thing." Christianity regards the decisive new thing
done by God to be the act of becoming incarnate in Jesus of Nazareth.
The idea that God continues to act in the world even after this decisive event is expressed by the Christian doctrine of the Holy Spirit.
Islam, while accepting these events of Hebrew and Christian history
as authentic acts of God, affirms another decisive act in the calling of
Mohammed to be God's prophet.

It is not only the biblically based religions, furthermore, that presuppose the notion of divine influence. This notion is assumed in most

primal religions, such as those of Native Americans and Africans. It is presupposed by theistic Hinduism, which is the type of Hinduism accepted by most Hindus. And if the notion of divine action is understood not in an overly anthropomorphic way but simply to mean *some* kind of divine influence in the world, it is even presupposed by many forms of Buddhism.[1]

Besides presupposing divine influence in the world, furthermore, most religious thought assumes that reference to this influence plays an essential role in our explanation of certain aspects of our world.

However, the modern scientific worldview, as now understood, allows for no divine activity, at least not if such activity is taken to provide an explanation of anything in particular. The notion of "God" or "divine influence" is almost universally said not be an acceptable explanation for any feature of the world. The worldviews of the scientific and the religious communities, accordingly, seem to be in irreconcilable conflict.

Scientific Naturalism

With regard to the other term in the title of this chapter, "scientific naturalism," its most basic connotation, I have argued, is simply the doctrine that there are no supernatural interventions in the world, with a "supernatural intervention" understood to be a *divinely caused interruption of the world's normal causal processes*.

Naturalism in this sense can be equated with philosophical *uniformitarianism*, which is the assumption that all events are connected to antecedent and subsequent events by universal, uniform causal principles. This uniformitarian naturalism, which came to be adopted by the scientific community in the nineteenth century, is now this community's most widely presupposed philosophical conviction.

NECESSARILY IN CONFLICT?

The question of this chapter is whether this scientific naturalism is compatible with the kind of divine activity in the world presupposed by most religious belief. My answer is Yes.

It is now widely assumed, however, that the answer to this question is No. In some circles, this answer is based on the equation of scientific naturalism with not merely the rejection of supernaturalism, as defined above, but also with an atheistic worldview. A thorough argument for the compatibility of scientific naturalism with belief in divine activity would need to challenge this equation, arguing that the kind of naturalism that is properly presupposed by science need not involve atheism. But the present book, rather than attempting a complete argument, deals only with certain dimensions of it.

Even with the question thus phrased, however, many thinkers would still answer No. By ruling out supernatural interruptions of the world's normal causal processes, these thinkers believe, scientific naturalism is necessarily in conflict with the notion of divine activity in the world. If this were indeed the case, the conflict between science and religion—at least most religions—would be permanent. One would need to choose between them. If one accepts the scientific worldview, with its naturalistic presupposition, one would have to conclude that religion is incurably false or at least mythological. This is, of course, a conclusion that many students feel forced to accept after a year or two at a college or university.

Not all students, of course, are led to this conclusion. Some retain, or develop, a religious worldview that presupposes divine interruptions of the web of natural causes. Although these students may accept many of the teachings and technological benefits of science, their religious beliefs put them in opposition to the most fundamental assumption of the worldview of the scientific community.

This is one of the central tragedies of contemporary higher education—that it seems to force reflective students to choose between being religious and being scientific. And this tragedy, of course, simply reflects the wider fact that late modern culture seems to force all reflective people, including college, university, and even seminary professors, to make this choice.

In the remainder of this chapter, I first review the standard attempts to overcome this problem, all of which, I suggest, are failures. I then point out how these failures are rooted in a traditional assumption about the relation between divine and worldly causation. Finally, I suggest another solution, which rejects that traditional assumption.

THE STANDARD SOLUTIONS

Philosophers and theologians have been suggesting solutions to the apparent conflict between scientific naturalism and divine causation for several centuries. Five of these solutions can be considered standard, in that they are known well enough to be widely discussed.

PANTHEISTIC IDENTITY OF DIVINE AND NATURAL CAUSATION

One of these solutions is based on a pantheistic worldview, according to which the terms "God" and "Nature" are simply different words for the same thing: the universe as a whole. In the seventeenth century, Spinoza affirmed this view with his famous phrase *deus sive natura* (God or Nature). Given this standpoint, anything can be looked at from two perspectives. On the one hand, everything that happens is produced by natural causes. There are no miracles, in the sense of interruptions of the chain of cause-effect relations. On the other hand, everything that happens can be considered an act of God. By thus affirming a pantheistic identity of natural and divine causation, Spinoza meant to reconcile scientific naturalism with divine activity.

The religious communities, however, have generally considered this pantheistic solution to be unacceptable. The religious sensitivity presupposes that not all events are *equally* acts of God. For example, Spinoza was Jewish, but most present-day Jews would reject the idea that the activities of Hitler were as fully caused by God as the activities of Moses, Amos, and Jeremiah. Religious believers, in other words, assume not only that God acts in the world, but that this divine activity is *variable*, rather than being the same at all times and places. This notion, that God acts differently in different events, was expressed in the previously quoted prophetic utterance, "Behold, I do a new thing" (Isaiah 43:19).

PARADOXICAL IDENTITY OF DIVINE AND NATURAL CAUSATION

A second solution was suggested by some existentialist theologians in the middle of the twentieth century, most notably New Testament theologian Rudolf Bultmann. He agreed with Spinoza that we should not think of acts of God as violations of the natural web of cause-effect relations. Bultmann's famous call to "demythologize" the message of the New Testament was based on his conviction that this idea of divine action is mythological. And he agreed with Spinoza that a non-mythological interpretation requires that we regard divine causation as somehow identical with natural causation.

He did not, however, agree with Spinoza's view that we can simply declare in advance that all events are acts of God. Rather, it is only in an existential moment of faith that one can speak of some particular event as an act of God. For example, if my sick child is healed, I may come to see the healing as an act of God, even though I know that the healing was produced by the medicine provided by the doctor. It is not that I think of it as *partly* caused by the medicine and *partly* by God. Rather, as a modern person, I accept the view that every event, even events of extraordinary healing, are *wholly* produced by purely natural causes. Nevertheless, I may also regard it as wholly produced by God.

Bultmann realized that this view is paradoxical. Indeed, he used the phrase "paradoxical identity" to describe the relation between divine and natural causation.[2]

This phrase points to the main problem with this solution, which is that we cannot understand what it *means* to say that, although all events are wholly caused by natural causes, some events can be said to be special acts of God. In philosophical language, an event cannot have more than one sufficient cause, because a *sufficient cause*, by definition, is a cause sufficient to bring about an effect.[3] If natural causes are sufficient to bring about a particular effect, there is no room for a supernatural cause.

Language about Divine Causation as Nonreferential

The first two attempts to reconcile belief in divine causation with scientific naturalism have both involved the notion of two perspectives: From one perspective, an event is purely natural, from another, it is an act of God. A third attempt speaks less of two perspectives than of two types of language: referential and nonreferential.

According to this view, much of our ordinary language *is* referential. That is, it is intended to refer to objects beyond our statements, as when we speak of rocks, trees, and planets. By contrast, religious language, especially language about God, is said to be nonreferential. For example, when we confess in reciting a creed that God created the world, our intention is not to refer to a supreme being who brought this world into existence, but to express our attitudes, such as our awe at the magnificence of the world. To say that God inspired the prophets is to say, perhaps, that one intends to live a life of justice.

But this view is problematic. One problem is that this account does not correspond with what most religious people really mean when they speak of divine activity, such as divine creation and inspiration. Another problem is that no religious community based on this understanding of religious language could be self-sustaining.

Religious language does, to be sure, have nonreferential functions, such as expressing attitudes and intentions. But those attitudes and intentions are taken to be *appropriate* because of beliefs, expressed in referential language, about the way the world really is. If language about God is said not to refer to anything, then we have no way of saying that particular attitudes, such as love and a concern for justice, are enjoined upon us.

This third solution, therefore, does not reconcile religious language about divine causation with scientific naturalism.[4]

SCIENTIFIC NATURALISM AS PURELY METHODOLOGICAL

The first three solutions assume the truth of scientific naturalism as usually understood, then seek to reconcile this doctrine with religion by reconceiving the religious belief in divine causation. A fourth standard solution takes a different approach, saying that it is the notion of scientific naturalism that needs to be reconceived.

According to this solution, scientific naturalism should be understood not as an ontological or metaphysical doctrine, according to which supernatural causation never occurs, but as a purely *methodological* doctrine, which deals with the nature of science, not the nature of the universe. To say that science is naturalistic is merely to say that science by definition—or at least by irreversible convention—restricts itself to tracing natural causes. Science as such, according to this view, neither affirms nor denies the reality of divine causation. It simply does not raise this question, because the restriction to natural causes is inherent in the scientific method.

In the thinking of most of its contemporary advocates, methodological naturalism is combined with the acceptance of supernatural causation. That is, these advocates believe that reference to divine causation is needed to explain various things, such as the existence and order of our universe, the rise of life, and various biblical miracles. They hold that the scientist *qua* scientist cannot refer to divine causation to explain these events, and this means that science cannot provide an adequate explanation for them. But this point simply illustrates the fact that science is an inherently *limited* enterprise. To have an adequate worldview, say these thinkers, we must place science, with its naturalism, *within* a supernaturalistic framework.[5]

But this solution is also problematic. Its main problem is that it fails to reconcile the worldview of the religious community with the worldview of the scientific community. The ideological leaders of the scientific community emphatically do *not* accept the view that their naturalism is purely methodological. They do not accept the contention that supernatural incursions into the world can be affirmed as long as one makes clear that such affirmations are not intended to be scientific statements. Rather, in affirming naturalism, the leading spokespersons of the scientific community affirm the ontological or metaphysical doctrine that no supernatural interruptions of the web of natural causation ever occur, so that all events are, at least in principle, explainable in terms of this web of natural causes.[6]

A second problem with this proposed solution is that, by returning to the idea of a God who can interrupt the world's causal processes at will, we would bring back the traditional problem of evil, which asks why an all-powerful God, who could interrupt natural and human causality, allows so much unspeakable evil.

REJECTION OF SCIENTIFIC NATURALISM IN FAVOR OF SUPERNATURALISTIC SCIENCE

A fifth standard solution casts an even more critical eye on the notion of scientific naturalism. Whereas the fourth solution accepted it as a methodological doctrine while rejecting it as a metaphysical doctrine, this fifth solution rejects scientific naturalism altogether. That is, it says that science, which simply means knowledge, should describe things as they really are. Therefore, if the world and many events within it came about through divine causation, then science, to "tell it like it is," must refer to divine causation.

The best science, in other words, would be a *theistic* science, by which is meant a *supernaturalistic* science. The most well-known version of this view is the fundamentalist position usually called "creation science" or "scientific creationism," which takes the first chapters of the Bible, understood literally, to be essentially accurate, so that the Earth is only a few thousand years old.

A less extreme version of theistic science has been represented most vigorously by attorney Phillip Johnson, whose book *Darwin on Trial* attracted much attention, and by well-known philosopher Alvin Plantinga.[7] In the Plantinga-Johnson version of theistic science, the scientific community's consensus that our world has come about over many billions of years is accepted, but a supernatural act of God is said to be the explanation for the origin of the universe, the rise of life, and the rise of every species of life thereafter. Arguing that this view provides the best explanation of these events, Plantinga and Johnson would overcome the conflict between scientific naturalism and divine causation by convincing the scientific community to reject naturalism in favor of supernaturalism.[8]

The main problem with this solution—ignoring here the question of its truth—is that there is virtually no chance that the scientific community will accept it, because the rejection of supernaturalism has become the most fundamental metaphysical conviction of the scientific community over the past 200 years. Also, this fifth solution, like the fourth, brings back the traditional problem of evil, which is, in fact, one of the reasons why this position has no appeal to the ideological leaders of the scientific community.

As this brief review of the standard positions suggests, they all fail to reconcile the worldview of the scientific community, with its naturalism, and that of the religious communities, with its notion of divine activity in the world. But why should this be the case? Why should it be impossible to have a notion of divine activity that would be religiously adequate without contradicting the scientific community's assumption that there are no interruptions of the world's normal causal processes? Why, in other words, can there not be a naturalistic notion of divine activity in the world, according to which divine influence is a normal part of the world's causal processes, not an interruption of those processes?

There *can be* and in fact *is* such a notion. But this alternative notion is not well known, due to the continuing impact, reflected in all the standard positions, of the way of understanding the relation between divine and natural causation that was dominant in the Middle Ages. I refer to the scheme of primary and secondary causation. I will briefly review this scheme in order to show how the conflict between divine activity and scientific naturalism arose.

The Scheme of Primary and Secondary Causation

According to the scheme of primary and secondary causation, God is the *primary* cause of all events. Being omnipotent, God's activity, as the primary cause of all events, makes God the *sufficient* cause of those events; no supplementation by other causes is needed. However, God usually does not bring events about unilaterally, but through *secondary* causes, now commonly called *natural* causes.

These secondary or natural causes are *also* sufficient causes—as long as attention is focused on the *nature* of the events that are brought about, on their *whatness*. If, by contrast, the question of the *thatness* of the events is raised—namely, why a world, with its chains of causal events, exists at all—one must then refer to God, as the creator and sustainer of the whole universe. But if one ignores this more radical question—of why there is anything rather than nothing—one need not refer to God to give a complete account of most events.

Divine causation, accordingly, is usually restricted to the invariable activity of sustaining the universe. It usually does not involve variable causation that is constitutive of the nature or whatness of worldly things and events. For the normal course of events, accordingly, a science limited to secondary or natural causes can in principle be complete.

THE APPEAL AND THE SNAG

This scheme has been very appealing to both scientists and theologians. On the one hand, it has allowed scientists to ignore theological ideas in developing their detailed accounts of how the world works. On the other hand, it has allowed theologians to defend the uniqueness of divine causation. Arguing that divine and natural causation occur on "different levels," theologians could say that "God is not one cause among others"—that divine causation is not to be treated as simply one more type of finite causation. This scheme, accordingly, allowed theologians and scientists to operate autonomously, with each protected from possible conflict with, and thereby interference from, the other.

There was, however, one snag. The doctrine, as I said, was that God *usually* brings about effects through secondary or natural causes. But in a *few* cases, God was said to bring about the effects directly, without using secondary causes as instruments.

The most obvious of such cases were the miracles in the Bible and the lives of the saints. Indeed, a miracle was *defined* as an event brought about directly by God as primary cause, without the employment of secondary causes. But the list of events produced directly by

God's primary causation also included events not usually classified as miracles, such as the creation of the world, the creation of life, the creation of the various species of plants and animals, the creation of the human soul, the inspiration of the prophets and the biblical writers, and the incarnation in Jesus. Given all these events that were not explainable in terms of natural causes, there could not really be a fully naturalistic science of either nature or history.

The God of the gaps

This is so because of the most fateful implication of the primary-secondary scheme for thinking about the relation between divine and worldly causation. According to this scheme, to speak of any divine influence that was constitutive of the nature of events in the world was *ipso facto* to speak of a *supernatural interruption* of the chains of natural causes and effects. Because most events were said to be fully explicable, at least in principle, without reference to any variable divine influence, the affirmation that some such influence played a constitutive role in particular events implied that this divine influence interrupted the causal principles involved in most events.

For example, to say that the prophet Jeremiah's experience of God's call was constitutive of his experience was to say that God's causal influence on Jeremiah in those moments was different in kind from God's causal influence in most human experience. Likewise, if we say that the creation of life involved divine activity beyond the undifferentiated divine influence that sustains all beings in existence, we had to say that the creation of life involved a kind of causation not involved in most events.

This position, which is embodied in the fourth and fifth of the standard solutions reviewed earlier, was widely accepted by scientists, philosophers, and theologians in the eighteenth and nineteenth centuries.

Those who were imbued with the spirit of the scientific enterprise, however, became increasingly reluctant to accept the idea that there were gaps in the chain of natural causes that needed to be filled by supernatural causation. These thinkers came, in other words, to reject the "God of the gaps." Given the primary-secondary scheme for thinking of the relation between divine and worldly causation, this denial of supernatural interruptions implied atheism, pantheism, or the deistic idea that, after creating the universe, God did *all* things through secondary or natural causes, never acting to fill a gap in the nexus of natural causes. This deistic solution was central to the uniformitarianism famously championed by Charles Lyell, according to which our explanations of past events should not assume any causal factors not operative today.

THE CONFLICT BETWEEN LYELL AND DARWIN

Lyell, however, illustrated the difficulty that thinkers had in fully leaving supernaturalism behind, given a worldview in which any affirmation of variable divine influence in the world entailed a supernatural intervention. Lyell believed that fresh divine influence was necessary to explain the origin of the human mind. Divine intervention, he said, added "the moral and intellectual faculties of the human race, to a system of nature which had gone on for millions of years without the intervention of any analogous cause." This meant that we must "assume a primeval creative power which does not act with uniformity."[9] Lyell, in other words, thought that there was still one gap to be filled.

On this point Charles Darwin broke with his older friend. In a letter to Lyell, Darwin rejected the idea of divine additions to explain the distinctive capacities of the human mind, saying: "I would give nothing for the theory of natural selection, if it requires miraculous additions at any one stage of descent."[10] Darwin still believed in a creator God, thinking evolution intelligible only on the assumption that God, having created the universe, had built in laws of evolutionary development. But Darwin insisted on a consistently deistic view, with not a single interruption of these laws.[11]

FROM DEISM TO ATHEISM

This rejection of supernatural causation, furthermore, was soon applied to the origin of the universe itself, so that Darwin's followers rejected his deism in favor of complete atheism. It is this late modern worldview, with its atheism, that is generally equated with scientific naturalism today. The denial of supernatural gap-filling is taken to mean the denial of *any* divine influence in the world.

It is this assumption that led thinkers to accept the first, second, or third of the three solutions reviewed earlier, in which the notion of "divine causation" is revised so radically that it is no longer recognizable by religious believers. And it is this same assumption that has led advocates of the fourth and fifth solutions to hold that, to do justice to religious belief, they must reject not only the atheism of the late modern worldview but also its naturalism, thereby reaffirming the medieval and early modern idea of supernatural interruptions of the world's normal causal processes. It was in these ways that the scheme of primary and secondary causation led to the present impasse, in which it seems impossible to do justice both to the scientific community's naturalism and the religious world's belief in variable divine influence in the world.

NATURALISTIC THEISM

I turn now to a new way of understanding divine causation that was developed in the twentieth century, a way that overcomes the impasse that resulted from the scheme of primary and secondary causation.

This new way was suggested by William James at the end of *The Varieties of Religious Experience*. I refer to the position that James, unfortunately, named "piecemeal supernaturalism." In calling it a version of supernaturalism, James was taking "naturalism" to be the doctrine that "nature," understood to be *the world knowable through sensory perception*, is all there is. Given this definition of naturalism, anyone who believes in the existence of something beyond nature thus defined, such as a Divine Actuality and/or a realm of ideal values, would *ipso facto* be a "supernaturalist." James did believe there was something beyond the world knowable through sensory perception, saying that we experience "ideal impulses" originating from an "unseen region."[12]

In calling his position *piecemeal* supernaturalism, James was contrasting it with "universalistic supernaturalism," by which he meant the doctrine of Hegelian transcendental idealists and others who "obey the Kantian direction enough to bar out ideal entities from interfering causally in the course of phenomenal events." This type of supernaturalism, in other words, does not take issue with the materialistic view, according to which the only causation exerted in the world is exerted by material bodies. This Hegelian supernaturalism accepts the idea that no ideal, nonactual, unseen entities, such as normative ideals or values, influence the course of the world.

This universalistic supernaturalism merely adds the proviso that, although a purely materialistic analysis is adequate from one perspective—the perspective taken by the sciences—it is not adequate from a perspective that asks about ultimate intelligibility. Such intelligibility can be achieved only by realizing that our world is a phenomenal appearance of an Absolute Reality. This universalistic supernaturalism is, in other words, a version of the doctrine that divine and worldly causation are identical. By affirming this position, its advocates said, one could give a religious gloss to the world without challenging the purely materialistic, deterministic analysis of natural and even historical processes.

James saw no need to resort to such a desperate doctrine in order to provide a religious interpretation of the world. He found, he said, "no intellectual difficulty in mixing the ideal and the real worlds together by interpolating influences from the ideal region among the forces that causally determine the real world's details." He rejected, in other words, the contention of the universalistic supernaturalists that "the world of the ideal has no efficient causality, and never bursts into the world of phenomena at particular points."[13] Explaining his reason for considering this universalistic supernaturalism religiously inadequate, James said:

> An entire world is the smallest unit with which the Absolute can work, whereas to our finite minds work for the better ought to be done within this world, setting in at single points. Our difficulties and our ideals are all piecemeal affairs, but the Absolute can do no piecework for us.[14]

James's own position, by contrast, was that the ideal world is, by means of "ideal impulses," able to "get down upon the flat level of experience and interpolate itself piecemeal between distinct portions of nature," thereby entering into "transactions of detail."[15]

James, as we have seen, defined naturalism in terms of sensory perception, so that anyone who thinks there is something beyond the world as known through sensory perception is a supernaturalist. But that is an unhelpful way of understanding the distinction between the view that normal causal processes can be interrupted and the view that they cannot. The main distinction, I have suggested, is between those who affirm violations of the normal causal processes and those who do not.

Given this way of distinguishing between naturalism and supernaturalism, James's position is a form of (theistic) naturalism, not supernaturalism: Thanks to James's panexperientialism,[16] he could affirm that the "ideal impulses" received by human beings are high-level forms of a kind of divine influence pervading "the whole universe."[17] That is, he could say that all things in the world, from atoms to human beings, are influenced by ideal impulses, coming from that "unseen region" that we call God, so that divine influence is a regular part of the world's normal causal transactions, never an interruption thereof.

However, given James's definition of "naturalism" as the view that there is nothing beyond the world known through sensory perception, his belief in an "unseen region" meant that his position had to be called a version of supernaturalism. As James himself put it: "If one should make a division of all thinkers into naturalists and supernaturalists, I should undoubtedly have to go . . . into the supernaturalist branch."[18]

This terminological choice was unfortunate, however, because it has led many interpreters to assume that James affirmed supernatural interruptions of the world's basic causal processes. For example, John Mackie, having defined miracles as "divine interventions which have disrupted the natural course of events," explicates James's piecemeal supernaturalism to mean that "the supernatural must enter into 'transactions of detail' with the natural—in other words, the sorts of interventions that we have defined miracles to be."[19]

RECONCILING VARIABLE DIVINE CAUSATION WITH SCIENTIFIC NATURALISM

The correct characterization of James, however, is that he was a naturalistic theist who, by virtue of his acceptance of divine "piecework," affirmed variable divine influence in the world. James therefore avoided the debilitating conclusion that God is on the side of evil as much as on the side of good.[20]

This kind of theism, which is naturalistic while allowing variable divine causation in the world, was worked out more systematically by Alfred North Whitehead. In the early modern view, the universe was thought of as a more-or-less fully self-sufficient machine, with God sustaining it from outside and perhaps intervening occasionally. In Whiteheadian theology, by contrast, God is the World Soul,[21] constantly interacting with all of its parts, somewhat as our minds or souls interact with our bodies.

To develop the analogy: In our bodies, each of the units is constantly receiving information from other parts: Cells, for example, receive information from molecules, from organelles, and from other cells. But they also receive information from our minds or souls. Likewise, our souls are constantly receiving information from our various bodily members and (telepathically) from other souls. If there is a mind or soul of the universe, it would be natural to assume that we are also constantly receiving influences from this source as well.

In terms of this framework, we can do justice both to scientific naturalism and to the religious belief in variable divine causation. Scientific naturalism is affirmed, because uniformitarianism is endorsed: No event is to be explained in terms of a type of divine causation that does not occur in all other events. Divine influence is *formally* the same in all events. Whitehead expresses this point in his technical language by saying that God provides an "initial aim" for each event. Receiving a divinely-rooted aim toward an ideal possibility, in other words, is part of the normal pattern of causal relations.[22] In this sense, divine action is uniform.

This view, nevertheless, can also do justice to the religious belief in divine causation. In the first place, process theology says that divine causation is a factor in every event in the universe—never a fully determining factor, to be sure, but a real causal factor.[23]

In the second place, although this divine causation is *formally* the same in all events, it is variable *substantively, that is, in content.* By analogy, your mind's influence on your body is formally always the same, as your mind provides instructive information to various parts of the body by means of influencing the brain. But this influence is variable in content, as your mind provides one instruction for your left hand, another for your right hand, another for your vocal cords, and still other instructions (usually unconsciously) for your heart, lungs, and stomach. In a similar way, the ideals or initial aims provided by God for different parts of the world would differ in content.

Whitehead expressed this notion by saying that the divine aim is always towards the best possibility for that particular situation.[24] This idea provides a basis for expressing the biblical notion that God does new things from time to time, and also the idea that some events are *special* acts of God, which express the divine character and purpose with special directness.[25]

NOTIONS RULED OUT BY NATURALISTIC THEISM

Process theology's naturalistic theism does rule out a few ideas that some religious people have believed. For example, it rules out the idea that God has acted in one religious tradition in a way qualitatively different from the way God has acted in other religions. But why, sinful arrogance aside, should anyone today want to maintain that idea, which has been the source of so much tragedy?

Process theism also rules out the idea that God can completely determine any particular event in the world. But that is the idea that has created an insoluble problem of evil, thereby being responsible for much of the agnosticism and atheism in the world.

This naturalistic theism also rules out the idea of miracles, *if* miracles are defined as supernatural interruptions of the world's normal causal processes. It does not, however, rule out the *kinds of events* that have usually been thought of as miracles, such as extraordinary healings,[26] so we need not, in the face of overwhelming evidence to the contrary, try to maintain that such events never happen. Process theism also does not rule out the notion that divine influence plays a role in such events. It merely holds that the divine influence in such events should not be thought to be formally different from that in all other events. Although such events are extraordinary, they are not supernatural. This is, in fact, the interpretation usually presupposed by those involved in parapsychological research.

Benefits of Naturalistic Theism

In discussing Whitehead's naturalistic theism, I have thus far been pointing out its benefits to the religious communities, suggesting that it, besides reconciling the religious belief in variable divine activity with scientific naturalism, can also avoid the problem of evil and overcome the primary basis for religious arrogance. But this version of theistic naturalism can be equally helpful to the scientific community.

This help is needed because the scientific community, insofar as it has equated scientific naturalism with atheism, has been unable to explain a wide range of phenomena. For example, this atheistic form of scientific naturalism cannot explain the extraordinary order of the universe, especially the apparent "fine-tuning" that made it possible for our universe to bring forth life. It cannot explain the directionality of the evolutionary process, in particular the direction toward richer modes of experience. It cannot explain the novelty that has kept appearing in physical, biological, and cultural evolution. With regard to human experience in particular, this atheistic version of naturalism cannot explain the objectivity of logic and mathematics, an issue that has been at the center of the philosophy of logic and mathematics in our century. It cannot explain the objectivity of moral experience. And, by virtue of denying the possibility of genuine religious experience, it cannot explain the universality and persistence of religion.

These controversial claims, simply stated baldly here, are discussed more fully in subsequent chapters.[27] For now, the central point is that I agree with Plantinga and Johnson that science could be improved by becoming theistic. My proposal differs from theirs, however, in rejecting a return to supernaturalism. What we need, I suggest, is a theistic science based on a *naturalistic* theism. If such a development were to occur while at the same time the theistic religious communities came to eschew supernaturalism in favor of a naturalistic form of theism, the apparent conflict between scientific naturalism and the religious belief in divine activity would be seen to be just that—merely apparent.

NOTES

1. Support for this assertion is provided in "The Two Ultimates and the Religions," Chap. 7 of my *Reenchantment without Supernaturalism.*

2. See Rudolf Bultmann, *Jesus Christ and Mythology* (New York: Charles Scribner's Sons, 1958), 12-15, 61-65, or *Kerygma and Myth: A Theological Debate,* ed. Hans Werner Bartsch, trans. Reginald H. Fuller (New York: Harper & Row, 1961), 120, 197-201. I have discussed Bultmann's view in "Paradoxical Identity of Divine and Worldly Action," in Griffin, *A Process Christology* (Philadelphia: Westminster, 1967; second edition (reprint with new preface), Lanham, Md.: University Press of America, 1990).

3. I argue this point in relation to bodily and "mental" action in my *Unsnarling the World-Knot: Consciousness, Freedom, and the Mind-Body Problem* (Berkeley: University of California Press, 1998; reprint, Eugene: Wipf and Stock, 2008), 29-30, 213, 222-23, and 232. The idea that this conclusion can be avoided by the idea that an effect can be

"overdetermined," I point out, works only if the effect is described in high abstractions, rather than in terms of its specific details.

4. I have argued against the adequacy of totally nonreferential interpretations of religious language in *Reenchantment without Supernaturalism*, especially the Introduction and Chapters 7 and 9.

5. See Ernan McMullan, "Natural Science and Belief in a Creator: Historical Notes," in R.J. Russell, W.R. Stoeger, and G.V. Coyne, eds., *Physics, Philosophy, and Theology: A Common Quest for Understanding* (Vatican City State: Vatican Observatory, 1988): 49-79, and "Plantinga's Defense of Special Creation," *Christian Scholar's Review* 21/1 (1991): 55-79; William Hasker, "Mr. Johnson for the Prosecution," *Christian Scholar's Review* 22/2 (December 1992): 177-86, and "*Darwin on Trial* Revisited: A Review Essay," *Christian Scholar's Review* 24:4 (May 1995): 479-88; and Howard Van Till, "Special Creationism in Designer Clothing: A Response to *The Creation Hypothesis*," *Perspectives on Science and Christian Faith* 47/2 (June 1995): 123-31, and "Basil, Augustine, and the Doctrine of Creation's Functional Integrity," *Science and Christian Belief* 8/2 (1996): 21-38. I discuss this position in "Harmonizing Science and Religion: Three Alternative Approaches," Chapter 3 of my *Religion and Scientific Naturalism*. Since my response to Van Till's essays, he has changed his position, saying that he is "learning to appreciate the ability of naturalistic theism to provide [him] with an effective conceptual vocabulary for reflecting on the experience of God's effective presence in everyday phenomena." See Van Till, "Foreword" to David Ray Griffin, *Two Great Truths* (Louisville: Westminster John Knox, 2004), vii-xviii, at xvii.

6. This problem is avoided by the consistently deistic version of this position, which says that, whereas God *could* interrupt the world's normal causal processes, God never in fact does so. This position was articulated a century ago by Rudolf Otto in *Naturalism and Religion* (London: Williams & Norgate; New York: G. P. Putnam's, 1907) and, more recently, and less wholeheartedly, by Peter Forrest in *God Without the Supernatural: A Defense of Scientific Theism* (Ithaca: Cornell

University Press, 1966). Although this position does avoid the most obvious conflict with scientific naturalism, it is still in conflict with it, insofar as naturalism affirms not only that supernatural interruptions never do occur but also that they are not even possible.

7. See Phillip E. Johnson, *Darwin on Trial,* 2nd edition (Downers Grove, Ill.: Intervarsity Press, 1993) and *Reason in the Balance: The Case Against Naturalism in Science, Law, and Education* (Downers Grove, Ill.: Intervarsity Press, 1993), which I have discussed in "Christian Faith and Scientific Naturalism: An Appreciative Critique of Phillip Johnson's Proposal" (*Christian Scholar's Review* 28/2 [Winter 1998]: 308-28). Plantinga states his position in "When Faith and Reason Clash: Evolution and the Bible" (*Christian Scholar's Review* 21/1 [1991]: 8-32), and "Evolution, Neutrality, and Antecedent Probability: A Reply to McMullin and Van Till" (*Christian Scholar's Review* 21/1 [1991]: 80-109). The Plantinga-Johnson position is treated in Chapter 3 of my *Religion and Scientific Naturalism.*

8. Although Johnson would probably have accepted this way of understanding the challenge, Plantinga articulates his position as a defensive strategy, aimed at justifying the right of conservative Christians to hold their beliefs without being able to show that they are more plausible than opposing beliefs. Johnson, by contrast, is more interested in trying to bring about a change in the scientific community.

9. Lyell's statements are quoted in R. Hooykaas, *Natural Law and Divine Miracle: A Historical-Critical Study of the Principle of Uniformity in Geology, Biology, and Theology* (Leiden: E.J. Brill, 1959), 114.

10. Francis Darwin, ed., *The Life and Letters of Charles Darwin,* 2 vols (New York: D. Appleton, 1896), II: 6-7.

11. Darwin's rejection of Lyell's exception had been anticipated by David Friedrich Strauss's rejection of an exception in Friedrich Schleiermacher's position. In one passage, Schleiermacher had said: "It can never be necessary in the interest of religion so to interpret a fact that its dependence on God absolutely excludes its being conditioned

by the system of Nature" (*The Christian Faith*, ed. H.R. Mackintosh and J.S. Stewart [New York: Harper, 1963], 178). However, in a passage in which he discussed the origin of the life of Jesus (ibid., 398-415), Schleiermacher maintained that Jesus' perfect God-consciousness is understandable only on the assumption that divine causation protected Jesus from the kinds of sinful influences to which the rest of us are subject. Strauss, who from his Hegelian-pantheistic position regarded any such exceptions to be impossible, criticized Schleiermacher for affirming one. While acknowledging that Schleiermacher "limits the miraculous to the first introduction of Christ into the series of existences, and allows the whole of his further development to have been subject to all the conditions of finite existence," Strauss argued that "this concession cannot repair the breach, which the supposition only of one miracle makes in the scientific theory of the world" (David Friedrich Strauss, *The Life of Jesus Critically Examined*, trans. George Eliot, ed. Peter C. Hodgson [Philadelphia: Fortress Press, 1972], 771).

12. William James, *The Varieties of Religious Experience* (New York: Longmans, Green, 1902), 520, 516.

13. Ibid., 520, 521.

14. Ibid., 522n.

15. Ibid., 521, 522.

16. Having described "a concrete bit of personal experience," James said: "It is a *full* fact, even though it be an insignificant fact; it is of the *kind* to which all realities whatsoever must belong." Speaking of the "feeling which each one of us has of the pinch of his individual destiny," James said that "it is the one thing that fills up the measure of our concrete actuality," and any would-be existent that should lack such a feeling, or its analogue, would be a piece of reality "only half made up." He then referred in a footnote to "Lotze's doctrine that the only meaning we can attach to the notion of a thing as it is 'in itself' is by conceiving it as it is *for* itself; i.e., as a piece of full experience" (ibid., 499). For a

discussion of James's panexperientialism, which he called "pluralistic panpsychism," see Marcus P. Ford, "William James," in David Ray Griffin et al., *Founders of Constructive Postmodern Philosophy: Peirce, James, Bergson, Whitehead, and Hartshorne* (Albany: State University of New York Press, 1993): 89-132, and *William James's Philosophy: A New Perspective* (Amherst: University of Massachusetts Press, 1982).

17. James, *The Varieties of Religious Experience*, 517.

18. Ibid., 520.

19. John Mackie, *The Miracle of Theism: Arguments for and against the Existence of God* (Oxford: Clarendon, 1982), 13, 182.

20. James, *The Varieties of Religious Experience*, 522n.

21. Although Whitehead himself did not use this term, or the related term "panentheism," Charles Hartshorne, in developing Whitehead's idea of God, used them both; see Hartshorne, *Man's Vision of God and the Logic of Theism* (New York: Harper & Row, 1941), 348, and *Omnipotence and Other Theological Mistakes* (Albany: State University of New York Press, 1984), 59.

22. Whitehead's doctrine that every actuality receives a divinely provided initial aim, which he originally called an "ideal consequent" (*Religion in the Making* [New York: Fordham University Press, 1996; reprint of 1926 edition], 156-58), seems to be his development of James's suggestion that God influences the world in terms of "ideal impulses." That Whitehead was, like James, affirming variable divine causation is shown by his statement that God provides "particular ideals relevant to the actual state of the world" (ibid., 159) and his later affirmation of "particular providence for particular occasions" (*Process and Reality* [orig. 1929], corrected edition, ed. [New York: Free Press, 1978], 351). Hartshorne explicitly connected this latter affirmation with "James's 'piece-meal supernaturalism'" (Hartshorne, "Whitehead's Idea of God," in *The Philosophy of Alfred North Whitehead*, ed. Paul Arthur Schilpp, 2nd edition [New York: Tudor, 1951]: 513-59, at 530).

23. James had already emphasized this point. Having said that "the unseen region is not merely ideal, for it produces effects in this world," James then said: "'God' is a causal agent as well as a medium of communion, and that is the aspect which I wish to emphasize" (*Varieties of Religious Experience*, 516, 517n).

24. Whitehead, *Process and Reality*, 84, 244.

25. I developed this idea in several essays, such as "Is Revelation Coherent" and "Relativism, Divine Causation, and Biblical Theology," as well as in my first book, *A Process Christology*. I have later modified the application of this idea to christology, as indicated in the new preface to the second edition of this book (1990).

26. It might be thought that my contention that James's position is *not*, according to my definition of supernaturalism, a species of it is contradicted by James's statement that his piecemeal supernaturalism "admits miracles" (*Varieties of Religious Experience*, 520). But in affirming miracles, James did not mean violations of the normal causal principles of the universe. Rather, having spent a significant portion of his life engaged with the phenomena of psychical research, he argued that we need a scientific worldview that would allow these phenomena to be regarded as fully natural, albeit exceptional, occurrences. He said, for example: "Science, so far as science denies such exceptional occurrences, lies prostrate in the dust for me; and the most urgent intellectual need which I feel at present is that science be built up again in a form in which such things may have a positive place" (*William James on Psychical Research*, 42). In my "Parapsychology and Philosophy: A Whiteheadian Postmodern Perspective" (*Journal of the American Society for Psychical Research* 87/3 [July 1993]: 217-88), I argued that Whitehead's philosophy provides the basis for a position that would fill this need. For an illuminating discussion of James's position from this point of view, see Marcus Ford, "James's Psychical Research and Its Philosophical Implications," *Transactions of the Charles S. Peirce Society* 34/3 (Summer, 1998), 605-26.

27. These claims are argued from additional perspectives in *Religion and Scientific Naturalism* and *Reenchantment without Supernaturalism*. The various problems related to evolution are treated in detail in the former book, while the remaining issues are treated in the latter.

CHAPTER THREE

Panentheism and Cosmic Design

In this chapter, I focus on the question, at the center of much of the science-and-religion debate these days, whether our cosmos or universe is designed. I suggest that, if faced with this question, Whitehead's answer, like the answer to most Yes-or-No questions about complex issues, would have been Yes and No. This ambivalent answer reflects the fact that the notion of a designed cosmos has many connotations, not all of which imply all the others. I will discuss eight possible meanings of this notion, suggesting that, from the perspective of Whiteheadian panentheism—here often called "Whiteheadian process theology" or simply "process theology"—the answer to six of them is No, but that there are two senses in which we can speak of our universe as designed.

SOME BASIC WHITEHEADIAN NOTIONS

An understanding of the position of process panentheism on this question requires an understanding of many basic Whiteheadian notions. Although some of those notions were introduced in the previous chapters, a discussion of the question of design requires a more complete and precise understanding than that so far provided. To fill in the remainder of the needed background, as well as to call to mind some of the salient points already introduced, I will here briefly summarize fourteen of the notions most central to the question at hand.

1. The universe's most fundamental units are *momentary spatiotemporal events.* Whitehead's ontology, in other words, is an event-ontology, in which the *actual entities*—the things that are actual in the fullest sense of the term—are spatiotemporal events, or happenings, rather than enduring things. He thereby rejects the traditional substance-ontology, according to which the actual entities are understood to be enduring substances.

He accepts this event-ontology for both philosophical and scientific reasons. Philosophically, it is fundamental to his defense of both pluralistic realism and his reconciliation of final and efficient causation and hence his defense of freedom. Scientifically, Whitehead saw that both quantum and relativity physics suggested that the fundamental units of the world are very brief events. (This idea is also supported by the discovery that some of the so-called elementary "particles" exist less than a billionth of a second, so they would more appropriately be called "events.") Whitehead also noted that both Buddhism and William James, in their phenomenological analyses of human experience, concluded that it comes in discrete "drops of experience." In order to emphasize this idea—that actual entities are spatiotemporal events rather than enduring things—Whitehead called them *actual occasions*.

2. Each momentary event is an embodiment of *creativity,* from which the physicist's energy is an abstraction. By enlarging the notion of energy to include all that Whitehead meant by "creativity," we could say that our universe is made up of energetic events. This is true even of so-called empty space, which means that Whitehead's ideas here are consonant with recent thinking about the ("virtual" or "false") vacuum. "Empty space," in other words, is not empty of events and hence not devoid of energy.

3. Creativity includes an element of self-determination, so that no energetic event is wholly determined by external forces. This is one respect in which creativity goes beyond "energy" as usually under-stood. The *epistemic* indeterminacy of the world at the quantum level reflects an element of *ontological* self-determinacy.[1]

4. **The energetic events are embodiments of in-formed energy.** They are, in other words, not simply embodiments of raw, unformed energy. The different types of things are different because they contain different forms, different in-formation.

5. **Each event *prehends* aspects of prior events, and thereby aspects of their in-formed energy, into itself.** The term "prehend" is simply "apprehend" without the prefix, meant to indicate that this response to other things need not be a *conscious* process. The crucial point here is that each event is *internally related* to prior events. That is, rather than being a solid piece of stuff, or a Leibnizian monad devoid of windows, each event is internally constituted by its rela-tions to prior events. Here Whitehead's view seems virtually identical with some Buddhist understandings of the "dependent origination" of all things.

6. *Enduring* **things, such as electrons, protons, and photons, exist because a particular form of energy is repeated by a long series of energetic events.** Such events can be repeated dozens, hundreds, thou-sands, millions, or even billions of times per second. That is, although each event is influenced by *all* prior events to at least some slight degree, an event in an enduring individual is *primarily* constituted by its prehension of, and thereby internalization of, the form of energy that was embodied by its predecessors in the enduring individual to which it belongs. The proton endures, in other words, because each of its protonic events essentially repeats the form of its predecessors, with this repetition going on, not quite endlessly, but for many billions of years. (I illustrate this point with protons, because they seem to have an especially high degree of tolerance for monotony.)

7. Low-grade enduring individuals can, in certain combinations, give rise to higher-level enduring individuals. Quarks and gluons, for example, give rise to protons and neutrons. These latter individuals combine with electrons to give rise to atoms and molecules. Still higher forms of enduring individuals include macromolecules, prokaryotic cells, organelles (which are evidently captured prokaryotic cells), eukaryotic cells, and animals, such as gnats, squirrels, and human beings.

These higher-level enduring individuals are, by hypothesis, not simply complex arrangements of lower-level individuals. Rather, they involve higher-level energetic events, with their own unity of response to their environments. This emergence of higher-level units is possible because of internal relations. That is, because each event is internally constituted out of the things in its environment, a more complex environment can provide the basis for more complex events and thereby "compound individuals," which are more complex enduring individuals compounded out of simpler ones.[2]

8. The most complex enduring individuals on our planet, evidently, are living human beings, with their psyches. There is no *ontological* difference between the psyches of humans and those of other animals, as some dualists hold, or between animal psyches and lower-level enduring individuals, as other dualists hold, or even between living and non-living individuals, as those dualists known as "vitalists" hold. But there are enormous differences *of degree* in terms of capacities for prehension and self-determination. Because our own existence is not entirely different from that of lower-grade enduring individuals, there are some features of our existence that can be generalized all the way down, to the simplest types of enduring individuals.

9. The most general of these generalizable features is *experience* (which is, of course, presupposed by previously mentioned general features: prehension and self-determination). This position can, accordingly, be called *panexperientialism*. This notion is one of the features of this position that is often thought to make it self-evidently subject to one-word refutations, such as "implausible,"[3] because we all know that sticks and stones have no experience and exercise no self-determination. However, the "pan" in panexperientialism, which means "all," does not mean all things whatsoever, but only *all true individuals*—the things I have been referring to as energetic events and enduring individuals.

Even then, the power of the modern worldview, which was adopted in the 17th century in opposition to views suggesting that matter involves sentience and spontaneity,[4] is such that most philosophers, scientists, and theologians refuse to entertain this idea seriously. One result of this refusal is that dualism and materialism, the two positions allowed by the modern worldview, have made little advance on the mind-body problem beyond the stand-off between Descartes and Hobbes three and a half centuries ago. I have recently shown that Whiteheadian panexperientialism can, at long last, resolve this problem, incorporating the strengths of dualism and materialism while avoiding their weaknesses.[5]

10. Another generalizable feature, both presupposed and implied by experience, is *time, temporal process*. Because each event prehends into itself aspects of prior events, *irreversible time* obtains even for the most elementary individuals. Time as we know it—that is, as an asymmetrical, irreversible process—did not have to wait for the emergence of human experience, as some think, or for life, as others think, or even for aggregations of atoms subject to entropy, as still others think. Rather, time as we know it is already real for individual atoms, even for their constituent electrons, protons, and quarks.[6]

11. Time is real even prior to the existence of enduring individuals. The ancient idea that the origin of our cosmos involved the emergence of a particular form of order out of chaos—an idea that was suggested by Plato, the book of Genesis,[7] and many other ancient cosmologies—is essentially correct. For Whitehead, the chaos would have been a situation in which extremely trivial energetic events happen at random, meaning that none of them would have been organized into enduring individuals, not even individuals as simple as quarks.

As pointed out in Chapter 1, when we speak of a "thing," we usually mean an *enduring* thing, which retains its identity through time, so the chaos prior to the creation of our world was a state of no-thing-ness. In *this* sense, we can say that our world was created out of nothing-ness. But, as also pointed out in Chapter 1, this was a state of *relative* nothingness, not *absolute* nothingness. The crucial implication of this distinction for the present discussion is that there would still have been time, or temporal process, in this chaotic situation, because each random event would have prehended prior events and been prehended by succeeding events.

Whitehead's position, therefore, rejects the view that, if our world began with some sort of "big bang," this was a "singularity," in the sense that, prior to it, there was no time whatsoever.[8]

12. In addition to all the local events, the universe involves an enduring individual comprised of an everlasting series of nonlocal, all-inclusive events.[9] Rather than existing outside the universe, in the sense of existing independently of any realm of finite entities, this nonlocal individual is *essentially* the soul of the universe, providing the unity that makes it a *uni*verse.

This everlasting individual is the home of all possibilities. By virtue of being prehended by all local events, this everlasting individual is the primary source of both order and novelty in our universe. Being good, in the twofold sense of having loving kindness and compassion for all sentient creatures,[10] as well as being ubiquitous, everlasting, and the source of the world's order, it can be considered divine.

13. The influence of this divine individual never involves super-natural interruptions of the world's normal causal processes. It is, instead, a *natural part of* these processes. The fact that process theology regards the God-world relation as a fully natural relation is due in part to its panexperientialism. One of the reasons for the decline of theism since the 17th century has been puzzlement as to how a cosmic mind could influence nature, understood in mechanistic or materialistic terms. The God-world problem was to some extent simply the mind-body problem writ large. Panexperientialism, by showing how our minds can influence our bodies, simultaneously shows how a Cosmic Mind could influence the physical world.

14. Although this divine individual, being ubiquitous, exerts influence on all finite events, it cannot fully determine either the inner constitution or the external effects of any of them. Although *creative power*, which is the twofold power to exercise self-determination and then to exert efficient causation on others, is embodied by this divine individual, this twofold power is also embodied by all finite events. The power of the divine individual in the world, accordingly, is the power to evoke and to persuade, never the power to coerce, in the sense of the power unilaterally to determine. This point, in conjunction with the two previous ones, constitutes the heart of Whiteheadian panentheism.

As this brief summary indicates, Whiteheadian process theology is not simple. As Whitehead himself observed, however, all simple theologies "are shipwrecked upon the rock of the problem of evil."[11] This point is central to our topic, because the decline in the belief that our cosmos is *in any sense designed* has surely resulted from the problem of evil as much as from any scientific developments. In any case, given these fourteen Whiteheadian notions, I turn now to the question of whether our universe is designed. I will begin with six senses in which, from a Whiteheadian perspective, our universe is *not* designed.

SIX SENSES IN WHICH OUR UNIVERSE IS NOT DESIGNED

1. *Not created out of absolute nothingness*. Sometimes the assertion that our cosmos or universe is designed means that it was brought into existence *ex nihilo*, with the *nihil* in this phrase taken to mean *absolute nothingness*, so that even the mere fact that there are finite actualities and temporal processes is due to divine design. Process theology rejects this view, holding instead that *our* universe, with its contingent laws of nature, is a particular instantiation of *the* universe, which exists eternally, embodying necessary metaphysical principles.

We can thereby give a "both-and" answer to the long-standing debate, often portrayed as a debate between Jerusalem and Athens, as to whether the universe had a beginning. On the one hand, by understanding "the universe" to mean our particular universe, we can endorse the view, associated with Jerusalem, that the universe had a beginning. On the other hand, by understanding "the universe" to refer to a multiplicity of finite actualities, whether ordered into a cosmos or existing in a state of chaos, we can endorse the idea, associated with Athens (and India), that the universe has always existed.

2. *Not created all at once*. Sometimes the idea that our universe is designed means that it, with all its present species of life, was created all at once, or at least virtually so. Process theology rejects this idea, agreeing instead with the consensus that the present form of our universe has come about through a long evolutionary process.

3. *Not progressively created out of nothing*. Sometimes, as in the thought of Alvin Plantinga and Phillip Johnson,[12] the idea that our universe is designed means that, although our present world came about over billions of years, each new species along the way was created *ex nihilo*. This view is sometimes called "progressive creationism" or, more fashionably, "punctuated creationism." This view is also at the central of the school of thought called "Intelligent Design"—a school that presents a fully supernaturalistic view of design.[13] This view is rejected by process theology, which accepts the evolutionary view that all new biological species have arisen through *descent with modification from prior species*. With regard to the twofold question as to why God created the world in such a simple state and then took so long to bring it to its present state, process theology's answer is that this is the only way that God could create a world.

4. *Not preprogrammed from the outset*. Some theists, such as Rudolf Otto early in the 20th century, have held that, although God has never intervened in the world since its creation, every detail of the evolutionary process was designed, because every evolutionary sequence was preprogrammed.[14] Even the thought of Charles Darwin, with its deism and determinism, implied this, although this implication of Darwin's thinking existed in strong tension with his belief in the contingency of evolutionary developments.[15]

Process theology rejects this notion of deistic design, holding more consistently than did Darwin to the contingency of every development in every evolutionary sequence, grounding this ubiquitous contingency in the doctrine that all individual events involve an element of self-determination. Evolutionary developments thereby involve chance in an ontological, not merely an epistemic, sense. Because the self-determination that exists at the quantum level is magnified, rather than being canceled out, in higher-level individuals, the contingencies increase in the later stages of evolution. The present world cannot, therefore, be considered, even approximately, as simply the inevitable outworking of a situation many billions of years ago, perhaps a Big Bang.[16]

5. *Not created solely for human beings.* Sometimes the idea that
our universe is designed means the anthropocentric notion—held by
William Paley, the utilitarian theologian studied by Darwin—that our
universe was designed solely or at least primarily for the sake of human
beings. According to this notion of design, the value of other species
is their utility for human beings.

Process theology rejects this anthropocentrism, holding instead
that every individual of every species has both intrinsic value, meaning
value in and for itself, and ecological value, meaning value for the eco-
system.[17] These two forms of value would have existed if human beings
had never appeared and will continue to exist after we have departed.

6. *Human beings not inevitable.* Sometimes the idea that our universe is designed means that it was designed to bring forth our own
species, just as it is. Process theology's rejection of this connotation is
implied by its insistence on contingency, rooted in the self-determination that has pervaded the evolutionary process. In the evolutionary
sequence that led to *Homo sapiens*, there were countless contingent
developments. If a different possibility had been actualized in any of
these cases, beings exactly like us would not exist. If a different possibility had been actualized in any of the more crucial cases, no beings
even remotely similar to us would exist.

Now, having discussed several senses in which, from the perspective of process theology, the universe is *not* designed, I turn to two
senses in which it *is*.

Two Senses in Which Our Universe Is Designed

The idea of divine "design" is not one that process theologians naturally
use, because it suggests that the creation of our cosmos came about
in accordance with a detailed blueprint, prepared in advance. But if
we understand the term "design" in a looser sense, to mean that our

universe reflects some sort of purpose, then process theologians *can* speak of our universe as designed, and this in two senses. First, the evolutionary process is viewed as reflecting a divine aim at increasing richness of experience—a directionality that is reflected in the rise of life and then the more complex forms of life. Second, the fact that our universe was able to bring forth life presupposed a basic cosmological order that can, with less qualification, be described as designed. I will discuss these two types of design in order.

1. *A Divine Aim Towards Richness of Experience.* Physicists, we are told, think of our universe as a physics experiment. Whitehead came to regard it as an *aesthetic* experiment, with the physics experiment being simply an aspect of this larger project. To explain: Experience is the only thing that is intrinsically valuable, meaning valuable in and for itself. Every individual, by hypothesis, has at least some slight degree of experience and thereby some slight degree of intrinsic value. But the intrinsic value of the simplest individuals, judged in terms of the aesthetic criteria of harmony, complexity, and intensity of experience, must be extremely trivial, compared with the intrinsic value of a human being, or even a bat. If, as Thomas Nagel has emphasized, we cannot imagine what it is like to be a bat,[18] far less can we imagine what it is like to be an atom, or even an amoeba. But this does not mean that it is not like *something* to be an amoeba, or even an atom.[19]

Compared with the career of a human being or even a squirrel, however, the career of an atom must involve an extremely trivial mode of existence. The divine aim, by hypothesis, has been to bring about conditions that allow for the emergence of individuals with more complex modes of experience and thereby the capacity for greater intrinsic value. This aim is reflected in the increasing complexity that, even allowing for all necessary qualifications, characterizes the evolutionary process.[20]

The *slowness* of this process reflects the fact that the power behind this aim is not omnipotent, in the traditional sense of being the only center of power.[21] Each event, having its own power of self-determination, can resist divinely proffered novel possibilities through which the present situation could be transcended. This present situation is supported, furthermore, by the power of the past, which weighs heavily on the present.

Charles Peirce and William James had suggested that the so-called laws of nature are really its most long-standing habits,[22] which would mean that any type of enduring individual, such as a proton, a DNA molecule, or a living cell, would be a more-or-less long-standing habit. Peirce held that the longer a habit persists, the stronger it tends to become. This idea led him to the conclusion that our universe would become increasingly deterministic, as the habits of nature became stronger and stronger, thereby imposing themselves more and more heavily on the present.

Whitehead, while endorsing the idea that the laws of nature are habits,[23] avoided the idea of increasing determinism partly by means of his doctrine of the divine reality as constantly presenting alternative possibilities. This divine influence, however, cannot unilaterally determine either what new possibility, if any, will be evoked or when this development will occur, because the divine evocative power is always competing with the power of the past as embodied in the habits of enduring individuals. It may take, accordingly, thousands, millions, or even billions of years for an alternative possibility to be evoked into existence.

Although this hypothesis is consistent with both the tempo and the direction of the evolutionary process, it might be thought that it goes against a scientifically established *randomness* in the process. But the idea that all variations are "random" has more than one meaning. I have already endorsed one possible meaning, which is that variations involve chance in the ontological sense, an idea that Darwin himself and some neo-Darwinists have rejected. A meaning that many neo-Darwinists do insist upon is that variations are random in every other possible sense, which would exclude their being due even in the slightest to any sort of aim that would give a bias toward variations of a particular sort, such as variations that lead to greater structural complexity and greater richness of experience.

But the neo-Darwinian insistence that evolution is random in *this* sense is simply philosophical dogma, not grounded in any empirical discovery. The randomness that is central to neo-Darwinism as a *scientific* theory is randomness in a third sense,[24] according to which there is no tendency for variations to be adaptational, that is, advantageous for survival in the environment in which they occur.

The kind of tendency that process theology posits is not in conflict with randomness in this strict sense, because there is no necessary correlation between increased richness of experience and success in the struggle for survival. To give a human example: The emergence of the capacity to do higher mathematics, while it may have increased the satisfaction of some early human beings on the savannas of Africa, would not have increased the likelihood of their sowing their wild genes. The criterion of greater richness of experience is not in tension with neo-Darwinian randomness, except insofar as this randomness is used as a pseudo-scientific front for antitheistic bias.

The divine aim towards greater richness of experience means that there is, in spite of what I said earlier about the contingency of human beings, a sense in which we can regard ourselves as intended. That is, insofar as human experience involves dimensions that give it the capacity for greater intrinsic value than that enjoyed by our evolutionary predecessors, we can say that we reflect the divine aim. Although human beings as such were not intended, human-*like* beings—meaning beings with the capacity to actualize high-level values—*were* intended, insofar as they were possible. This would mean that, on other planets with the conditions for life to emerge and to evolve for many billions of years, we should expect there to be some with creatures that, no matter how different in physical constitution and appearance, would share some of our capacities, such as those for mathematics, music, and morality, or, more generally, truth, beauty, and goodness.

These capacities, however, imply the capacities for falsehood, for ugliness, and for immorality, such as genocide and ecological destruction. Must we not conclude, therefore, that the divine individual of process theology is as responsible for evil as was the deity of traditional theism? It is true that process theology's deity is responsible for evil in one sense—namely, that if human beings had not been evoked into existence, the world would have been free from all the evils caused and experienced by human beings. The question of theodicy, however, is whether the divine reality is responsible in such a way as to be *indictable*, that is, blameworthy.

With regard to this question, process theism differs from traditional theism in two crucial respects. In the first place, given the omnipotence attributed to the deity of traditional theism, that deity could have created beings who were identical to us in virtually all respects, having the capacity for realizing most of the values we enjoy, differing only by having much less, or even no, power to bring about evil. Because this traditional deity created our world *ex nihilo*, all the principles of our world were freely chosen. There were no metaphysical principles lying in the nature of things, beyond divine volition.

In process theology, by contrast, such principles do exist, and one of these principles is that an increase in the capacity for richness of experience is impossible without a correlative increase in freedom and the power to affect other beings. This principle means that every increase in the capacity for good entails an equal increase in the capacity for evil. Any being with our capacities to experience and create good, therefore, would necessarily have our capacities to experience and cause evil. Insofar as we think of the divine individual as confronting a choice with regard to the existence of human-like beings, the choice was only between having beings approximately like us, with our capacities for evil as well as for good, or no human-like beings whatsoever. The deity of process theology could be indicted because of human evil, therefore, only by those who could honestly say that our planet would have been better without human-like beings altogether.

A second crucial difference between the two types of theism is that, according to traditional theism, every instance of evil that has occurred could have been unilaterally prevented by God. One version of traditional theism, to be sure, says that God gave us genuine freedom, so that we can freely choose to do evil.[25] It remains the case, however, that the deity of traditional theism could always intervene either to determine our decisions or to cancel out the natural effects thereof—hence the strong hostility to theism by many morally sensitive people

In process theism, by contrast, the divine power cannot do either of these. Although the human degree of freedom would not exist if the divine power had not led the evolutionary process to bring human beings into existence, now that we do exist the divine power cannot cancel out our power to make our own decisions and to inflict them on others. The sense of meaning that comes from seeing the evolutionary process as divinely influenced is not, therefore, undermined or rendered horrible by the conclusion that the "divine" influence is indifferent or even demonic.[26]

2. The Establishment of the Most Fundamental Contingent Principles of Our Cosmic Epoch. I conclude by briefly explaining the second sense in which process theology can regard our universe as designed. This second sense involves the much-discussed idea that our universe from the outset evidently embodied a number of "cosmic constants" that give the impression of being finely tuned in relation to each other, because if any of them were slightly different, life could never have evolved. These constant constants, furthermore, do not seem to be simply "habits," as usually understood—that is, to be modes of behavior that have developed gradually and are only usually, rather than always, followed.[27]

Some traditional theists have used this fact as new evidence that our universe is the product of Omnipotent Intelligence. Such theists might argue that, even if process theism, with its non-omnipotent deity, can do justice to the world's evil, it cannot do justice to the best scientific account of how our universe originated. A divine being whose power can be resisted by the creatures could not, they might argue, have imposed all of these mathematical values with sufficient precision to pull off an initial creative event, such as a Big Bang, that would bring about all the conditions necessary for life in portions of the resulting universe. Although that conclusion might at first glance seem to follow from what I have said, I argue that it does not.

Purely persuasive divine influence could bring about such an initial event because, in a chaotic state prior to the beginning of our cosmic epoch, the two reasons why there is usually so much resistance to divine persuasion would not apply. One of these reasons is that, as the evolutionary process increasingly brings forth more complex individuals, the world thereby has creatures with increasingly greater capacity for self-determination and thereby increasingly greater capacity to resist divine influence. In a chaotic state between cosmic epochs, however, the events would be extremely trivial, with a vanishingly small capacity to exercise self-determination.

The second reason why divine influence usually encounters so much resistance is that the divine intention to instill new ideals, meaning new possible modes of being and interacting, is usually in competition with the power of the past, the modes of being that constitute the essence of enduring individuals. However, in the postulated chaos between the running down of one cosmic epoch and the starting up of another, there would, by definition, be no enduring individuals, therefore no entrenched modes of being to force themselves upon present events. The chaos would not be absolute, to be sure, because events would still exemplify the *metaphysical* principles, which by definition obtain in all possible worlds, including the relatively chaotic periods between cosmic epochs. But there would be no contingent *cosmological* principles constituting well-entrenched habits. In this situation, therefore, the divine influence, in seeking to get a set of contingent principles embodied in our universe, would have no competition from any other contingent principles.

In the first instant of the creation of a particular universe, accordingly, divine evocative power could produce quasi-coercive effects. A divine spirit, brooding over the chaos, would only have to think "Let there be X!"—with X standing for the finely tuned set of contingent principles embodied in our world at the outset.

To say this is *not* to suggest that this effect would necessarily have occurred immediately. It is also not to deny the possibility that our universe might have been preceded by a number of brief universes, which were not sufficiently fine-tuned to last very long. (Like many physics experiments, the physics part of this divine experiment may have had to be carried out more than once before it succeeded, not because of any impotence on the part of the divine experimenter, but because of the iota of self-determination in the materials.) But it *is* to suggest an alternative to the three major ways of thinking of the laws of physics of our universe: that they are necessary, that they exist purely by chance, or that they are the product of an Omnipotent Designer.

This alternative possibility is that a creator without coercive power could, in a chaotic situation, produce *quasi*-coercive effects. From then on, however, the divine persuasive activity would always face competition from the power embodied in the modes of being reflecting these contingent principles, so that divine power would never again, as long as the cosmic epoch exists, be able to produce quasi-coercive effects. In this way, process theism, while maintaining that God's agency *in* our universe is always persuasive, can nevertheless account for the remarkable contingent order *on* which our particular universe is based. This suggestion, I should add, will not be found in Whitehead's writings. But it does seem consistent with his position.

SUMMARY AND CONCLUSION

Although Whiteheadian process theology, with its panentheistic vision of reality, shares with late modern thought the rejection of many of the senses in which our universe had traditionally been thought to be designed, it can speak of our universe as designed in two significant senses. In doing so, furthermore, it can arguably do justice to the best scientific evidence about cosmic and biological evolution without being undermined by the horrendous evils that have resulted from the creation of life, especially human life.

The way in which process panentheism avoids the traditional problem of evil is explained more fully in the following chapter.

NOTES

1. The idea of indeterminacy in quantum physics came as a great shock to many physicists and philosophers, given the long-held assumption that the world—at least the "physical world"—is a fully deterministic system, so that an omniscient being, knowing all the facts about the present state of the world, would be able perfectly to predict all of its future states. Many physicists and philosophers, still clinging to this belief, have held that the indeterminacy revealed by quantum physics is a purely epistemic matter, meaning that it is simply a matter of

the human inability to know the present state of the world perfectly. Whitehead's view was that the indeterminacy is also ontological, rooted in the nature of the world, so that even an omniscient being could not know the future.

2. See Hartshorne, "The Compound Individual," in *Philosophical Essays for Alfred North Whitehead*, ed. Otis H. Lee (New York: Longmans Green, 1936), 193-220; reprinted in Hartshorne, *Whitehead's Philosophy: Selected Essays 1935-1970* (Lincoln: University of Nebraska Press, 1972), 41-61. I have discussed this idea in "Compound Individuals and Freedom," Chap. 9 of my *Unsnarling the World-Knot: Consciousness,* Freedom, and the Mind-Body Problem* (Berkeley: University of California Press, 1998; reprint, Eugene: Wipf and Stock, 2008).

3. I have discussed the allegation that panexperientialism (usually discussed under the term "panpsychism") is implausible in "Fully Naturalizing the Mind: The Neglected Alternative," Chap. 7 of *Unsnarling the World-Knot.*

4. The theological and sociological motives behind the modern notion of matter as inert and insentient are discussed in "Religion and the Rise of the Modern Scientific Worldview," Chap. 5 of my *Religion and Scientific Naturalism.*

5. See *Unsnarling the World-Knot,* especially Chaps. 6, 8, and 9.

6. See the Introduction to David Ray Griffin, ed., *Physics and the Ultimate Significance of Time: Bohm, Prigogine, and Process Philosophy* (Albany: State University of New York Press, 1986), and my "Time in Process Philosophy," *KronoScope: Journal for the Study of Time* 1/1-2 (2001): 75-99.

7. On the fact that the doctrine of *creatio ex nihilo* is not a biblical doctrine, see the following chapter.

8. Whitehead does share one of the presuppositions that view, which is the assumption that time is a relational matter: that there could be

no time apart from actual entities that are involved in temporal, time-generating processes. But he rejects the other assumption, which is that there was state in which there were no actual entities, or at least no actual entities engaged in time-generating processes. Whitehead's view is that there have always been actual occasions, and that these prehend prior occasions and are in turn prehended by succeeding occasions.

9. For arguments for the existence of a divine reality as conceived by Whiteheadian process theology, see "Natural Theology Based on Naturalistic Theism," Chap. 5 of my *Reenchantment without Supernaturalism*. For my argument that this reality should be understood, with Charles Hartshorne, as an everlasting *temporal society* of actual entities, rather than, with Whitehead himself, as a single everlasting actual entity, see "Naturalistic Dipolar Theism," which is Chap. 4 of the same book.

10. In speaking of "loving kindness" and "compassion," I am using Buddhist terminology for what Whitehead calls God's "primordial nature" and "consequent nature," respectively. I elsewhere have used the more Christian language of "creative love" and "responsive love" ("God as Creative and Responsive Love," Chap. 3 of Cobb and Griffin, *Process Theology*). Implicit in this ascription of compassion or responsive love to God is, of course, a rejection of traditional Christian theism's acceptance of the idea that God is wholly "impassible," hence devoid of sympathy or compassion for the world.

11. Alfred North Whitehead, *Religion in the Making* (New York: Fordham University Press, 1996 [reprint of 1926 edition]), 77. I have summarized my own Whiteheadian solution to the problem of evil in the following chapter.

12. See note 7 of Chapter 2, above.

13. See William A. Dembski and Michael Behe, *Intelligent Design: The Bridge between Science and Theology* (Downers Grove Ill: Intervarsity, 1999); William A. Dembski and Charles W. Colson, *The Design Revolution: Answering the Toughest Questions about Intelligent Design*

(Downers Grove, Ill: Intervarsity, 2004); William A Dembski and Jonathan Wells, *The Design of Life: Discovering Signs of Intelligence in Biology* (Foundation for Thought and Ethics, 2007); and William A. Dembski and Jonathan Wells, *Intelligent Design Uncensored: An Easy-to-Understand Guide to the Controversy* (IVP Books, 2010).

14. See Rudolf Otto, *Naturalism and Religion* (London: Williams & Norgate; New York: G. P. Putnam's, 1907) and "Darwinism and Religion," in Otto, *Religious Essays: A Supplement to "The Idea of the Holy,"* trans. Brian Lunn (London: Humphrey Milford, 1931), 121-39. I have discussed Otto's position in "Harmonizing Science and Religion: Three Alternative Approaches," Chap. 3 of *Religion and Scientific Naturalism*.

15. On Darwin's deism and determinism, see "Creation and Evolution," Chap. 8 of *Religion and Scientific Naturalism*.

16. In *A Brief History of Time: From the Big Bang to Black Holes* (New York: Bantam, 1988), Stephen Hawking, while giving up the older ideal of a completely deterministic science, still said that the goal of science should be "the discovery of laws that will enable us to predict events up to the limits set by the uncertainty principle" (173). He evidently held, furthermore, those limits to be purely human, epistemic limits, as he suggested that we can "still imagine that there is a set of laws that determines events completely for some supernatural being, who could observe the present state of the universe without disturbing it" (55).

17. I have developed this distinction, showing its relevance to the debate about the "egalitarianism of value," in "Whitehead's Deeply Ecological Worldview," published in Mary Evelyn Tucker and John Grim, eds., *Worldviews and Ecology: Religion, Philosophy, and the Environment* (Maryknoll: Orbis Books, 1994). This essay has been reprinted, in slightly revised form, in Griffin, *Whitehead's Radically Different Postmodern Philosophy: An Argument for Its Contemporary Relevance* (Albany: SUNY Press, 2007).

18. Nagel's "What Is It Like to Be a Bat?" is contained in his *Mortal Questions* (London: Cambridge University Press, 1979).

19. This more radical question was broached, Whitehead points out, by Leibniz. Whereas Lucretius and Newton told us "what an atom looks like to others," Leibniz "explained what it must be like to be an atom" (*Adventures of Ideas* [1933; New York: Free Press, 1967], 132).

20. For discussions of whether we can speak of progress in the evolutionary process, see Matthew H. Nitecki, *Evolutionary Progress* (Chicago & London: University of Chicago Press, 1988). I have discussed this issue in "Creation and Evolution," Chap. 8 of my *Religion and Scientific Naturalism.*

21. It might be objected that this was not traditional theism's view, because it held that God had voluntarily given power to the creatures, including the power of self-determination to human beings. That, however, is just the point—that the creatures were said to have power only by virtue of a voluntary gift. Power belonged essentially—by essence—only to God. In process theism, by contrast, power belongs by essence both to God and to the world. The fact that we human beings have such a high degree of power *is* due to God, because without God's stimulation of the evolutionary process over billions of years, no high-grade creatures such as us would exist. But the fact that there is a world of actual entities with *some* power is not contingent upon a divine decision.

22. See William James, *The Principles of Psychology* (New York: Dover, 1950), I: 104-05, and Peter Ochs, "Charles Sanders Peirce," 67-68, 73-75.

23. Alfred North Whitehead, *Modes of Thought* (1938; New York: Free Press 1968), 154.

24. I have discussed these different meanings of "randomness" in *Religion and Scientific Naturalism*, 252-53.

25. I have compared process theism and traditional free-will theism with regard to their adequacy for Christian faith in "Process Theology and the Christian Good News: A Response to Classical Free Will Theism," in John B. Cobb, Jr., and Clark H. Pinnock, eds., *Searching*

for an Adequate God: A Dialogue between Process and Free Will Theists (Grand Rapids: Eerdmans, 2000), 1-38.

26. Antitheists sometimes charge that revisionary theists can overcome the problem of evil only by revising the conventional understanding of theism so drastically that the resulting position is no longer intelligibly called "theism," because the resulting referent of the word "God" has been redefined out of all recognition. That charge does indeed apply to many modern theologies (see my discussion in *God and Religion in the*✈ *Postmodern World* (Albany: State University of New York Press, 1989), 58-61). However, I have argued, this charge does not apply to process theism, because the deity of process theism embodies all the features of what can be called the "generic idea of God" in cultures primarily shaped by biblically-based religions (*Evil Revisited*, 10-12).

27. See, however, the evidence summarized in Rupert Sheldrake, *Seven Experiments That Could Change the World: A Do-It-Yourself Guide to Revolutionary Science* (London, Fourth Estate, 1994), that some of things that have been considered cosmic constants, such as the gravitational force, show signs of slight fluctuations. This evidence lends support to the thesis that all of the (contingent) laws of nature are habits, which Sheldrake supported in "The Laws of Nature as Habits: Postmodern Basis for Science," in David Ray Griffin, ed., *The Reenchantment of Science: Postmodern Proposals* (Albany: State University of New York Press, 1988: 79-86); *The Presence of the Past: Morphic Resonance and the Habits of Nature* (New York: Times Books, 1988); an expanded version, published as *Morphic Resonance: The Nature of Formative Causation* (Park Street Press, 2009); and "Are the Laws of Nature Fixed?" Chap. 3 of *The Science Delusion: Freeing the Spirit of Enquiry* (Philadelphia: Coronet Books, 2012). Confirmation of this evidence for slight fluctuations would mean that there are no exceptions to the idea that all features of our world, beyond its strictly metaphysical principles, have resulted from divine-creaturely co-operation. That is, our particular cosmic epoch would still presuppose divinely fine-tuned "constants" established at the outset,

but these "constants" would leave room for slight variations, so that the exact values at any time would be settled by the world.

The notion of the "fine-tuning" of the "constant contents" of the universe has been fiercely debated. See, for example, John Gribbin and Martin Rees, *Cosmic Coincidences: Dark Matter, Mankind, and Anthropic Cosmology* (Bantam, 1989); Richard Swinburne, "Argument from the Fine-Tuning of the Universe," in *Physical Cosmology and Philosophy*, ed. John Leslie (Collier Macmillan), 154–73. Luke A. Barnes, "The Fine-Tuning of the Universe for Intelligent Life," Cornell University Library, 11 June 2012; David H. Bailey, "What Is the Cosmological Constant Paradox, and What Is Its Significance?" Sciencemeetsreligion.org, 1 January 2014.

CHAPTER FOUR

Panentheism and the Problem of Evil

I n the previous chapters, I have touched repeatedly on the problem of evil. This problem, as illustrated by the fact that I found it necessary to refer to it repeatedly, has been one of the major reasons for the decline in the belief in divine activity—a reason at least equal in importance with the fact that naturalism$_{sam}$ has become equated with the scientific worldview. No discussion of divine activity can be complete, therefore, without a direct and extensive treatment of evil—understood most broadly as any things or occurrences that are less good than they might have been.

Things that are "less good than they might have been" can at times, of course, be unspeakably horrible. Evils are of two basic kinds: Evils caused by human beings, and evils that are not produced by human agency, usually called "natural evils." Evils of either type can be horrendous.

It might be argued that so-called natural evil, such as suffering caused by earthquakes, hurricanes, and tornadoes, is not really evil, because, one might argue: "Earthquakes, hurricanes, and tornadoes are not evil. They are simply inevitable consequences of the way in which our world was created—probably the only way. Likewise, the sufferings produced in humans and other sentient creatures by earthquakes and other natural processes also cannot be called evil, because such sufferings became inevitable once sentient beings were created."

This argument would be sound from the perspective of atheism or any other naturalistic perspective. But from the perspective of traditional theology, the world was created by a Divine Creator who has unlimited power, and hence could have created a world that (a) has human beings and other sentient creatures but (b) contains no earthquakes, hurricanes, or tornadoes—or any other "natural" processes that would produce great death and destruction. From that perspective, the sufferings produced by earthquakes and other natural processes are indeed evil, because they cannot be justified as necessary.

Traditional theism, therefore, is inconsistent: The world is said to be the creation of a good and omnipotent creator; but things happen that such a being would not allow; the position, accordingly, cannot possibly be true. In the present chapter, I argue that Whitehead's panentheism, which has previously been shown to conform to scientific naturalism$_{ns}$, also, by virtue of that very fact, provides a concept of divine activity that is not falsified by the horrendous evils of our world. I will also document in some detail the historical point, mentioned earlier, that panentheism's rejection of the traditional doctrine of *creatio ex nihilo* is, far from being a rejection of the biblical view, a return to it. I will, indeed, begin with this latter point.

CREATION OUT OF CHAOS OR CREATIO EX NIHILO

"When God began to create the heaven and the earth, the world was without form and void." According to most scholars of the Hebrew Bible, this is the best translation of Genesis 1: 1-2a.[1] Most Bibles, however, have translated it, "In the beginning God created the heaven and the earth. The earth was without form and void." The latter rendition, by indicating that the earth's being "without form and void" comes *after* God's initial creative activity, suggests that our universe was created *ex nihilo*. The former rendering suggests a version of the view articulated not only in most cosmogonies of the Ancient Near East but also in Plato's *Timaeus*, namely, that our universe was created out of a primeval chaos.

These alternative ways of understanding the origin of our universe suggest different conceptions of divine power. "Creation out of chaos" suggests that the "material" from which our world was created had some power of its own, so that it would not be wholly subject to the divine will. Plato explicitly makes this point, saying that the creator willed that everything should be good "as far as possible."[2] By contrast, the idea that our universe was created out of nothing suggests the doctrine that the divine creator is absolutely omnipotent. This doctrine often, to accommodate Genesis 1:1-2, involves a "two-stage" theory, according to which God first created the raw material out of nothing, then used it to create our world.

According to this view, the basic elements of the world, owing their existence wholly to the creator's will, would have no *inherent* power with which to offer any resistance. This understanding is expressed by Millard Erickson, a contemporary Calvinist theologian, who says:

> God did not work with something which was in existence. He brought into existence the very raw material which he employed. If this were not the case, God would . . . have been limited by having to work with the intrinsic characteristics of the raw material which he employed.[3]

Erickson's view, that God is *not* limited by anything, is expressed in his conviction that "God's will is never frustrated. What he chooses to do, he accomplishes."[4]

The difference between these two views is crucial for the question whether the world's evil is compatible with the idea that it is the product of a perfectly good creator. The idea of divine power suggested by *creatio ex nihilo* makes it difficult to give an affirmative answer. If, as Erickson says, God's will is never frustrated, then the Jewish Holocaust, in which millions of Jews were murdered, must ultimately have been in harmony with the divine will. It was Jewish theologian Richard

Rubenstein's realization of this point that led him to declare that *After Auschwitz* no Jew—and, by implication, no person who is morally sensitive—should believe in the God who determines the course of history.[5] The idea of creation out of chaos, by contrast, suggests that the creatures have some power that is not fully controllable by divine power, so that we should not expect the course of history to wholly reflect the divine will.

The theodicy developed in this essay is a version of this latter view. I hope that it will be found helpful by Jews, Muslims, and Christians, as well as members of other theistic traditions. It is widely assumed, however, that such a theodicy should be considered unacceptable by adherents of the biblically based religions, because the doctrine that our universe was created out of absolutely nothing is the biblical position. In the first section, I will show otherwise. In the second section, I will suggest that the doctrine of creation out of absolute nothingness makes a satisfactory solution to the problem of evil impossible. In the final section, I will lay out a theodicy based on the philosophy of Whitehead, who returned to the idea of creation out of chaos, which had been affirmed by Plato and, unbeknownst to Whitehead, the Bible and many early Christian theologians.

THE ORIGIN OF THE DOCTRINE OF CREATIO EX NIHILO

Although it has been widely assumed that the doctrine of *creatio ex nihilo* is the biblical doctrine, or is at least reflected in some biblical passages, this view is now rejected by leading scholars. I will here employ the books of two such scholars, Jon Levenson's *Creation and the Persistence of Evil* and Gerhard May's *Creatio Ex Nihilo.*[6]

CREATIO EX NIHILO NOT A BIBLICAL DOCTRINE

If "properly understood," says Levenson, Genesis 1:1-2:3 "cannot be invoked in support of the developed Jewish, Christian, and Muslim

doctrine of *creatio ex nihilo*."[7] One problem with the traditional translation of the opening verse—"In the beginning God created the heaven
and the earth"—is that later verses say that the heaven was created on
the second day, the earth on the third.[8] This inconsistency, Levenson
points out, is removed if the first verse is taken as a temporal clause,
"When God began to create the heaven and the earth," and the second
verse as saying that the world was then a formless waste.[9] Another
count against the idea that Genesis 1 implies *creatio ex nihilo* is the fact
that the waters and the darkness are not said to have been created.[10]

With regard to the Hebrew Bible more generally, Levenson argues
that the assumption that it is based on the idea of *creatio ex nihilo*
has led to the distorted, overly optimistic, view that God is in complete control.[11] "The persistence of evil" in the title of Levenson's book
reflects the idea that chaos was only circumscribed, not annihilated,
with the result that it constantly threatens to erupt.[12]

Gerhard May also argues, independently of Levenson,[13] that the
doctrine of *creatio ex nihilo* is nowhere to be found in the Hebrew
Bible. Because that judgment is now commonplace, far more important is May's conclusion that this doctrine is also not found in inter-
testamental Judaism. The main evidence for the contrary view has
always been 2 Maccabees 7:28, which says that God created the world
and humanity "out of non-being."

May argues, however, that this formula does not necessarily imply
creatio ex nihilo in the strict sense.[14] In the fourth-century B.C.E., for
example, the Greek philosopher Xenophon said that parents "bring
forth their children out of non-being," and in the first century C.E., the
Hellenistic Jewish philosopher Philo spoke of God as creating "out of
non-being," even though Philo accepted the existence of a pre-existent
matter alongside God.[15] The formula *creatio ex nihilo*, in other words,
was simply an "unreflective, everyday way of saying that through the
act of creation something arose which did not previously exist."[16] As

such, it did not imply the doctrine of *creatio ex nihilo* in the strict sense, according to which the very stuff of which this world is composed was itself created out of nothing (which is the sense in which *creatio ex nihilo* will be used in the remainder of this chapter).

This denial that *creatio ex nihilo* was developed in the pre-Christian Jewish tradition is especially important, because many scholars have argued that "primitive Christianity found the doctrine ready-made in the Jewish tradition," so that "[o]ne would be able to presuppose it for the New Testament."[17] On this basis, several passages in the New Testament, such as John 1:3, Romans 4:17, Colossians 1:16, and Hebrew 11:3, have been taken as evidence that the doctrine of *creatio ex nihilo* was held by first-century Christians. Having undermined this basis, May argues that neither these nor any other passages in the New Testament provide evidence for this doctrine.[18] May's testimony is especially important because he cannot be suspected of slanting the biblical evidence to support his own position.

THE DOCTRINE OF *CREATIO EX NIHILO* NOT NECESSITATED BY CHRISTIAN FAITH

May's own position is that, although the doctrine of *creatio ex nihilo* is nowhere explicitly formulated in the Bible, it is implicit in the biblical view, in the sense that once biblically-based thinkers were exposed to the Greek idea that our world was formed by the creator out of some pre-existent stuff, the doctrine of *creatio ex nihilo* was seen to be necessary to protect the biblical view of divine power.[19]

The exposure to this Greek idea came in the form of Middle Platonism, according to which, although the *ordered* cosmos originated in time, there are "three principles"—namely, God, the Ideas, and Matter—that are co-eternal.[20] May's contention is that "as soon as Christian thought engaged in a critical debate with the philosophical doctrine of principles," the contrary doctrine of *creatio ex nihilo* "sooner or later had to be drawn from the biblical belief in creation."[21]

May's contention, however, begs the question of *why* Christian thinkers came to engage in "critical debate" with Middle Platonism's doctrine
of principles. Although May claims that the rejection of the Platonic
doctrine of principles in favor of the doctrine of *creatio ex nihilo* reflected
an "inner necessity,"[22] this claim is contradicted by his own account.

One problem with May's claim is that the idea of creation out of
chaos was accepted by Jewish thinkers for many centuries. Nothing in
May's account challenges Levenson's view that creation out of chaos was
the standard Hebraic position. May points out, furthermore, that the
theology of Hellenistic Judaism in general, and of Philo in particular, saw
no contradiction between the biblical doctrine of God's power and "the
acceptance of a matter that had not originated in time."[23] May points out,
in fact, that *creatio ex nihilo* was not accepted by Jewish thinkers until
the Middle Ages.[24] May's contention that the Platonic view contradicts
the true biblical view can be maintained only by means of the question-
begging claim that these Jewish thinkers were insufficiently critical.[25]

Although May believes that Christian thinkers had reason to be
more critical,[26] he points out that many second-century theologians
who were considered "orthodox" by later standards—including Justin
Martyr, Athenagoras, and Clement of Alexandria—held that the "acceptance of an unformed matter was entirely reconcilable with biblical
monotheism."[27] Justin even argued that Plato "took over the doctrine
that God made the cosmos out of unoriginate matter from the opening verses of Genesis."[28] May contends that when Christian theologians
finally developed the doctrine of *creatio ex nihilo*, they did so "partly
to express opposition" to Middle Platonism.[29] But if there had been
something about Middle Platonism as such that was antithetical to the
monotheism of the Bible in general and Christian faith in particular,
we should expect opposition to have been expressed from the outset.

May's own account shows that, when some Christian theologians began rejecting the idea of creation out of chaos in the latter

part of the second century, they did so because of the threat raised by Marcion's version of gnosticism.[30] Besides accepting the eternity of matter, Marcion regarded it as *evil*. Our world is filled with evil, argued Marcion, because it was formed out of evil matter by the Hebrew Bible's creator-God, who is different from the supreme God revealed in Jesus.[31] Marcion thereby contradicted not only the monotheism of Christian faith but its view of the world as *essentially* good, only contingently evil. As May points out, it was because of Marcion that the church not only began to fence itself off from heretical tendencies but also to include among those tendencies the idea that our world was created out of unformed matter.[32]

Endorsing this inclusion, May says: "Marcion's teaching that matter and the world created from it were bad and hateful could only make it obvious in an impressive way what dangerous dualistic consequences could develop from the philosophical doctrine of the pre-existence of matter."[33] The phrase to emphasize here is "*could* develop." That philosophical doctrine did not *necessarily* have any "dangerous dualistic consequences."

May himself points out, in fact, that most philosophers who affirmed the existence of uncreated matter defined it as being "without qualities," so that it could not coherently be said to be essentially either good *or* evil.[34] Marcion's idea that matter is essentially evil was, far from being a logical implication from the idea of formless matter, actually an *incoherent addition* to it. Thanks to Marcion, nevertheless, the idea of uncreated matter became subject to guilt by association, with the result that Christian theologians began attacking the idea of uncreated matter as such.[35]

HERMOGENES: THE UNRECOGNIZED HERO OF CHRISTIAN FAITH

The Platonic Christian theologian who was the primary victim of this development was Hermogenes, who otherwise might be recognized as one of the greatest Christian thinkers of the period. Hermogenes, May points out, was "emphatically anxious to ensure the absolute goodness of the creator God."[36] In employing the idea of unoriginate matter, his primary concern was to explain the origin of evil in a way that protected that absolute goodness.[37] Although Hermogenes' own writings are no longer extant, his basic idea seems to have been that "the ground of the evil present in the world" is "the trace of the original disorder of matter remaining in every created thing."[38]

If, by contrast, we supposed God to have created our world out of nothing, Hermogenes held, we could have no coherent explanation, "because as perfect Goodness [God] could only have created good, so the origin of evil would not be explained."[39] The idea of *creatio ex nihilo*, by saying that God is the source of literally everything, including evil, would threaten the perfect goodness of God.

Besides showing that the doctrine of creation out of chaos protected the absolute goodness of the Creator, Hermogenes argued that it was otherwise perfectly acceptable from the perspective of Christian faith. His contention that Genesis 1:2 supported creation out of chaos followed, May points out, "a widespread expository tradition."[40] Also, far from regarding matter itself as evil, Hermogenes pointed out that "matter before its ordering is without qualities" and therefore "neither good nor evil."[41]

If Hermogenes' theology is to be called "dualistic," therefore, it was clearly not the Manichean, Marcionite type of dualism. It was not even dualistic in a weaker sense: "Hermogenes emphatically declared that matter cannot be a principle of equal rank ontologically with God. God is Lord over matter."[42] Apart from the polemical, fencing-off mind-set created by the Marcionite episode, accordingly, there was evidently nothing in Hermogenes' position that would have provoked charges of heresy.

As it was, however, "When Hermogenes put forward his ideas, literary polemic against him seems to have begun almost immediately."[43]

May's account shows that Hermogenes' position never had a chance:

> In the last decades of the second century the process by which
> the Catholic Church fenced itself off from the gnostic heretics
> was in full swing, and with it there was a critical reaction against
> philosophical reinterpretations of Christian doctrine and espe-
> cially against all forms of intellectual syncretism. In this histori-
> cal situation a synthesis of Christianity and Platonism, such as
> Hermogenes was attempting, could no longer be pursued; to
> undertake it was, in the atmosphere of anti-gnostic theology,
> immediately to incur the verdict of heresy.[44]

The reverse side of this rejection of Platonic Christianity was the
adoption of the fateful doctrine of creation out of nothing: "Theophilus
of Antioch, the earliest opponent of Hermogenes, is the first church
theologian known to us—and this is certainly no accident—to use
unambiguously the substance and the terminology of the doctrine of
creatio ex nihilo."[45] Theophilus's polemical writings on this issue influenced not only Hippolytus and Tertullian,[46] but probably also Irenaeus,
the other founder—along with Theophilus himself—"of the church
doctrine of *creatio ex nihilo*."[47] This rejection of creation out of chaos,
which had been the understanding of the biblical tradition for over a
millennium, occurred very suddenly: "For Tertullian and Hippolytus
it is already the fixed Christian position that God created the world
out of absolutely nothing."[48]

Given the context and suddenness of this change, we should ask
if it was precipate. In spite of being in favor of the change, May makes
many comments that suggest that its implications were insufficiently
thought through. For example, after pointing out that the doctrine
of *creatio ex nihilo*, "which removes all restrictions on God's creative
activity by declaring the free decision of God's will [to be] the sole
ground of creation," was bound to make the biblical concept of God "a
philosophical problem," May adds: "But this is a question far beyond

Theophilus."[49] Also, May does praise Irenaeus' rejection of the Platonic view that God can only will "the best possible," in favor of the "the absolute freedom and omnipotence of the biblical God," which "must rule and dominate in everything" so that "everything else must give way to it."[50] And yet May adds: "Beyond the demands of the controversy with gnosticism cosmological questions scarcely worried Irenaeus." And May adds that Iranaeus' position was "only attainable because Irenaeus is quite unaware of philosophical problems."[51]

The move to the doctrine of creation out of absolute nothingness, I suggest, *was* precipitate. It was spearheaded by theologians who, besides being uninterested in taking a circumspect view because of their single-minded focus on the threat from Marcionite gnosticism, they were perhaps intellectually unequipped to do so. Moreover, their adoption of *creatio ex nihilo* was made without due regard to the warning by Hermogenes about the threat to Christian faith implicit in this doctrine: the threat to the perfect goodness of God.

The history of theodicy would bear out the warning of Hermogenes that, if God is said to have created the world out of absolute nothingness, the origin of evil cannot be explained, at least without implying that God's goodness is less than perfect.

CREATIO EX NIHILO *AND TRADITIONAL THEISM'S PROBLEM OF EVIL*

In line with widespread usage, I use the term "traditional theism" to refer to the doctrine of God as a personal being whose attributes include not only perfect goodness but also omnipotence (all-powerfulness), with the nature of this omnipotence clarified by the assertion that this divine being created our universe out of absolute nothingness. A central question of critics of this doctrine is whether the perfect goodness is contradicted by the implications of the omnipotence in light of the world's evil. This "problem of evil" can be formulated thus:

1. God is, by definition, omnipotent and perfectly good.

2. Being omnipotent, God *could* unilaterally prevent all evil.

3. Being perfectly good, God would *want* to prevent all evil.

4. However, evil does occur.

5. Therefore, God (thus defined) does not exist.

The special difficulty created for traditional theism by its acceptance of the doctrine of *creatio ex nihilo* is indicated by the word "unilaterally" in the second premise. Without that doctrine, the idea that God is *all*-powerful could be taken to mean, for example, that God is the only being who exerts power over all other things; that God is the *supreme* power of the universe, far more powerful than anything else; or even that God is *perfect* in power, having all the power that it is *possible* for one being to have.

None of these definitions would entail that God essentially has *all* the power in the universe, so that any power possessed by any other beings would be wholly derivative from, and thereby wholly controllable by, God's power. Accordingly, any or all of these conceptions of "divine omnipotence" could be held without implying that God could *unilaterally* prevent all evil. Evil could be explained, as Hermogenes suggested, in terms of power to resist the divine will inherent in the creatures, a power that they have by virtue of the "primordial stuff" from which they were made.

The doctrine of *creatio ex nihilo*, however, closes off that option by implying that (1) the creatures have no inherent power with which to offer any resistance to the divine will, and that (2) there are no metaphysical principles, inherent in the nature of things, descriptive of the kinds of relations that necessarily obtain either between God and the creatures, or among the creatures themselves.

These two implications lie behind the traditional doctrine of omnipotence, according to which God can unilaterally bring about any possible state of affairs, providing that such states of affairs do not contain (1) anything self-contradictory, such as round squares, or (2) anything that could not without self-contradiction be unilaterally brought about by God, such as the free decisions of creatures.

The most important implication of this view is that God could unilaterally bring about a world that is just like ours except for being free of at least most of those things that we normally consider unnecessary evils, such as cancer, earthquakes, hurricanes, nuclear weapons, rape, murder, genocide, and global warming. Traditional theism's problem of evil is this: If the divine power is unlimited, why does our world have these (and many other) seemingly unnecessary evils? In considering the possible answers, we need to distinguish between two versions of traditional theism: the all-determining and the free-will versions.

TRADITIONAL ALL-DETERMINING THEISM

According to the all-determining version of traditional theism, as its name indicates, literally every event and feature of the world—whether in the physical world or the human mind—is fully determined by God. Although advocates of this position affirm that human beings are free in the sense of being responsible for their actions, their freedom is said somehow to be compatible with their actions, thoughts, and feelings being fully determined by God. How can advocates of this position, such as Augustine, Aquinas, Luther, Calvin, Leibniz, and Karl Barth, avoid the conclusion of the above argument, namely, that "God does not exist"? I can here give only summary statements of their approaches, which I have discussed at length elsewhere.[52]

One approach has been to reject the third premise—that God would *want* to avoid all evil. Many evils, such theologians point out, lead to great goods that would have been impossible without the evils:

Pain created by the dentist is necessary for healthy teeth later on; poverty provides the opportunity for charity; sin against others provides them the opportunity for forgiveness; suffering can promote compassion; and so on. Although this answer may initially seem convincing, it really amounts only to the observation that many things that seem evil at first glance, which we can call *prima facie* evils, are not *genuine* evils, defined as occurrences that make the universe worse than it might have been, all things considered. Many *prima facie* evils, in other words, are *only apparently* evil. This is certainly true.

But this observation would provide a solution to the problem of evil only if it were persuasively claimed that *every* instance of *prima facie* evil is only apparently evil, so that there would be *no* genuine evil. With that claim, however, the all-determining theist would be denying not the third premise, but the fourth one—that "evil does occur."

The confusion as to what is being denied can be avoided by inserting the word "genuine" before "evil" in premises 2, 3, and 4. While this insertion will not affect the second premise, it turns the third premise into a truism, because a perfectly good being is *by definition* one who would want to prevent all genuine evil, meaning anything that would make the world worse than it might have been. All-determining theists can logically avoid the conclusion that God does not exist, therefore, only by denying the fourth premise—that "genuine evil exists"—which is what Leibniz did in declaring this to be "the best of all possible worlds."[53]

However, as I have argued elsewhere,[54] this denial is not one that we can make consistently—that is, without contradicting what we presuppose in practice—because in our daily living we all presuppose that less than optimal events occur. The same is true for the closely related idea that we have genuine freedom (which all-determining theism denies in effect by redefining freedom to make it compatible with divine determinism): We all in practice presuppose that we have a degree of freedom in the sense that, after we choose A, it is true that we could have chosen B or C.

The denial that any genuine evil occurs also contradicts the very nature of religion, which, in providing a way to overcome (genuine) evil, presupposes that it occurs. Because we cannot help presupposing that genuine evil occurs even if we verbally deny it, all-determining theism, by implying that God has unnecessarily brought about genuine evil, in effect denies the perfect goodness of God, as Hermogenes warned.

The only way to avoid this implication is to deny that the ordinary rules of logic apply in theology. This approach has been employed in Christian theology by Karl Barth and Emil Brunner and in Jewish theology by Emil Fackenheim.[55] One problem with this approach is that it gives up the very task of theo-logy, which is that of applying logos, or rational thought, to our image of God. Also, if we exempt our own thinking from the basic rules of logical implication, we must, in fairness, do this for opposing schemes of thought. Rational argumentation would no longer be possible.

TRADITIONAL FREE WILL THEISM

Some traditional theists, recognizing that all-determining theism cannot provide a satisfactory answer to the problem of evil, have developed a free-will version. It holds that although God *essentially* has all the power, God has, through a self-limitation on this power, *voluntarily* given freedom to at least some of the creatures—human beings and perhaps some other rational creatures, such as angels—freedom with which they can act contrary to the will of God. This idea of a voluntary self-limitation on divine omnipotence is necessary to have a rational position, because free-will theists (rightly) reject the "compatibilism" of all-determining theism (according to which creaturely freedom is somehow compatible with divine determinism).

The basic idea of free-will theism is that, although creaturely freedom allows genuine evils to occur—namely, sin and the evils resulting therefrom—*the fact that* such evils occur is itself not genuinely evil, because a world with genuinely free creatures, who can freely choose the right and the good and thereby freely develop moral and religious virtues, is a better world than a world that, while sin-free, is devoid of the values made possible by genuine freedom.

This version of traditional theism, by allowing for both genuine freedom and genuine evil, can provide a more satisfactory answer to the problem of evil than can the all-determining version. But it still has several problems. I will mention three.

First, given the idea, usually accepted by advocates of traditional free will theism, that human beings are the only Earthly creatures with freedom, free-will theism—with its notion that God essentially has all the power—provides no answer to the question of what is usually called "natural evil," meaning the forms of evil that are not due to human volition, such as the suffering in the pre-human evolutionary process. This type of theism also provides no answer to the fact that the face of our planet is susceptible to earthquakes, tornadoes, and hurricanes; the fact that human beings and other animals are susceptible to cancer and other diseases; and the fact that Earth contains the elements to produce nuclear weapons and other weapons of mass destruction. The doctrine of *creatio ex nihilo* implies that God could have created a world supportive of human life that would not have had all these dangers. For example, Dale Aukerman, a conservative, pacifist, Christian theologian, has said in a chapter entitled "Why the Possibility for the Bomb?":

> God certainly could have created the universe and the earth without uranium and thus without the possibility of these technological breakthroughs that have given human beings the capability of turning the planet into an uninhabitable waste. . . . God set us in the midst of a creation which

contained that very hidden and most terrible possibility. Why?—when He could so easily have withheld it from us.[56]

Of course, traditional free-will theists can speculate, as does Aukerman, that God did this in order to accentuate the fact that we are doomed unless we turn to God. The fact remains, however, that the nuclear and climate perils are evils that were not required by human freedom as such but that God, according to traditional theism's construal of divine power, freely chose to allow.

A second problem is that, according to the hypothesis of traditional free-will theism, God could intervene to prevent any specific instance of evil. God could have diverted every bullet headed toward a human being "too young to die." God could have prevented any of the massacres that have occurred. God could, in fact, prevent any sinful human intention from producing its intended effects. And God could prevent any disease or any natural disaster from producing permanent injury or premature death. This position, therefore, retains the assumption of traditional theism that has led millions to question the existence or at least the goodness of a divine being. If there were a Superman who could prevent all these kinds of events but refused to do so—perhaps on the grounds that doing so would "prevent opportunities for human growth"—we would certainly question his moral goodness. A Superman, of course, could not prevent all genuine evils, because, being finite, he could not be everywhere at once. But the God of traditional theism, being ubiquitous, does not have this excuse. (As mentioned in Chapter 1, Stendahl's well-known conclusion was that "God's only excuse is that He does not exist.")

A third problem for traditional free-will theism is based on its position that even the freedom of human beings is an entirely gratuitous gift of God, not necessitated by anything in the nature of things (except the purely logical point that only genuinely free creatures can develop virtues that presuppose freedom). According to this position, God could have created beings identical with ourselves in all respects except for one thing: they would not really be free to sin. They could have enjoyed all the kinds of values that we enjoy, from friendship and family to music and philosophy, except those that involve or presuppose genuine evil. They could even have believed that they were really acting freely while always doing good. Only God would know otherwise. It is only God, accordingly, who gains anything from the fact that creatures have genuine freedom. Granting this freedom, from which most of the world's ills result, would arguably seem to be a selfish decision.

Even if we granted that our world, with its genuine freedom and correlative genuine evils, was the best choice, it would still be the case—to return to the second problem—that this freedom could always be temporarily interrupted. Defenders of this position rightly point out that, given our normal understanding of human beings as genuinely free, God's interruption of someone's freedom would mean that that person in that moment would not be fully human. To have violated Hitler's freedom would have violated his full humanity.

In response, however, the critic can ask: Would not this violation have been a small price to pay to have prevented Hitler from violating the freedom and humanity of millions of other people? A similar question arises every time human beings use their freedom to rob, injure, rape, murder, and otherwise violate the freedom and humanity of other human beings: Can we consider perfectly good and loving an omnipotent being who, having the power to prevent such acts, does not do so?

Faced with these problems, some classical free will theists simply say that, although they cannot explain why God allows so much evil, they need not do so. "If God is good and powerful as the theist believes," says Alvin Plantinga, "then he will indeed have a good reason for permitting evil; but why suppose the theist must be in a position to figure out what it is?"[57]

Plantinga's answer here is part of his claim that theists need not offer a *theodicy,* which would attempt to provide a *plausible* explanation for the world's evils, but can rest content with a *defense,* which merely shows that there is *no logical contradiction* between holding that "evil exists" and that "God is omnipotent, omniscient, and wholly good." As long as a proffered explanation shows how these two propositions *might* be consistent, says Plantinga, the fact that it is implausible "is utterly beside the point."[58]

The main problem with this approach is that its contentment with such a minimalist view of theological rationality seems to be based on the assumption that traditional theism is somehow in a privileged position. I have argued, by contrast, that traditional theism is no longer in such a position, so that it must, like any other position, commend itself in terms of plausibility as well as self-consistency.[59] But that is what it has been unable to do—at least without smuggling in assumptions that are inconsistent with the doctrine of *creatio ex nihilo.*[60]

Neither version of traditional theism, in sum, provides a position that shows the world's evils to be compatible with the perfect goodness of God.

A *PROCESS THEODICY*

Having suggested that traditional theism has an insoluble problem of evil because of its acceptance of the (postbiblical) doctrine of *creatio ex nihilo,* I will now show how the process panentheism being articulated in this book can, by virtue of its rejection of that doctrine, provide a satisfactory theodicy.[61] This panentheism has much in common with traditional theism, affirming the existence of a personal creator who is perfect in both power and goodness. But it is nontraditional in affirming a contemporary version of the biblical and Platonic notion of creation out of chaos and thereby a different understanding of divine power. Although the brief account provided here will necessarily leave many questions unanswered, the interested reader can consult the more extensive accounts that I have provided elsewhere.[62] I will first explain how creation out of chaos is understood, then lay out some implications for the problem of evil.

CREATION OUT OF CHAOS: A PROCESS VERSION

In the ancient visions of creation out of chaos, the "stuff" out of which our world was created was generally thought of as passive matter. As such, it could be understood to offer resistance to the divine will and thereby to provide a reason for imperfections in the natural world. But it provided little if any basis for explaining distinctively human evil.

In process theism, by contrast, the stuff out of which our world was created is not what we normally think of as "stuff" at all, but creative activity. This idea is based in part on recent physics, according to which what we think of as "matter" consists of energy. Generalizing the notion of energy, Whitehead, as we saw in the previous chapter, refers to the stuff embodied in all things as "creativity." On this basis, the long-standing dualism between "physical nature" and "human experience" can be overcome: All things, from subatomic particles to living cells to human beings, could be understood as embodiments of creativity, or creative activity.

A crucial feature of this nondualistic worldview is a new understanding of the basic units of which the world is composed. In line with the view that the "stuff" of which things are composed is not stuff-like, Whitehead also held that the basic "things" are not thing-like: Rather than being enduring substances, as we have seen, they are momentary *events*.

The creative activity embodied in each event takes two forms. One form is the influence of an event on subsequent events, which involves what physics describes as the transfer of energy. This creative activity is *efficient causation*, the causal influence of one actuality on others. After these other events receive this causal influence, they then exercise the other kind of creativity, which is *final causation*, in the sense of self-determination, insofar as they decide precisely how to respond to the various causal influences upon them. These decisions then become the basis for their efficient causation upon subsequent events.

We are aware that we make such decisions in every moment, insofar as we hold ourselves responsible for how we respond to the various situations we confront. We also commonly attribute a degree of spontaneity to other animals. Whitehead's view is that we can intelligibly attribute at least some iota of such spontaneity all the way down, to the subatomic level, suggesting that it accounts for the lack of complete determinism discerned by quantum physics.

Accordingly, rather than an absolute dualism between "humanity," with its freedom, and "nature," assumed to be rigidly determined, process philosophy suggests, in line with the evolutionary nature of our world, a series of more or less radical differences of degree. In other words, the evolutionary process, in successively bringing forth atoms, molecules, prokaryotic cells, eukaryotic cells, multicellular animals, mammals, and human beings, has brought forth beings with increasingly greater freedom.

Given this initial overview of the position, we can now ask how it conceives the beginning of our universe as the bringing of order out of chaos. If the ultimate units of our world are not enduring things, but momentary events, then enduring individuals—such as electrons, photons, and quarks—would already constitute an evolved type of order, in which a particular form of existence is repeated rapidly.

Prior to the emergence of these "enduring objects"—better called "enduring individuals"—the realm the realm of finitude would have consisted entirely of extremely trivial events—at least as trivial as the types of events of which quarks now consist—happening at random. To say that these events are extremely trivial means that they have very little intrinsic value, meaning value for themselves, and very little extrinsic value, meaning value for others (including God). It also means that they have very little power, either to exercise self-determination or to influence future events. To say that these events happen "at random" is to say that they do not belong to enduring individuals. Without enduring individuals, the development of higher forms of existence, with more value and power, would have been impossible. Accordingly, the creation of elementary enduring individuals, such as quarks, photons, electrons, protons, neutrons, and neutrinos, was the necessary first step in the creation of our universe.

Prior to the emergence of these enduring individuals, there would have been no "things," in the ordinary sense of *enduring* things. For those who like the phrase, then, it can be said that our world was created out of "no-thing." It was not, however, created *ex nihilo* in the sense that this phrase took on in postbiblical times, to mean the absolute beginning of finite existence. Finite events were happening, but they constituted a chaos, not a cosmos, because none of the events were yet ordered into the contingent forms of order lying at the root of our universe.

The realm of finitude did not, accordingly, have forms of energy such as quarks, electrons, and photons (which would be a contemporary way of understanding the suggestion of Genesis 1:2 that the world was "formless"). The realm of finitude was, however, not devoid of power or energy in the most general sense. Rather, each of the events embodied creativity, understood as the most fundamental type of power or energy, having the potential to be transmuted into the contingent forms of energy constituting our universe. This description of the pre-cosmic chaos still applies, in fact, to most of the universe today, insofar as it mostly consists of "empty space," meaning space that is empty of standing enduring individuals (as distinct from forms of radiation passing through). Whitehead's view that it is *not* empty of events embodying creative power is consistent with the view of recent physics that the "vacuum" contains enormous energy.

Those whose thinking has been shaped by the idea of *creatio ex nihilo* will be inclined, at this point, to ask where this chaos of events came from. They may contend that it must have been created by God. What, however, is the self-evident truth behind this *must*? It cannot be simply that "everything that exists must have been created," or else we would have to ask who created God. We do not ask this question, however, because part of what we mean by "God" is "a being who exists necessarily." This point leads to the correct formulation of the self-evident truth involved, which is that "everything that exists contingently, rather than necessarily, must have been created." Traditional theists are quite right to hold that *something* must exist necessarily: Given the intuition that *ex nihilo nihil fit*, which implies that a universe could have never arisen out of a complete absence of anything actual, there must be something actual that exists eternally and thereby necessarily. The question, however, is what this something is.

Western minds have been shaped by many centuries of traditional theism to assume that this something was God alone, without a realm of finitude. One can at least equally well assume, however, that what exists necessarily is God-with-a-realm-of-finite-existents. In fact, as May points out, Hermogenes used the biblical designation of God as "Lord" to support this view, arguing that "God was in his unchangeableness always Lord, and so there must have been from eternity something for him to be Lord of."[63]

Whitehead's position embodies an analogous idea: that it is the very nature of God, as the supreme embodiment of creativity, to interact with finite embodiments of it, both influencing and being influenced by worldly events. Or, in Charles Hartshorne's language, it belongs to the very nature of God to be the soul of the world.[64] The necessary existence of God, therefore, implies the necessary existence of a world—not of *our* world, of course, and not even a world in the sense of an ordered cosmos, but simply a realm of finite existents, which can exist either in an ordered or a chaotic state.

DIVINE POWER AS PERSUASIVE, NOT CONTROLLING

One implication of this view is that power is always shared power. If God is the supreme but never the only embodiment of creativity, then God never has a monopoly on power. Also, because the creativity embodied in finite beings is inherent to the realm of finitude, rather than freely bestowed by a creator to whom all creativity essentially belongs, it cannot be withdrawn or overridden.

This rejection of free will theism does not, however, imply a rejection of the idea that human freedom is a gift from God. Although at least an iota of self-determination is inherent in finitude itself, all the higher degrees of self-determination are due to God. Our human freedom is a result of billions of years of evolution, each advance of which was divinely inspired. But because it was evoked out of the capacity for self-determination that is inherent to the world, this human freedom, now that it exists, cannot be simply withdrawn or overridden by God.

This view of shared power implies, in turn, that divine power is persuasive, not controlling. God, by hypothesis, influences every finite event, but God cannot wholly determine how any event will use its own creativity and thereby its twofold power to exert both self-determination and causal influence. This point applies all the way down: Because living cells, viruses, bacteria, macromolecules (such as DNA and RNA), ordinary molecules, atoms, subatomic particles, and quarks have the twofold power to respond with spontaneity and then to influence other things (for good or ill), we should not suppose that there is some level of the world that fully reflects the divine will— as if, for example, God for some mysterious reason wanted there to be cancer, AIDS, and genetically deformed babies. Rather, as Plato suggested, our creator would have at each level brought about the best order that was then possible.

A clarification is needed: The idea that all things have some degree of spontaneity, which has thus far been suggested, is true not of all things whatsoever, but only of *all genuine individuals*. This distinction, between things with and without spontaneity, reflects two basic ways in which enduring things can be organized: into "compound individuals," such as cells and animals, and into mere "aggregational entities," such as rocks and stars.

In humans and other animals, the organization of the cells supports the existence of a higher-level actuality—which we call the *anima*, psyche, or soul—which exerts a dominating influence over the organism as a whole, enabling it to coordinate the spontaneities of its various members into a unified, self-determining response. Something analogous occurs, by hypothesis, in living cells and even lower-level individuals, such as atoms and electrons.

Rocks and stars, by contrast, have no dominant member, so that the spontaneities of their various members cancel each other out, so that the rock or star as such is devoid of spontaneity.

Having made this clarification, I move now to an implication related to the fact that, within the hierarchy of true individuals, the power of self-determination can range from the extremely minimal to the enormous. This implication develops the basic insight of the traditional free-will theists, that there is a correlation between freedom and the higher types of value, but does so in the context of the rejection of the doctrine *creatio ex nihilo*. The point made above, that the finite individuals have at least some iota of nonoverridable power—so that the divine power is persuasive, not coercive—explains why the perfect goodness of God is compatible with there being *some* genuine evil in the world. The point to be developed now answers the further question of why there can be so *much* evil, including *horrendous* evil, in the world.

Necessary Correlations between Value and Power

If the doctrine of *creatio ex nihilo* is rejected, it makes sense to suppose that there are some necessary principles, inherent in the very nature of things, about the nature of finite actualities, their relations to each other, and their relations to God. I have already suggested one such set of principles—namely, that in any world that God could create, the ultimate actual units would be events, that all such events would embody creativity, in the sense of the twofold power to exert self-determination and to influence subsequent events, and that God could influence but never interrupt or override the creatures' exercise of this twofold power. Another principle is that a positive correlation necessarily obtains among the following variables: (1) The capacity to enjoy positive value. (2) The capacity to suffer negative value (evil). (3) The power of self-determination. (4) The power to influence others, for good or ill. To say that a positive correlation exists means that, as one variable increases, all the others increase proportionately.

It is evidently an empirical fact that the correlations obtain in our world. For example, human beings can enjoy positive values of which their pets have no inkling, but they can also suffer forms of evil from which their cats and dogs are free. We are surely right to assume that dogs enjoy more, and also suffer more, than do the fleas in their fur, which in turn must be superior to the cells of which their bodies are composed. This hierarchy of positive and negative value is also a hierarchy of power. We manifestly have far more power of self-determination, far more freedom, than dogs. We also have far more power to shape things around us for both good and ill, as illustrated by art and medicine, on the one hand, and warfare and pollution, on the other. To the extent that other types of individuals have less of this twofold power, they also seem to have less power to realize positive values and to suffer evil.

From the perspective of process theism, these correlations are not merely empirical, but reflect principles that would necessarily obtain in any world that God could create. Unlike traditional free-will theists, therefore, we need not ask why God did not create beings who could enjoy all the positive values of which we are capable but were not so subject to suffering. Such beings are, by hypothesis, metaphysically impossible. We also need not ask why God did not create beings just like us, capable of all the physical, aesthetic, and intellectual pleasures enjoyed by human beings, but with far less freedom, in the sense of the capacity to act contrary to the divine will. The same is true of the question as to why God did not create beings just like us but with far less power to be destructive of other people and the rest of life.

The idea that God could not have created such beings is, of course, a speculative hypothesis. But it is no more speculative than the contrary hypothesis, which says that God *could* have created such beings.

This contrary hypothesis is, in fact, *more* speculative, because we know that a world in which these correlations obtain is a possible world, but we have no knowledge that a world in which they do not obtain is possible. The only reason for supposing such a world to be possible, in fact, is the doctrine of *creatio ex nihilo*, which we also do not know to be possible. It arose as a purely speculative hypothesis, originally suggested by a few men who, employing it polemically against an intellectual threat to faith in the goodness of our creator, evidently did not realize that their solution would pose an equal threat.

Therefore, in judging between these two hypotheses – "creation out of chaos" and "creation out of absolute nothingness"—we should be primarily guided not by the concern to be faithful to the (postbiblical) tradition, but by the concern to do justice, in a self-consistent, plausible way, to all the relevant considerations. Two such considerations are the reality of genuine evil and, as Hermogenes emphasized, the absolute goodness of our creator. These considerations, I have suggested, support a contemporary version of the position shared by Plato and the Bible.

Another relevant consideration is the need for an intelligible idea of how God could have created our world, which also supports a return to creation out of chaos.[65]

Still another consideration, which has played a large role, is the need for a doctrine of divine power that supports an adequate eschatology, especially life after death. Since the time of Tertullian—who, May says, was "the first to adduce creation out of nothing as a proof that God had the power to awaken the dead"[66]—many theologians have argued that faith in resurrection requires the kind of divine power that goes with *creatio ex nihilo*.[67] As I have argued elsewhere, however, hope for salvation in a life beyond death is fully supportable in terms of persuasive divine power, so that this issue need not block us from enjoying the benefits, for theodicy and intelligibility more generally, of returning to the biblical notion of creation out of chaos.[68]

Conclusion

Whiteheadian panentheism, besides providing a concept of divine activity that is not in conflict with the kind of naturalism that is properly presupposed by the sciences, is also, by virtue of the rejection of supernaturalism, not falsified by the evils of our world. Insofar as these two issues have provided the major reasons for the rejection of theism of all forms in intellectual circles, this twofold conclusion is of incomparable importance. Among the reasons for this importance is that it allows intellectuals who accept a naturalistic worldview to regard religious experience as cognitive, as telling us something important about the nature of reality. Taking religious experience seriously means, in turn, that the question of the relation among the religions becomes again an important intellectual issue, as well as one that is of vital importance for the future of the planet. The discovery of an idea of divine activity that is not vetoed by either scientific naturalism or the problem of evil also provides a basis for reversing the modern "disenchantment of the world," so we in our public life can again see moral norms as grounded in the nature of things. These issues will be discussed in the following chapters.

NOTES

1. Jon D. Levenson, *Creation and the Persistence of Evil: The Jewish Drama of Divine Omnipotence* (San Francisco: Harper & Row, 1988), 5, 121, 157 n.12.

2. Plato, *The Timaeus*, 30A.

3. Millard J. Erickson, *Christian Theology* (Grand Rapids: Baker Book House, 1985), 374.

4. Ibid., 277.

5. Richard L. Rubenstein, *After Auschwitz: Radical Theology and Contemporary Judaism* (Indianapolis: Bobbs-Merrill, 1966), 46, 64-65, 153. For an analogous argument, see William R. Jones, *Is God a White Racist? A Preamble to Black Theology* (Garden City: Anchor Press, 1973).

6. Jon Levenson, *Creation and the Persistence of Evil*; Gerhard May, *Creatio Ex Nihilo: The Doctrine of "Creation out of Nothing" in Early Christian Thought*, trans. A. S. Worrall (Edinburgh: T. & T. Clark, 1994).

7. Levenson, *Creation and the Persistence of Evil*, 121.

8. Ibid., 5, 121.

9. Ibid., 121, 157 n.12.

10. Ibid., 4, 123.

11. Ibid., xiii, 49, 50.

12. Ibid., 12, 26, 122-23.

13. Whereas Levenson's book was published in 1988, May's book was originally published in German in 1978.

14. May, *Creatio Ex Nihilo*, xi-xii, 7.

15. Ibid., 7-8, 11, 16.

16. Ibid., 21.

17. Ibid., xi.

18. Ibid., 27.

19. Ibid., viii, xii, 25-26, 77, 161, 174.

20. Ibid., 3-4.

21. Ibid., 150.

22. Ibid., 77.

23. Ibid., 6, 12.

24. Ibid., 25.

25. Ibid., 12, 25.

26. Ibid., 25.

27. Ibid., xiii, 61, 74.

28. Ibid., 122.

29. Ibid., 4.

30. Ibid., xiii, 24.

31. Ibid., 40, 56.

32. Ibid., 43.

33. Ibid., 61.

34. Ibid., 56n., 152.

35. Ibid., 151. (It is also important to note that, when the doctrine of *creatio ex nihilo* was affirmed by the Fourth Lateran Council in 1215, it was directed against Catharism, which held Manichean doctrines of matter and creation similar to those of Marcion. See Jeffrey Burton Russell, *Lucifer: The Devil in the Middle Ages* (Ithaca: Cornell University Press, 1984), 189.

36. Ibid., 146.

37. Ibid., 140, 145.

38. Ibid., 142.

39. Ibid., 141.

40. Ibid., 144.

41. Ibid., 142.

42. Ibid., 141.

43. Ibid., 140.

44. Ibid., 146.

45. Ibid., 147.

46. Ibid., 147.

47. Ibid., 159, 178.

48. Ibid., 178.

49. Ibid., 161.

50. Ibid., 167-68, 174.

51. Ibid., 174, 177.

52. Griffin, *God, Power, and Evil: A Process Theodicy* (Philadelphia: Westminster Press, 1976; reprinted with a new preface, Lanham, Md.: University Press of America, 1991; reprinted with a newer preface, Westminster John Knox (Louisville, Ky., 2004), Chaps. 6-7, 9-12.

53. Ibid., Ch. 11.

54. Griffin, *Reenchantment Without Supernaturalism: A Process Philosophy of Religion* (Ithaca: Cornell University Press, 2001), Chap. 6.

55. *God, Power, and Evil*, Chaps. 12 and 15.

56. Dale Aukerman, *Darkening Valley: A Biblical Perspective on Nuclear War* (New York: Seabury, 1981), 160-61.

57. Alvin Plantinga, "Reply to the Basingers on Divine Omnipotence," *Process Studies* 11 (Spring 1981), 25-29, at 28.

58. Ibid., 26-27.

59. *Evil Revisited: Responses and Reconsiderations* (Albany: State University of New York Press, 1991), Chap. 2.

60. Ibid., Chap. 5.

61. My first articulation of a process theodicy in *God, Power, and Evil* (1976) received several extensive critiques, to which I replied in *Evil Revisited: Responses and Reconsiderations* (1991). Several critiques of my position, along with responses from me, are also available in *Encountering Evil*, ed. by Stephen Davis. There are also a few pages in Marilyn McCord Adams, *Horrendous Evils and the Goodness of God*. However, her critique deals primarily with the position of Charles Hartshorne and, insofar as it deals with my position, takes account only

of my 1976 book, showing no apparent awareness of the "responses and reconsiderations" in my 1991 book, some of which are directly relevant to the issues she raises. Also, in her most extensive critique of my position, she suggests that my position "seems to confuse *having power* with *exercising power*" (75). But most and perhaps all of my critiques of traditional theism have emphasized the distinction between traditional *all-determining* theism, according to which God both *has* and *exercises* all the power of the universe, and traditional *free-will* theism, according to which God *essentially* has all the power but freely allows some of the creatures to have some.

62. See *Evil Revisited*. For a briefer account, see *God, Power, and Evil*, Chs. 17-18, or *Reenchantment Without Supernaturalism*, Chs. 3-7.

63. May, *Creation Ex Nihilo*, 141.

64. Charles Hartshorne, *Man's Vision of God and the Logic of Theism*. New York: Harper & Row, 1941), 174-87; *Omnipotence and Other Theological Mistakes* (Albany: State University of New York Press, 1984), 56-62.

65. I have argued this point in *Reenchantment Without Supernaturalism*, Chs. 4 and 5.

66. May, *Creation Ex Nihilo*, 137.

67. May himself suggests that Christianity's Easter faith was one reason that Christian theologians adopted the doctrine of *creatio ex nihilo* more quickly than did Jewish thinkers (ibid., 25, 129, 137).

68. On the possibility of life after death within process thought, with supporting empirical evidence, see my *Parapsychology, Philosophy, and Spirituality*. For briefer discussions, see "Parapsychology, Science, and Religion" (Ch. 7 of *Religion and Scientific Naturalism*) and the section on eschatology in "Evolution, Evil, and Eschatology" (Ch. 6 of *Reenchantment without Supernaturalism*).

CHAPTER FIVE

Scientific Naturalism and Religious Experience

The present chapter focuses on an issue that has been only briefly treated in previous chapters: the fact that the acceptance of scientific naturalism has created difficulties for the idea of religious experience. The discussion again involves the distinction between naturalism in the generic sense (naturalism$_{ns}$) and the specific form in which, for various contingent historical reasons, this generic naturalism came wrapped (naturalism$_{sam}$). I begin this discussion by explaining how all three dimensions of naturalism$_{sam}$—its sensationism, atheism, and materialism—play a role in ruling out the possibility of genuine religious experience, especially religious experience of the theistic type.[1] The second section then explains why naturalism$_{sam}$, although promulgated in the name of science, is inadequate for science itself. The final section explains how Whitehead's naturalism$_{ppp}$ allows religious experience to be taken seriously as a direct experience of Something Holy.

HOW NATURALISM$_{SAM}$ RULES OUT RELIGIOUS EXPERIENCE

SENSATIONISM

The sensationist doctrine of perception was primarily implanted in modern thought through the philosophies of John Locke, David Hume, and Immanuel Kant. This doctrine says that all our experience of the world beyond our own minds is by means of our bodily sensory organs, which are stimulated only by physical objects. There can, accordingly, be no nonsensory perception, no perception of anything other than physical objects.

This sensationist doctrine obviously rules out the possible genuineness of the "extrasensory perception" studied by parapsychologists. But it also rules out any genuine theistic experience, understood in the traditional sense as a perception of a Divine Subject distinct from the perceiver. Although Kant did not affirm naturalism~sam~,[2] he did insist on the sensationist doctrine of perception, which led him to deny the possibility of genuine theistic experience. To believe in a "feeling of the immediate presence of the Supreme Being," said Kant, would be a "fanatical religious illusion," because it would be to affirm "a receptivity for an intuition for which there is no sensory provision in man's nature."[3]

The assumption that there could be no direct experience of a Holy Reality raised the question as to how religion came to exist and why it continues to persist. It is not surprising, therefore, that the nineteenth century gave birth to numerous psychological and sociological theories of religion that tried to explain why people always and everywhere have been religious, even though genuine religious experience is impossible. As Emile Durkheim put it, the primary problem for the scientific understanding of religion is "explaining the sacred"—that is, explaining why religious people think in terms of the distinction between the "sacred" and the "profane," even though "nothing in sensible [sensory] experience seems able to suggest the idea of so radical a duality to them."[4] Durkheim, who simply presupposed the sensationist theory of perception, assumed that any explanation, to be scientific, would have to be in terms of sensory experience.

This assumption is now widespread among intellectuals. For example, J.J.C. Smart said that "if mystical experiences are not mere aberrations of feelings, that are explicable in naturalistic terms, then they must be in some way miraculous"—by which Smart meant impossible. Smart's assumption was that a naturalistic account of "getting in touch" with things meant having responses to physical stimuli from things, such as rabbits or electrons. Given this assumption, no naturalistic account could be given of getting in touch with something nonphysical. Since "mystical cognition of the supernatural" is supposed to involve getting in touch with something nonphysical, concluded Smart, all apparent mystical experience must be illusory.[5]

Although the widespread rejection of genuine religious experience in intellectual circles is due primarily to the specific type of naturalism that I am calling naturalism$_{sam}$, scientific naturalism in the generic sense, with its rejection of supernaturalism, has also played an essential role. Although thinkers such as Locke and Kant rejected nonsensory perception and thereby genuine religious experience, they still affirmed traditional theism, even if in a more or less deistic form. They could assume, therefore, that religion existed because it had been divinely implanted in the human mind. Kant derived religion from morality, which he explained in terms of a divinely implanted a priori category of the human mind.

Other thinkers said that religion had its own a priori category. In *The Idea of the Holy*, Rudolf Otto, who stood in this neo-Kantian tradition, explained the existence of religion in terms of the divinely implanted category of the holy.[6] Mircea Eliade, evidently influenced by Otto, famously—or notoriously—said that "the 'sacred' is an element in the structure of consciousness."[7]

But those who have adopted scientific naturalism cannot accept such an explanation, with its implicit supernaturalism. For example, Samuel Preus, in his book *Explaining Religion*, wrote: "[I]n an academic setting where other scholars are struggling with the evolutionary emergence of our species, one legitimately wants to know how Eliade's remarkable 'element in the structure of consciousness' might have gotten there."[8] Preus's critique on this point will be endorsed by everyone who accepts scientific naturalism in the generic sense.

Preus, however, also illustrated the fact that many students of religion affirm not only this generic naturalism but also naturalism$_{sam}$. This more restrictive doctrine does not merely reject all explanations that rely on supernaturalist versions of theism. By virtue of its atheism, naturalism$_{sam}$ leads its proponents to reject *any* explanation that involves the idea of a Holy Reality distinct from the totality of finite entities, events, and interactions. Given this dimension of naturalism$_{sam}$, it goes beyond naturalism$_{ns}$, which merely rejects the idea of supernatural interruptions of natural processes. It also affirms that "nature is all there is," with "nature" here understood to mean the totality of finite entities, events, and interactions.

Naturalism in this sense can be called naturalism$_{nati}$ (with "nati" meaning "nature is all there is"). This "nati-naturalism" denies not only traditional Western theism but also the more general idea, shared by most of the religious traditions of the world, that there is a divine actuality that is distinct from the world and exercises agency in the world. Preus, accordingly, said that the naturalistic analyst rejects the account that religious believers give of their religious experiences, "because the analyst does not believe their explanation that mysterious transcendent powers beyond the realm of natural causation . . . really create this experience."[9] Proponents of naturalism in this sense assume that the academic student of religion must, in Preus's words, "explain religions—that is, their universality, variety, and persistence until now," on the assumption that "God is not given."[10] In the same vein, Robert Segal, in *Explaining and Interpreting Religion*, said that social scientists should assume that "believers never encounter God."[11]

This assumption, shared by Preus and Segal, is based on the twofold idea that there is no Divine Actuality and that, even if there were, we would be unable to experience it, because we can experience things beyond ourselves only through our sensory organs. This twofold idea is held not only by many scholars involved in the academic study of religion. It has also been held by some theologians, such as Gordon Kaufman, who agreed with Kant's insistence that all perception is *sensory* perception. Accepting not only Kant's less controversial point, shared by empiricists of all stripes, that concepts without percepts are empty, Kaufman also accepted Kant's sensationist point that percepts are exclusively sensory. On this basis, Kaufman said, in response to the question of what the word "God" might refer to: "Certainly not to anything we directly experience." Kaufman therefore said that the idea of God, not being at all similar to the idea of a perceptual object, such as a table or a person, is "constructed imaginatively in the mind."[12]

The atheism and sensationism of naturalism have led to the view, articulated by Preus, that a naturalistic approach is necessarily "reductionistic," so that religious experiences must be explained without recourse to the categories of "transcendence" and "the sacred."[13] The most prevalent way of carrying out this program has been to understand religious experiences purely as the result of cultural beliefs.

For example, Wayne Proudfoot, in his *Religious Experience*, argued for "a historical or cultural explanation of religious experience."[14] What William James called a religious *sense*, said Proudfoot, is really a *thought*.[15] Proudfoot's point was that what constitutes an experience as a *religious* experience is the interpretive framework that the individual brings to the experience, not something inherent to the experience itself. People have historically explained the existence of religious beliefs, at least partly, in terms of religious experiences. But, said Proudfoot, we are to explain the occurrence of religious experiences wholly in terms of religious *beliefs*, which are themselves to be wholly explained in nonreligious terms. Proudfoot's analysis exemplified Segal's stipulation that, for an explanation of religion to count as a *scientific* explanation, it must say that religion has "a naturalistic *rather than* divine origin."[16] It also exemplified what Preus called the program of explaining and interpreting religion in terms of a "naturalistic paradigm" understood as "an altogether nonreligious point of view."[17] This analysis thereby exemplifies the ideal of bringing the study of religion into line not only with scientific naturalism in the generic sense but also with the sensationism and atheism of naturalism$_{sam}$.

MATERIALISM

This approach is reinforced and expanded by the materialism of naturalism$_{sam}$. *Materialism can be defined as the twofold doctrine that (1) the ultimate units of the world are devoid of both experience and spontaneity and that (2) nothing exists except such units and aggregations of them.* Materialism thereby denies that you have a mind or soul that is distinct from your brain.

This denial is called "identism," which says that what we call the mind is (numerically) identical with the brain. Identism, in other words, says not only that the mind and the brain are ontologically the same, in the sense of being made of the same "stuff," but also that they are numerically the same, being literally the same thing (just as, to use a well-worn example, "Evening Star" and "Morning Star" are two names for the same thing). This materialistic identism reinforces the idea that your mind has no way of perceiving the universe beyond itself except by means of the brain's sensory system.

Materialism also asserts that the universe has no nonphysical realities—no Divine Reality, not even any ideal ("Platonic") forms, such as normative values. Materialism thereby denies that religious and normative experiences can be genuine in the sense of reflecting a distinct realm or dimension of reality.

Materialism also rules out the genuineness of another kind of experience that is often considered a type of religious experience: experiences suggestive of life after death. For example, some people experience apparitions of persons who have died (the reported post-crucifixion appearances of Jesus would fit into this category).[18]

Also, some people have out-of-body experiences, in which they seem to be viewing the world from a perspective outside of their physical bodies. The out-of-body experiences that have been studied most intensely in recent years are *near-death* out-of-body experiences, which occur in situations, often in hospitals, when the persons are physically near death. The equation of the "scientific view" with materialism often leads thinkers simply to dismiss reports of such experiences as obviously fraudulent, mistaken, or pathological.

For example, Richard Blacher, a physician who classified the near-death out-of-body experience as a "fantasy of death," rejected out of hand all interpretations that accept at face value the experiencers' statements that they were out of their bodies. Blacher defended this a priori rejection by saying that it would be unscientific to "accept the ideas of spirits wandering around the emergency room."[19] Philosopher Susan Blackmore agreed, saying that science supports the materialistic view that "mental phenomena depend upon, or are an aspect of, brain events."[20] It would be unscientific, she held, to believe that we have a soul that could survive death, because "[s]cience tells us that death is the end."[21]

Like many others, Blacher and Blackmore have confused scientific naturalism$_{sam}$, which is simply the philosophical worldview that is currently dominant in the scientific community, with science itself.

As we have seen, the acceptance of scientific naturalism, identified with naturalism$_{sam}$, has led to reductionistic interpretations of religious experiences, according to which they signify something radically different from what most of those having such experiences take them to signify. Although many of those who offer such interpretations may consider it unfortunate that their interpretations diverge so radically from the interpretations of those who have had the experiences, they assume that this divergence is unavoidable, because they believe that only an interpretation that is consistent with naturalism$_{sam}$ can be considered scientific or even academic.

IS NATURALISM$_{SAM}$ GENERALLY ADEQUATE?

This assumption is based, in turn, on the further assumption that naturalism$_{sam}$ has proved to be a satisfactory basis for explanations in science and in life more generally. Given this further assumption—that naturalism$_{sam}$ has proven itself adequate for virtually everything except religious experience—it would certainly make sense to try to bring the interpretation of religious experience into line with it.

DOMAIN UNIFORMITARIANISM

The intellectual ideal behind this move can be called "domain uniformitarianism," which says that we should try to interpret every intellectual domain in terms of the same basic principles. If one accepts this ideal, as I do, the crucial question is whether the further assumption is true. That is, has naturalism$_{sam}$ proven itself, in fact, to be adequate for all other types of experiences?

Although the assumption that it has indeed proven itself generally adequate seems to be very widespread in intellectual circles, the truth is quite otherwise. Each aspect of naturalism$_{sam}$ makes this worldview inadequate for science in particular and for experience more generally.

ADEQUACY TO INEVITABLE PRESUPPOSITIONS

To measure the "adequacy" of any theory, we must, of course, have some criteria. Although it is now argued in some philosophical circles that there are no universal criteria in terms of which to judge the adequacy of theories, Whitehead disagreed. The "metaphysical rule of evidence," he said, is "that we must bow to those presumptions which, in despite of criticism, we still employ for the regulation of our lives."[22]

In referring to presuppositions involved in "the regulation of our lives," Whitehead was referring to what is often called "practical reason." However, rather than accepting, with Hume and Kant, the idea that these presuppositions can diverge from the ideas that we employ in "theoretical reason," Whitehead argued that theoretical reason must be brought into line with the presuppositions of practical reason. Whereas Hume said that we have various "natural beliefs," such as the belief in an external world, which we necessarily presuppose in practice but cannot affirm in philosophical theory. Whitehead said:

> Whatever is found in 'practice' must lie within the scope of the metaphysical description. When the description fails to include the 'practice,' the metaphysics is inadequate and requires revision. There can be no appeal to practice to supplement metaphysics.[23]

If one were to ask why the inevitable presuppositions of practice should be taken as the final authority, the answer is that, if they are *inevitably* presupposed, then any verbal denial of them involves one in a self-contradiction. This is because one would be both (implicitly) affirming while (explicitly) denying one and the same proposition. Such a self-contradiction is "absolutely self-refuting" in the sense clarified by John Passmore: "The proposition *p* is absolutely self-refuting, if to assert *p* is equivalent to asserting *both p and not-p*."[24]

Jürgen Habermas and Karl-Otto Apel have both called such a self-contradiction a "performative contradiction," because the *performance* of making the statement contradicts the statement's *meaning*.[25] For example, if I say that I doubt your existence, the fact that I am addressing you contradicts my professed doubt.[26] Like Passmore, Habermas, and Apel, Whitehead stated that our theories must seek to avoid such self-contradictions by avoiding "negations of what in practice is presupposed."[27]

COMMON SENSE

In enunciating this criterion, Whitehead thereby stood in the tradition of "commonsense" philosophy. The term "common sense," however, is now often used quite differently, to refer to ideas that, although widely held at a certain time and place, are false. Science, in fact, is often described as a systematic assault on common sense, undermining such "commonsense" ideas as the flatness of the Earth, its centrality in the universe, and the solidity of matter.

To avoid confusion with regard to the meaning of "common sense," I refer to the two types of common sense as *soft-core* and *hard-core* common sense. Soft-core common sense is illustrated by the belief that matter is solid and any other beliefs that, while they may be widely held at a certain time and place, are not inevitably presupposed. Hard-core commonsense ideas are those that people inevitably presuppose.

It was common sense in the hard-core sense that Whitehead had in mind in referring to his "endeavor to interpret experience in accordance with the overpowering deliverance of common sense."[28] Commonsense notions of this hard-core type are "overpowering" because we cannot help presupposing them, even in the act of verbally denying them. They thereby must serve as the primary criteria for testing the adequacy of any theory, whether that theory be called scientific, philosophical, or theological.

I will now point out how each aspect of naturalism$_{sam}$ results in an overall theory that cannot do justice to many of our hard-core commonsense assumptions, which are presupposed by scientists in their scientific work as much as by anyone else. I will begin with the sensationism of naturalism$_{sam}$.

SENSATIONISM

Science claims to be an *empirical* enterprise, which includes the idea that its basic notions are based on experience. The sensationist version of empiricism, however, does *not* provide an experiential basis for several notions presupposed by the scientific enterprise.

External World: One of these notions, first, is the idea of an external world. "The belief in an external world independent of the perceiving subject," declared Albert Einstein, "is the basis of all natural science."[29] But Hume's analysis of sensory perception notoriously showed that it provides us knowledge only of sense data, not of an actual world beyond these perceptual data. Although Hume pointed out that *in practice* he necessarily presupposed such a world, his philosophical *theory* entailed solipsism. I am a solipsist if I hold that, for all I know, I am the only being that actually exists, with everyone and everything else being mere figments of my imagination.

The fact that no one really believes this position is illustrated by an old joke: A philosopher, in the midst of a lecture, announces that he is a solipsist. "Thank God," says a voice from the back of the room, "I was afraid I was the only one." The point of the joke, of course, is that both of its speakers show, by speaking to each other, that they do not really doubt the existence of other human beings. In claiming to be solipsists, therefore, they are guilty of "performative contradictions," contradicting the content of a proposition in the very act of uttering it.

Philosopher Willard Quine's position can be used to illustrate the irrationalism to which sensationism leads. Quine insisted that "whatever evidence there *is* for science *is* sensory evidence,"[30] so that "our statements about the external world face the tribunal of sense experience."[31] Quine also agreed with Hume that we have no knowledge of physical objects, so that they are in the same boat as Homer's gods. But, said Quine, "I believe in physical objects and not in Homer's gods."[32]

Quine thereby continued Hume's irrational separation of theory and practice, holding a philosophical theory while recognizing that it provided no basis for beliefs he inevitably presupposed in practice.

That is, although Quine rightly said that we should be empiricists, in that our beliefs should be based on experience, and recognized that he could not help believing in the existence of things such as rocks, he endorsed the sensationist form of empiricism even while admitting that sense perception provides no more basis for believing in rocks than it does for believing in Homer's gods, the existence of which he rejected out of hand.

Time: Sensationism also provides no experiential basis for our distinction between the past and the present and thereby our concept of time. Philosopher George Santayana famously pointed out that the consequences of the sensationist doctrine of perception are even worse than Hume acknowledged, because this doctrine implies not merely solipsism but also "solipsism of the present moment."[33] This is so because sense perception provides no knowledge of the existence of a past. With no knowledge of the distinction between past and present, we would have no knowledge of time.

The problem pointed out in Santayana's famous analysis, however, was ignored by Quine. Acknowledging the fact that sensory experience gives us only the "specious present," Quine asked how we make the "momentous" step involved in "the transcending of the specious present." But he then said that we begin with "a state of language that is limited to the specious present *and to short-term memories and expectations.*"[34] Quine thereby simply assumed the knowledge of temporality that he was supposed to explain.

Causation and Induction: Besides presupposing the external world, the past, and time, science also presupposes efficient causation and the validity of induction. But as Hume famously showed, sensory perception provides no basis for affirming efficient causation, in the sense of the real influence of one thing on another. Sensory perception therefore provides no basis for affirming a necessary connection between "cause" and "effect," hence no basis for scientific induction—the assumption that an experiment performed today in New York will turn out the same way tomorrow in Edinburgh. This problem threatens the very rationality of science, Hans Reichenbach pointed out, because it suggests that science "is nothing but a ridiculous self-delusion."[35]

A.J. Ayer asserted that we should "abandon the superstition that natural science cannot be regarded as logically respectable until philosophers have solved the problem of induction."[36] He thereby illustrated the fact that the problem is widely regarded as insoluble among philosophers who presuppose naturalism~sam~.

Mathematics: The philosophy of mathematics reveals a fourth problem created for science by sensationism. Mathematics seems to deal with a "Platonic realm" of nonphysical objects, which by definition cannot be perceived by the senses. One famous mathematician, Kurt Gödel, said that our knowledge of these objects comes through a nonsensory type of perception, called "mathematical intuition." Most philosophers of mathematics, however, have rejected this suggestion. For example, Quine's Harvard colleague Hilary Putnam, insisting that "we think with our brains, and not with immaterial souls," declared: "We cannot envisage *any* kind of neural process that could even correspond to the 'perception of a mathematical object.'"[37]

This reaffirmation of the view that we have no source of knowledge about reality other than sensory perception leaves only three alternatives with regard to mathematics. One option is to affirm formalism, according to which mathematics is merely a game with meaningless symbols. However, given the fact that most mathematicians are Platonic realists in practice,[38] this option entails a complete divergence of theory from practice.

A second possibility is to overcome the problem of "unobservable Platonic entities" by stipulating that mathematical objects are part of the physical world, so that they can be perceived by sensory perception. But this attempt, besides being desperate, is merely verbal.[39]

A third alternative is simply to ignore the problem, which was Quine's response. Being a "physicalist" in the sense of one who takes physics as the final arbiter of ontology, Quine affirmed the existence of the abstract entities of mathematics on the grounds that they are indispensable for physics. But he simply, in Putnam's words, "ignores the problem . . . as to how we can know that [these] abstract entities exist."[40] Putnam himself later took the same approach.

None of those solutions is acceptable if we think science should be a rational enterprise.

Logic: Because, as Putnam points out, "the nature of mathematical truth" and "the nature of logical truth" are one and the same problem,[41] the problem that sensationism creates for mathematical truth is equally a problem for logical truth—without which science would obviously be impossible.

At one time, Putnam had endorsed Quine's denial that there are any a priori truths, different in kind from empirical truths, which created an insuperable problem for affirming the reality of logical knowledge. But Putnam later declared, in "There Is at Least One A Priori Truth," that the principle of noncontradiction is an absolutely unrevisable a priori truth.[42] This gave Putnam a basis for affirming logical truth. But Putnam's continued acceptance of sensationism forced him to ignore the question of how he could possibly know this truth.

Moral Objectivity: One more problem created by sensationism— the fact that much scientific activity presupposes the objectivity of moral ideals, while sensationism says that we can have no knowledge of moral principles or ideals—will be discussed in Chapter 7.

MATERIALISM

Having now discussed several ways in which the sensationism of naturalism$_{sam}$ creates problems for science, I turn now to some ways in which the materialism of naturalism$_{sam}$ makes some hard-core commonsense presuppositions unable to pass the test of adequacy.

Materialism was defined above as "the twofold doctrine that (1) the ultimate units of the world are devoid of both experience and spontaneity and that (2) nothing exists except such units and aggregations of them." Although this doctrine creates problems for at least a dozen notions presupposed by science,[43] I will here discuss only five.

Experience. One of these is how things with experience could have emerged out of things wholly devoid of experience. Some philosophers, to be sure, argue that this constitutes no problem, since it is simply one more example of "emergence." Berkeley philosopher John Searle, for example, has argued that just as liquidity emerges when hydrogen and oxygen molecules, none of which separately have liquidity, form H_2O, experience emerges when cells, none of which individually have experience, are organized into a living brain.[44] This argument, however, commits what I have called the "emergence category mistake."[45]

The problem is that, although Searle suggests that the two cases of alleged emergence are analogous, they are not. Liquidity is a property of things *as they appear* to us—*as they are experienced* by us—whereas experience is what something is *for itself*. Things without experience—such as, in Searle's view, molecules—are nothing for themselves. To suggest that things *without* experience give birth, through being organized in a particular way, to something *with* experience is to say that a combination of things that are nothing for themselves can result in something that exists *for itself*.

To imagine an emergence of this type is to affirm something that is categorically different from an unproblematic type of emergence—such as a when *things that do not feel wet to us* produce *things that do feel wet to us*. This latter type of "emergence" involves merely different external appearances, whereas the former involves the alleged emergence of things with an "inside" out of things that had nothing but an "outside."

Thomas Nagel, using the French term *pour soi* for something that, having experience, exists "for itself," and the term *en soi* for something that, being devoid of experience, merely exists "in itself," has stated the problem clearly:

> One cannot derive a *pour soi* from an *en soi*. . . . This gap is logically unbridgeable. If a bodiless god wanted to create a conscious being, he could not expect to do it by combining together in organic form a lot of particles with none but physical properties.[46]

Colin McGinn, building upon Nagel's analysis, declares "the problem of consciousness" to be insoluble in principle, saying that we have no understanding of how "the aggregation of millions of individually insentient neurons [constituting the brain] generate subjective awareness."[47] McGinn even says that at this point "scientific naturalism runs out of steam," because "[i]t would take a supernatural magician to extract consciousness from matter."[48]

McGinn thereby gave inadvertent support to the position of his former colleague at Oxford University, Richard Swinburne, who has long included an "argument from consciousness" in his cumulative case for the existence of an omnipotent, supernatural deity.[49] But as a naturalist, McGinn, of course, cannot accept this solution, so he is left with a problem that, by his own admission, is insoluble in principle. McGinn, furthermore, is only one of several philosophers in the materialist tradition who have come to this conclusion.[50]

Freedom: Materialism also renders difficult the *freedom* that we all presuppose. Although Searle fails to grasp the radical difficulty that the emergence of consciousness presents for materialism, he has provided an especially clear analysis of the problem of freedom. On the one hand, says Searle, science "allows no place for freedom of the will,"[51] because science teaches that the world "consists entirely of

mindless, meaningless, physical particles."[52] Explicitly affirming identism by rejecting any numerical distinction between the mind and the
brain, Searle says of the human head that "the brain is the only thing
in there."[53]

This identist doctrine means that animals, such as dogs and human
beings, are *structurally* or *organizationally* similar to things such as
rocks, telephones, and typewriters, in which there is no dominant
member that can make decisions for the thing as a whole. Dualists,
by contrast, had said that there was such a dominant member, called
the *psyche* or the *anima*, this being what made animals different from
plants and inorganic things. Materialists, however, deny that animals,
including human beings, have a dominant member. Daniel Dennett,
for example, says that the human head contains only billions of "mini-
agents and microagents (with no single Boss)."[54]

The implication is that the behavior of human beings is to be
explained, like the behavior of all other aggregations of physical particles,
such as rocks, in terms of "bottom-up causation."[55] To explain human
beings in this reductionistic way, using only bottom-up causation, means
that the human mind, with all its feelings and decisions, is to be explained
entirely in terms of brain processes; that these brain processes are to be
explained entirely in terms of the activities of the individual brain cells;
that the activity of each cell is to be explained entirely in terms of the
activities of its organelles and macromolecules; and that these are to be
explained entirely in terms of their atoms and subatomic particles.

In accordance with this reductionistic view, Searle says that we
must assume that "the psychological facts about ourselves, like any
other higher level facts, are entirely causally explicable in terms of . . .
elements at the fundamental micro-physical level."[56] This means that
the causal relations behind our experiences "are entirely a matter of
neurons and neuron firings at synapses."[57] Consciousness, as an emer-
gent property of the brain, cannot exert any additional causal influence.

It cannot, therefore, "cause things that could not be explained by the causal behavior of the neurons."[58] Human behavior must, therefore, be assumed to be entirely determined by occurrences at the microphysical level, just as we assume this with regard to the behavior of billiard balls and telephones. That is all on the one hand.

On the other hand, Searle insists, this deterministic conclusion is not a position any of us can live with in practice: "Our conception of ourselves as free agents," Searle points out, "is fundamental to our overall self-conception." Accordingly, "we can't act otherwise than on the assumption of freedom, no matter how much we learn about how the world works as a determined physical system."[59]

Some materialists, to be sure, try to reconcile these two conclusions in terms of the position called "compatibilism," which involves redefining freedom so that it is compatible with physical determinism.[60] For example, an act might be said to be a "free act" as long as the agent wanted to perform it, even if the fact that the agent *wanted* to do it was determined by the agent's physical-chemical make-up. We could say that "Jones did X freely," therefore, even though Jones could not have acted otherwise. Searle, however, rightly rejects this move, pointing out that the freedom that we all presuppose involves "the belief that we could have done things differently from the way we did in fact do them."[61]

Searle is left, therefore, with an irreconcilable contradiction between scientific theory and the presuppositions of human practice. On the one hand, the scientific worldview, as he understands it, implies that human behavior, including human thinking, is as determined as the movements of billiard balls. On the other hand, he says that none of us can live with this deterministic view in practice. Insofar as Searle seeks to overcome this contradiction, he does so by giving more authority to his scientific theory than to his hard-core commonsense assumption about freedom. While pointing out that he cannot help presupposing freedom, the fact that it is not reconcilable with scientific materialism means, he suggests, that it must be an illusion.[62] This conclusion, which is accepted by virtually all materialistic philosophers, provides another example of how naturalism$_{sam}$ leads to an irrationalist philosophy of science.

Mental Causation: The materialism of naturalism$_{sam}$ also renders the notion of mental causation problematic. We all presuppose in practice that our thoughts, especially our decisions, exert "downward causation" on our bodies. For example, we know that we walk to the water fountain *because* we want a drink. Materialist philosophers, however, have been unable to explain how this is possible, given their commitment to the idea that the microlevel of the world studied by physics is causally sufficient for all effects, so that all vertical causation is *upward* causation.

An example is provided by Brown University's Jaegwon Kim, a highly respected materialist philosopher of mind who has worked for many years on this issue. Kim said early on that for a position to affirm epiphenomenalism, according to which "our reasons and desires have no causal efficacy at all in influencing our bodily actions," would constitute a *reductio ad absurdum* of that position.[63] Kim eventually realized, however, that materialism could not avoid epiphenomenalism, at which point he declared that materialism seemed to be "up against a dead end."[64]

Rational Activity: Materialism is perhaps most clearly in conflict with that aspect of mental causation that we call *rational activity*.[65] According to the materialist worldview, all causation is *efficient* causation, the influence of one thing or event on another. The rational activity of a philosopher of science is, however, action in terms of some norm, such as the norm of self-consistency. Rational activity is, in other words, an example of *final* causation, causation in terms of a norm or goal. But the materialist worldview has no room for such activity, because the mind is equated with the brain and the brain's activities are said to be, like everything else, determined by the causal activities of their most elementary parts, which are assumed to consist entirely of sequences of efficient causation.

McGinn raises this problem by asking "how a physical organism can be subject to the norms of rationality. How, for example, does *modus ponens* get its grip on the causal transitions between mental states?"[66] McGinn admits that materialism can provide no answer, thereby illustrating Putnam's charge that most science-based philosophies are self-refuting because they "leave no room for a rational activity of philosophy."[67]

Ideal Entities: Materialism, as the doctrine that nothing exists except physical particles and aggregations thereof, creates a fifth problem for science by entailing the nonexistence of ideal entities. As we saw earlier, however, Quine affirmed the real existence of mathematical objects on the grounds that physicists presuppose them. Quine said, accordingly, that his physicalism "is materialism, bluntly monistic except for the abstract objects of mathematics," because he assumed the existence of "abstract objects over and above the physical objects."[68] Although Quine was right to say that physics presupposes the existence of mathematical objects, his affirmation of their existence was arbitrary, because he did not explain how these abstract or ideal entities could exist in an otherwise materialist universe.

ATHEISM

Just as the sensationism and materialism of naturalism$_{sam}$ create insoluble problems, so does its atheism. In other chapters of this book and elsewhere,[69] I have argued that atheistic cosmologies are unable to give intelligible accounts of a wide range of features of our world, including the metaphysical and cosmological order underlying the evolutionary process; the repeated occurrences of novelty; the upward trend in the evolutionary process; and our inevitable presuppositions about ultimate truth and importance. In Chapter 7, I develop an additional point, which is that atheism also cannot account for our inevitable presuppositions about mathematical objects, logical principles, and moral norms.

In sum: If we view together all of the problems created by sensationism, materialism, and atheism, we can see that naturalism$_{sam}$ is not even close to providing a worldview adequate for our experience in general or science in particular. In light of the fact that those who endorse this version of naturalism cannot account for our presuppositions about the external world, the past, time, causation, induction, rational activity, conscious experience, mental causation, freedom, logical principles, moral norms, and mathematical objects, there is no reason to try to bring our understanding of religious experience into line with it.

Indeed, the fact that naturalism$_{sam}$ cannot allow for genuine religious experience, rather than being a reason to doubt such experience, is simply one more reason to consider this version of naturalism a woefully inadequate framework for interpreting human experience in general and scientific experience in particular. The reason this is the case is that by not being able to accept the reality of genuine religious experience—defined as experience in which Something Holy is experienced *as* Holy—social scientists presupposing naturalism$_{sam}$ cannot account for the origin and persistence of religion. This point will be developed in the following chapter. For now, the point is that the general inadequacy of naturalism$_{sam}$ means that there is no good reason to try to explain religious experience within its constraints.

SCIENTIFIC NATURALISM$_{ppp}$

This conclusion does not imply, however, that our interpretation of religious experience should not be naturalistic in the broad sense of conforming to naturalism$_{ns}$. For one thing, naturalism in this generic sense, which is simply the rejection of the possibility of supernatural interruptions of the world's normal pattern of causal relations, is presupposed by the scientific community more widely and deeply than is naturalism$_{sam}$. Unlike naturalism$_{sam}$, furthermore, naturalism$_{ns}$ does not contradict any of our inevitable presuppositions. It also does not, at least arguably, contradict any well-documented phenomena. Although some religious thinkers would claim that scientific naturalism$_{ns}$ is contradicted by numerous miracles, I have argued that the alternative version of naturalism recommended here can, in light of the science of parapsychology, accommodate various kinds of phenomena traditionally called miracles.[70]

Yet another consideration is the fact that it is simply very difficult, given the infinitely complex ways in which events are interwoven in the causal web of the world, to imagine how this web could be broken here and there. Insofar as we accept domain uniformitarianism, in any case, it is not unreasonable to expect that explanations of religious experience provided in intellectual circles would be naturalistic in the generic sense.

When this point is conjoined with the arguments against naturalism$_{sam}$, the implication is that we need a new version of naturalism$_{ns}$. The kind of naturalism we need, I argue, has been provided by Whitehead.[71] In Whitehead's version of naturalism, which I have called naturalism$_{ppp}$, the sensationism of naturalism$_{sam}$ is replaced by a prehensive doctrine of perception, the atheism is replaced by panentheism, and the materialism is replaced by panexperientialism.

PANEXPERIENTIALISM WITH ORGANIZATIONAL DUALITY

It is important to emphasize, as already mentioned in Chapter 1, that this third doctrine, "panexperientialism with organizational duality,"[72] does *not* attribute experience and spontaneity to all things whatsoever.

It cannot be quickly dismissed, therefore, by simply pointing out that there is no good reason to think of rocks as having experience. Experience is attributed only to true individuals—whether simple individuals, such as quarks, or compound individuals, such as animals—not to aggregational societies of individuals, such as sticks and stones, which show no signs of spontaneity. Given this version of naturalism, we can account for all those notions that we presuppose in practice to which naturalism$_{sam}$ cannot do justice.

Thanks to the panexperientialism of naturalism$_{ppp}$, we can understand how our conscious experiences can arise out of our brains, enjoy a degree of free self-determination, and then act back upon our brains and thereby upon the larger world.

The materialistic view that the mind must be numerically identical with the brain resulted from the failure of dualistic interactionism, articulated most famously by Descartes. Because Descartes thought of the brain, along with the rest of nature, as composed of bits of matter devoid of both spontaneity and experience, he necessarily thought of the human mind, with its freedom and conscious experience, as different in kind from the brain's components, which we now call neurons. He could explain the interaction between brain and mind, therefore, only by appealing to God's supernatural power.

Materialism, wanting to avoid this appeal to a *deus ex machina*, rejected the idea of a mind that is numerically distinct from the brain. It is primarily this idea, that the mind and the brain are numerically identical, that makes it impossible for materialists to do justice to our presuppositions about freedom, rational activity, and mental causation, and to accept the possibility of nonsensory perception and out-of-body experiences.

Panexperientialism, by contrast, allows us to return to the idea that mind and brain are numerically distinct—but without affirming the problematic idea of dualistic interactionism. Because the brain's neurons are thought to have their own experience and spontaneity, we can think of the mind or soul as a distinct actuality that arises out of the brain and, on the basis of its own partially self-determining experience, acts back upon it. This is a return to interactionism, but it is a *nondualistic* interactionism, so it is intelligible without supernatural assistance. With this panexperientialism, we also avoid the impossible question of how experience emerges out of nonexperiencing things; we can take our experiences of freedom, rational thought, and mental causation at face value; and we can conceive of the possibility of non-sensory perception and even out-of-body experiences.

Panentheism

Given the panentheism of naturalism$_{ppp}$, we can reaffirm the idea of divine influence in the world. We can thereby explain those features of the world, mentioned in passing earlier, that an atheistic cosmology cannot explain: the world's order; the novelty and upward trend in its evolutionary process; our presuppositions about ultimate truth and importance; and the existence and efficacy of mathematical, logical, and moral principles.

This reaffirmation of divine influence does not, however, bring back the problem of evil, which was created by supernaturalistic theism. Within this panentheistic vision, divine influence is understood as part and parcel of the world's normal causal relations, never an interruption thereof. With regard to the topic at hand, the most important fact about panentheism is that it says that there is a Holy Actuality, distinct from the world, which could in principle be experienced *as* Holy, resulting in genuine religious experience.

Prehensive Doctrine of Perception

To see further how this is possible, we need to turn to the final element of naturalism$_{ppp}$, its *prehensive, nonsensory doctrine of perception*.

With this doctrine of perception, we can, in the first place, understand why we inevitably presuppose the reality of the external world, the past, time, and causation. It is because we have a direct, nonsensory experience of them.[73]

We can likewise understand our mathematical, logical, moral, and aesthetic intuitions as reflecting, at least to some extent, patterns really existing in the nature of things, because these patterns exist in God and we experience them, even if dimly, by virtue of our prehension of God.

In these ways, this prehensive doctrine of perception, taken in conjunction with the panentheistic doctrine of the universe, can account for most of our hard-core commonsense assumptions. The division between theory and practice, or theoretical and practical reason, which has plagued modern philosophy since the writings of Hume and Kant, is overcome. Naturalism$_{ppp}$ thus proves itself to be far more adequate for interpreting our experience, including our scientific experience, than naturalism$_{sam}$.

RELIGIOUS EXPERIENCE

With regard to the topic of this chapter in particular, the adequacy of naturalism$_{ppp}$ is further illustrated by the fact that its prehensive doctrine of perception, combined with its panentheism, is able to explain why people always and everywhere have given testimony to a distinctive type of experience that we call religious experience. It is distinctive in that it involves the experience of a Holy Reality—of something that is real and seems to have the unique quality that we call the "sacred" or the "holy," because our awareness of it evokes in us feelings with this quality.

According to Whitehead's prehensive doctrine of perception, which both supports and presupposes panexperientialism, we directly perceive other actual entities, all of which are occasions of experience. We most directly perceive them not through our sensory organs—sensory perception is a very indirect mode of perception. Rather, we directly prehend them in a nonsensory manner, as when I directly prehend my brain cells and my past occasions of experience. This direct prehension is a *feeling*—the present experience directly feels the feelings of the prior experiences. As the term "feeling," used interchangeably with "prehension," is meant to suggest, perception in this mode involves not only an object, which is *what* is felt, but also a subjective form, which is *how* the object is felt.

For our present purposes, the most important feature of this idea is that the subjective form of a present experience tends to sympathize with, and hence conform to, the subjective form of the feeling that it is prehending. For example, if the cells in my arm have been injured, so that they are feeling pain, I will feel their pain painfully. Likewise, if I am intensely worried or angry, my bodily cells will prehend my experiences with negative subjective forms, which, if chronic, may result in bodily illness. But if I am happy, my bodily cells will feel my experiences with positive subjective forms.

According to the panentheistic view of reality, we are related to God somewhat as our brain cells are related to us. We are, therefore, directly prehending God all the time, just as our brain cells are directly prehending us. Assuming that God truly is, as theistic interpretations of religious experience suggest, characterized by the quality that we call "holiness," then we would be feeling this divine holiness all the time. Given this account, the question would no longer be why people occasionally report having "religious" or "mystical" experiences. The question would be why they report having them only occasionally, instead of all the time.

The answer to this question is provided by another feature of Whitehead's account of perception, which is that we are conscious of only a tiny portion of the things that we experience, and that we tend *not* to be conscious of the things that we directly prehend. For example, I am conscious of the tree outside my window, which I see only by means of a highly indirect process, involving billions of photons and then billions of events in my eyes and my brain's optic system. But I am not conscious of my brain cells, which I prehend directly, and by means of which I see the tree. As this example illustrates, consciousness primarily illuminates the products of sensory perception, tending to leave the objects of our more fundamental, nonsensory perception in the dark. Using "prehension in the mode of causal efficacy" for this nonsensory prehension and "prehension in the mode of presentational immediacy" for our perception of sensory data, Whitehead says:

> [C]onsciousness only dimly illuminates the prehensions in the mode of causal efficacy, because these prehensions are primitive elements in our experience. But prehensions in the mode of presentational immediacy are among those prehensions which we enjoy with the most vivid consciousness.[74]

Our prehensions of God, like our prehensions of our brain cells, are prehensions in the mode of causal efficacy, and hence are ordinarily not illuminated by consciousness.

In certain extraordinary moments, however, our prehensions of God can rise to the level of consciousness. After such moments, we say that we had a "religious" experience, an "experience of God," or an "experience of the holy." What was extraordinary about those moments, however, was not that we perceived God; we are doing that all the time. What was extraordinary was only that this perception, with its subjective form of holiness, rose to the level of consciousness.

On this basis, we can see that theistic religious experience can involve a direct experience of a Holy Actuality, in whom we live, move, and have our being. And on this basis, in turn, we can understand why human beings always and everywhere have been religious, orienting their lives around the idea of something holy or sacred.

This position can thereby be used to explain, without presupposing occasional divine interruptions of our normal perceptual processes, why people in all times and places, evidently, have reported occasional extraordinary experiences, which we now usually call religious or mystical experiences.

Also, the idea that everyone is experiencing a Holy Actuality all the time can explain why people in general, even if they have never had one of these extraordinary experiences, have religious feelings and understand the meaning of religious terms, such as "God" and "the holy." That is, in addition to the extraordinary kind of experience, to which the label "religious experience" is usually applied, we can also speak of a general "background religious experience," through which all people are, more or less dimly, aware of the reality of something holy. From this awareness arises our knowledge that something important is going on, so that, somehow, life is ultimately significant.

CONCLUSION

Insofar as this explanation of the existence and persistence of religion is based on a naturalistic worldview that is more adequate and coherent than naturalism$_{sam}$, it should be regarded as superior from an academic, including a scientific, point of view. If our culture would shift from naturalism$_{sam}$ to naturalism$_{ppp}$, it would have an intellectual framework that is far more adequate to our experience and practice in general and to our scientific experience and practice in particular. It would also no longer be teaching people—whether explicitly or only implicitly—that the naturalism properly presupposed by the scientific community rules out the possibility of genuine religious experience. This issue of the best framework for scientific interpretations of religion will be continued in the next chapter.

NOTES

1. I have discussed the distinction between theistic and nontheistic religious experiences in "The Two Ultimates and the Religions," Chap. 7 of *Reenchantment without Supernaturalism*.

2. Kant did contribute to the scientific community's acceptance of naturalism$_{sam}$, however, insofar as he argued that scientific (theoretical) reason had to presuppose not only a sensationist doctrine of perception but also a deterministic, nontheistic worldview.

3. Kant, *Religion within the Limits of Reason Alone,* trans. Theodore M. Greene and Hoyt H. Hudson (New York: Harper & Row, 1960), 163.

4. Emile Durkheim, *The Elementary Forms of the Religious Life*, trans. Joseph Ward Swain (New York: Free Press, 1963), 57.

5. J.J.C. Smart, "Religion and Science," in Stephen H. Phillips, ed., *Philosophy of Religion: A Global Approach* (Fort Worth: Harcourt Brace, 1996: 217-24).

6. Rudolf Otto, *The Idea of the Holy*, trans. John H. Harvey (New York: Oxford University Press, 1958), 175.

7. Mircea Eliade, *History of Religious Ideas,* trans. W.R. Trask (Chicago: University of Chicago Press, 1978), Vol. I: xiii.

8. J. Samuel Preus, *Explaining Religion: Criticism and Theory from Bodin to Freud* (New Haven & London: Yale University Press, 1987), xix.

9. Ibid., 174.

10. Ibid., xv.

11. Robert A. Segal, *Religion and the Social Sciences: Essays on the Confrontation* (Atlanta: Scholars Press, 1989), 71.

12. Gordon D. Kaufman, *In Face of Mystery: A Constructive Theology* (Cambridge: Harvard University Press, 1993), 415, 323.

13. Preus, *Explaining Religion*, ix n.2, xx, xxi.

14 Wayne Proudfoot, *Religious Experience* (Berkeley & Los Angeles: University of California Press, 1985), 223; cf. 197, 215.

15. Ibid., 161.

16. Segal, *Explaining and Interpreting Religion*, 19.

17. Preus, *Explaining Religion*, xiii, xiv.

18. In *The Easter Enigma: An Essay on the Resurrection with Special Reference to the Data of Psychical Research*, Michael C. Perry argues for this point even though he holds to a traditional, supernaturalist interpretation of the resurrection of Jesus.

19. Richard S. Blacher, "Near-Death Experiences," *Journal of the American Medical Association* 244 (1980), 30.

20. Ibid., 47.

21. Susan J. Blackmore, *Dying to Live: Near-Death Experiences* (Buffalo: Prometheus Books, 1993), xi.

22. Whitehead, *Process and Reality*, 151.

23. Ibid., 13.

24. John Passmore, *Philosophical Reasoning* (New York: Basic Books, 1961), 60.

25. See Martin Jay, "The Debate over Performative Contradiction: Habermas versus the Poststructuralists," in Jay, *Force Fields: Between Intellectual History and Cultural Critique* (New York & London: Routledge, 1993), 25-37.

26. In "Cogito, Ergo Sum: Inference or Performance," Jaakko Hintikka has shown that Descartes' argument involved the notion of a performative self-contradiction. If I say, "I doubt herewith, now, that

I exist," explains Hintikka, "the propositional component contradicts the performative component of the speech act expressed by that self-referential sentence" (*Philosophical Review* 71 [1962], 3-32, at 32).

27. Whitehead, *Process and Reality*, 13.

28. Ibid., 50.

29. Albert Einstein, "Maxwell's Influence on the Development of the Conception of Physical Reality," in J.J. Thomson et al., *James Clerk Maxwell: A Commemorative Volume* (Cambridge: Cambridge University Press, 1931), 66-73, at 66.

30. Willard V.O. Quine, *Ontological Relativity and Other Essays* (New York: Columbia University Press, 1969), 75.

31. Quine, *From A Logical Point of View* (Cambridge: Harvard University Press, 1953), 41.

32. Ibid., 44.

33. George Santayana, *Scepticism and Animal Faith* (New York: Dover, 1955), 14-15.

34. Quine, *From Stimulus to Science* (Cambridge: Harvard University Press, 1995), 36; emphasis added.

35. Hans Reichenbach, *Experience and Prediction* (Chicago: University of Chicago Press, 1938), 346.

36. A.J. Ayer, *Language, Truth, and Logic* (New York: Dover, 1952), 49.

37. Hilary, Putnam, *Words and Life*, ed. James Conant (Cambridge: Harvard University Press, 1994), 503. (The quotation comes from an essay originally published in 1979, when Putnam still held a materialist worldview, with a functionalist, cybernetic view of the mind.) Gödel's suggestion was also derisively rejected by Charles Chihara in "A Gödelian Thesis Regarding Mathematical Objects: Do They Exist? And Can We Perceive Them?" (*Philosophical Review* 91 [1982]: 211-17, at 217.

38. Reuben Hersh, *What is Mathematics, Really?* (New York: Oxford University Press, 1997), 7; Penelope Maddy, *Realism in Mathematics* (Oxford: Clarendon Press, 1990), 2-3.

39. Maddy, *Realism in Mathematics*, 44, 59, 178.

40 Putnam, *Words and Life*, 153.

41. Ibid., 500.

42. Putnam, *Reason, Truth, and History* (Cambridge: Cambridge University Press, 1981), 98-114.

43. See Chap. 1 of my *Reenchantment without Supernaturalism.*

44. John E. Searle, *The Rediscovery of the Mind* (Cambridge: MIT Press, 1992), 14.

45. See my *Unsnarling the World-Knot*, 64-67.

46. *Mortal Questions* (London: Cambridge University Press, 1979), 189.

47 McGinn, *The Problem of Consciousness: Essays Toward a Resolution* (Oxford: Basil Blackwell, 1991), 1.

48. Ibid., 45.

49. Swinburne, *The Existence of God* (New York: Oxford University Press, 1979), 161, 197-73; *The Evolution of the Soul* (Oxford: Clarendon, 1986), 198-99.

50. Analyses similar to McGinn's can be found in (besides Thomas Nagel's *Mortal Questions*) William S. Robinson's *Brains and People: An Essay on Mentality and Its Causal Conditions* (Philadelphia: Temple University Press, 1988), William Seager's *Metaphysics of Consciousness* (London & New York: Routledge, 1991), and Galen Strawson's *Mental Reality* (Cambridge: MIT Press, 1994)—although Strawson in this book and Seager in later works proposed panexperientialist [which they called "panpsychist") solutions. For a summary of this discussion, see the

Introduction and Chap. 6 of my *Unsnarling the World-Knot*, or Chap. 6 of my *Religion and Scientific Naturalism*.

51. Searle, *Minds, Brains, and Science: The 1984 Reith Lectures* (London: British Broadcasting Corporation, 1984), 92.

52. Ibid., 13.

53. Searle, *The Rediscovery of the Mind* (Cambridge: MIT Press, 1992), 248.

54. Dennett, *Consciousness Explained* (Boston: Little, Brown & Co., 1991), 458.

55. Searle, *Minds, Brains, and Science*, 93.

56. Ibid., 98.

57. Ibid., 93.

58. *The Rediscovery of Mind,* 63. The idea of statistical indeterminacy at the quantum level also provides no basis for affirming freedom, Searle adds, because all such indeterminacy is canceled out in macro-objects, such as billiard balls and human bodies, and "the human mind can[not] force the statistically-determined particles to swerve from their paths" (*Minds, Brains, and Science,* 87).

59. Ibid., 86, 97.

60. See, for example, William G. Lycan, *Consciousness* (Cambridge: MIT Press, 1987), 113-18. I have discussed Lycan's position in *Unsnarling the World-Knot*, 212-17.

61. Searle, *Minds, Brains, and Science*, 92.

62. Ibid., 5, 94, 98. I have discussed Searle's position on freedom more fully in *Unsnarling the World-Knot*, 38-40, 163-70, and in *Religion and Scientific Naturalism*, 151-57. An analysis of the problem of freedom and determinism similar to Searle's is provided by Thomas Nagel, *The*

View from Nowhere, 110-23, and by philosopher of law Lloyd Weinreb, *Natural Law and Justice*, vii, 9-12, 263-65, and "The Moral Point of View," 202-04.

63. Kim, *Supervenience and Mind: Selected Philosophical Essays* (Cambridge: Cambridge University Press, 1993), 104-06.

64. Ibid., 367. Chapter 10 of my *Unsnarling the World-Knot* is devoted to a critique of Kim's position. This chapter is reprinted, in slightly revised form, as "Materialist and Panexperientialist Physicalism: A Critique of Jaegwon Kim's *Supervenience and Mind*," in *Process Studies* 28 (Spring-Summer 1999), followed by a response from Kim and a counter-reply from me. For a collection of essays on the problem, see John Heil and Alfred Mele, eds., *Mental Causation* (Oxford: Clarendon, 1995).

65. Kim points out that thinking of ourselves as capable of mental causation is closely related to thinking of ourselves "as reflective agents capable of deliberation and evaluation—that is, ...as agents capable of acting in accordance with a norm" *(Supervenience and Mind*, 215).

66. McGinn, *The Problem of Consciousness*, 23n.

67. Putnam, *Realism and Reason* (New York: Cambridge University Press, 1983), 191.

68. Quine, *From Stimulus to Science*, 14; *Theories and Things*, 14-15.

69. Especially *Reenchantment without Supernaturalism*, Ch. 5.

70. See my *Parapsychology, Philosophy, and Spirituality: A Postmodern Exploration* (Albany: State University of New York Press, 1996). For a more thorough discussion of the philosophical possibility of parapsychological phenomena, see "Parapsychology and Philosophy: A Whiteheadian Postmodern Perspective." On the question of whether parapsychology should be taken seriously, rather than rejected as a mere "pseudo-science," see Chap. 7 of *Religion and Scientific Naturalism*.

71. Whitehead was, incidentally, Quine's teacher, so one might think that Quine had explicitly rejected Whitehead's argument. However, Quine said that he paid little attention in Whitehead's classes except when the latter was dealing with logic and mathematics ("Autobiography of W.V. Quine," in *The Philosophy of W.V. Quine*, ed. Lewis Edwin Hahn and Paul Arthur Schilpp [Library of Living Philosophers 18. LaSalle, Ill.: Open Court: 1986], 9-10).

72. The point of the term "organizational duality" is that we can account for the obvious duality in the world—between things that have a unified experience, and therefore the capacity for spontaneity or self-determination, and things that do not—without positing Descartes' *ontological dualism* between mental and physical substances, which created an insuperable mind-body problem and a host of related difficulties.

73. In Ch. 10 of *Reenchantment without Supernaturalism*, I have contrasted this Whiteheadian view of these Humean "natural beliefs," according to which we presuppose them because we always experience them, with Alvin Plantinga's position that such beliefs are "properly basic" even though they are not experientially rooted--a position that he uses to support his claim that belief in an omnipotent deity can be properly basic for a Christian.

74. Whitehead, *Process and Reality*, 162.

CHAPTER SIX

Scientific Naturalism and the Study of Religion

I n this chapter, I continue the discussion of the relation between scientific naturalism and religious experience, here focusing on the way in which scientific naturalism has shaped the modern study of religion in the academy. For this purpose, I extensively explore the positions of two well-known interpreters of religion, Robert A. Segal and J. Samuel Preus.

Robert Segal, in *Religion and the Social Sciences* (henceforth *RSS*) and *Explaining and Interpreting Religion* (henceforth *EIR*),[1] has portrayed an antithesis between the "social scientific" approach to religion, which he favored, and the approach of those he calls "religionists," by which he meant thinkers who defend the truth and thereby the "religiosity" of religion (*RSS* 1; *EIR* 1). The first book, in fact, is subtitled *Essays on the Confrontation*.

Samuel Preus, in *Explaining Religion* (henceforth *ER*),[2] drew an equally strong opposition between "the modern study of religion," which he advocated, and all "theological" and "religious" approaches, which he rejected.[3]

For both authors, the difference was that the approach that they advocated explains religion in "naturalistic" terms, whereas religious approaches resist naturalistic explanations. These "religious" approaches are of two fundamental types. One type rejects causal explanations altogether, saying that religion is a phenomenon to be "interpreted," not explained. The other type of approach, while agreeing with Preus and Segal that an explanation is needed, offers a *religious* explanation. The type of religious explanation primarily targeted by Preus and Segal was *theological* explanation, which explains religion, at least theistic religion, in terms of a genuine religious experience of a holy actuality distinct from the totality of finite things. But Preus and Segal also rejected all other religious explanations, such as those that explain religion in terms of an innate religious sense and those that explain nontheistic religions in terms of a genuine experience of a nonpersonal religious ultimate, which some might call Nirvana, Emptiness, Nirguna Brahman, or the Tao.

Although Preus spoke of the "modern" or "naturalistic" study of religion and Segal of the "social scientific" study of religion, they both were clearly advocating the same approach. For example, they illustrate the approach said to be appropriate for the academic study of religion with the same exemplars, such as Auguste Comte, E.B. Tylor, Emile Durkheim, and Sigmund Freud. Also, Segal said of Preus's book that it traces "the emergence of the social scientific, or naturalistic, explanation of religion" (*EIR* 123), thereby showing that he saw Preus's "naturalistic" approach to be equatable with the "social scientific" approach that he advocated. And Preus, regarding David Hume as the thinker who completed the paradigm shift in the study of religion to a thoroughgoing naturalism, said that he prefers "to label Hume as the founder of the scientific study of religion" rather than of the philosophy of religion (*ER* xi, 84 n.1). Therefore, although Preus did not characteristically use the term "social scientific," he was, no less than Segal, saying that the academic study of religion should be equated with, or at least based on, the social scientific study of religion.[4]

Thus understood, the common position of Segal and Preus involves three distinguishable claims: (1) The academic study of religion should not avoid the task of explaining the origin and persistence of religion. (2) Any explanation, to be acceptable in the academy, must be a social scientific explanation. (3) Any explanation, to be considered a social scientific explanation, must be "naturalistic" in their sense of the term.

Any of these three claims can, of course, be challenged. The first claim can be rejected by those who believe that the task of the academic study of religion is to *interpret* it, rather than to explain it. This position may be held on the basis of a methodological distinction between the *Geisteswissenschaften*, which properly *interpret* their phenomena, and the *Naturwissenschaften*, which properly *explain* their phenomena. This distinction may in turn be based on the assumption that "explanations" are necessarily reductionistic. Or one might simply believe for some other reason that the attempt to give causal explanations for religion is somehow inappropriate, perhaps sacrilegious.

In any case, although this division—on whether the study of religion should focus primarily on interpretation or explanation—has probably been the major division within the academic study of religion, I will not here directly discuss this complex issue,[5] except to register my agreement with Preus and Segal that the task of attempting to explain the origin and persistence of religion should not be avoided. While agreeing on the need for explanation, however, I reject their view, as expressed in the second and third claims, as to the only academically acceptable type of explanation.[6]

This Preus-Segal view seems to be rather widely accepted among those engaged in religious studies. That is, although many religion scholars reject the task of explaining religion or at least do not devote their own energies to this task, the negative implication of the Preus-Segal position seems to be widely assumed—namely, that insofar as causal explanations *are* proffered, academicians involved in the study of religion cannot, by definition, argue for the truth of religion in the sense of holding that the best explanation for the existence of religion is that it arises from a response to something holy in the nature of things. One can remain neutral on this question, by not raising it or by endorsing methodological agnosticism. Or one can advocate a negative answer, as do Preus and Segal. But one cannot, at least in one's academic work, argue for the truth of religion in the aforementioned sense.[7] Although a more complete critique of this position would need to consider both theistic and nontheistic understandings of the "something holy," I will here limit my discussion to the theistic understanding.

My argument against the shared position of Preus and Segal develops as follows. In the first section, I lay out the Preus-Segal claim that academic explanations of religion, being naturalistic, are necessarily in opposition to theistic accounts of religion.

In the second section, I point out that, although Preus uses the term "naturalism" as if it had a single meaning, his discussion actually employs the term with eight distinguishable meanings. The question thereby raised is whether all of these meanings of "naturalism" are really implied by the rejection of supernaturalism. I answer this question in the negative, denying in particular that the rejection of supernaturalism requires what I call naturalism$_{sam}$, meaning the sensationistic, atheistic, materialistic version of naturalism.

In the third section, I argue that the only valid reason for advocating the employment of this version of naturalism in the academic study of religion would be a *philosophical* conviction as to its truth, while I argue, in the fourth section, that the acceptance of this form of naturalism is *not* philosophically warranted.

The overall purpose of my argument is to undermine the widespread assumption, expressed especially clearly by Preus and Segal, that the academic study of religion necessarily excludes all theistic explanations of religion. I turn now to my argument against the Preus-Segal claim that to accept a naturalistic view of religion means rejecting a theological explanation.

Naturalistic Versus Theological Explanations

The academic study of religion, both Preus and Segal argued, should take a "naturalistic" and *thereby* antitheological approach. Preus, speaking of an "essential contradiction" between "theology" and "the study of religion" (*ER* xvi), located this contradiction in the former's being supernaturalistic, the latter, naturalistic.

The naturalistic approach, he said, "is the decisive feature which distinguishes the study of religion from theology" (*ER* 205). The study of religion could not emerge, Preus said, "as long as a supernatural (or some objective, transcendent) ground of religion was assumed as the really existent referent and generative source of religious language" (*ER* xvi). Although this statement might seem to allow for a distinction between a "supernatural" and an "objective, transcendent" ground of religion, Preus regarded the two as equally objectionable. Identifying "the study of religion" with a "naturalistic approach," he contrasted it with "theology" and a "religious approach" (*ER* xi). And, referring to "two rival paradigms," he equated "the naturalistic paradigm" with "an altogether nonreligious point of view," which rejects "the absolutes of confessional and natural theology" (*ER* xi, xiii, xiv). The naturalistic approach, he indicated, is "reductionistic," claiming that "transcendence" is not the best answer to the question of the cause of religion (*ER* ix n.2, xx). This naturalistic, reductionistic approach has "its own explanatory apparatus," in which the categories of "transcendence" and "the sacred" are absent (*ER* xxi). Preus clearly indicated, therefore, that a properly academic approach to religion could not hold that religion might have a ground that is objective, in the sense of being transcendent to one's experience, even if this objective ground would not properly be called "supernatural."

The naturalistic approach to religion, in other words, begins with the assumption that there is no *genuine* religious experience, in the sense of an experience of a divine reality distinct from the totality of finite causes. The naturalistic analyst of religion, says Preus, *rejects* the religious participants' own account of their religious experience, "because the analyst does not believe their explanation that mysterious transcendent powers beyond the realm of natural causation . . . really create this experience" (*ER* 174). The same point is made by Preus's succinct statement of the central question for the academic study of religion: "if 'God is not given,' how is one to explain religions—that is, their universality, variety, and persistence until now?" (*ER* xv)

As these statements show, what Preus means by the academic study of religion excludes not merely confessional theology but any position that is "theological" in the sense of explaining the origin and persistence of religion in terms of genuine religious experience of, and thereby causal influence by, a divine reality distinct from the totality of finite causes. To be academic, the study of theistic religion must consider it false.

Segal makes essentially the same point. To be sure, Segal came to focus his critical attention in his later writings (those in the second of his two books) on those "religionists" who deny the propriety of explaining religion in favor of "interpreting" (more than on those who offer religious explanations for it). Indeed, Segal even came to criticize as "outdated" Preus's "concentration on a religious cause" (*EIR* 124-25). The fact that Segal came to think the major battle to lie elsewhere does not, however, imply any retraction of his view that the social scientific and thereby the academic study of theistic religion, to be such, must consider it false.

For example, assuming that to attribute religion to "the experience of god" is to speak of a "supernatural origin," Segal said that every social scientific explanation of religion involves "a naturalistic rather than divine origin" (*RSS* 76, 81; *EIR* 19). In one place, in fact, Segal said that "any naturalistic explanations . . . *are* social scientific ones" (*RSS* 78), thereby seeming to say that being naturalistic is a sufficient as well as necessary condition for an explanation to count as (social) scientific. Should it not, one might ask, also have some other characteristics, such as self-consistency and reasonable adequacy? In any case, the social scientist's naturalistic (read "nonreligious") explanation of religious experience, said Segal, intends to be a *sufficient* explanation, obviating the need for any divine cause (*RSS* 82). The naturalist, Segal said, argues that "believers never encounter God" (*EIR* 71). Social scientific explanations thereby deny the genuineness of religious experience.

Given my exposition of the positions of Preus and Segal thus far, it would seem that they completely equated the academic study of religion with a naturalistic approach and this with a wholly nonreligious approach. And that was, indeed, their overwhelmingly dominant tendency. In a few passages, however, they both allow for a more nuanced understanding. Segal granted that some (unconventional) social scientists have given a "social scientific affirmation of the truth of religion" (*RSS* 15, 107). And Preus pointed out that some early members of the naturalistic tradition gave theistic explanations of religion (*ER* 23-28, 206, 211). If one can be a theist and yet be a naturalistic social scientist, "naturalism" must be multidimensional, with some dimensions being more essential than others. I turn now to this issue.

VARIOUS DIMENSIONS OF "NATURALISM"

A careful reading of the writings of Segal and Preus, especially the latter, reveals that their advocated naturalism, which at first sight seems to be a simple notion that one must either affirm or reject wholesale, is actually a very complex notion, with many dimensions, not all of which are entailed by the rest. It might be possible, accordingly, to affirm some aspects of their naturalism while rejecting others, with the consequence that an approach that is theological as well as naturalistic might be possible.

I will carry out this analysis in terms of Preus's treatment of naturalism, which was far more extensive than Segal's. The basic distinction to be made is between the *epistemic* and *ontological* dimensions of the full-fledged naturalism his discussion advocated. Each of these dimensions, furthermore, contains four distinguishable doctrines. Preus himself did not draw attention to these distinctions, which may help account for his simple division between naturalistic and supernaturalistic approaches. The distinctions, nevertheless, are there to be seen. I will lay out the four epistemic meanings of "naturalism," then the four ontological meanings.

1. The most obvious meaning of epistemic naturalism is the *denial of epistemic supernaturalism,* which would hold that some ideas are to be accepted because of their alleged mode of origin in an infallible revelation, according to which a divine being supernaturally overrode the fallibility that characterizes most human thought, thereby making the message error-free. The denial of this doctrine can be called *epistemic naturalism$_{nsr}$* (with "nsr" indicating "no supernatural revelation").

The acceptance of this view puts one within the naturalistic tradition, at least partly, Preus indicated, by saying that the work of Jean Bodin and Herbert of Cherbury represented "a paradigm shift—for although they stayed firmly within a religious mode of explaining religion . . . , they put reason above the alleged revelations as the norm for religious truth, and they rejected the authority of confessional groups" (*ER* 206). Preus further illustrated the importance of epistemic naturalism$_{nsr}$ in referring to Tylor's criticism of "the refusal of theologians to give up the fight for a theological or revelational scheme to answer questions that belong to natural science" (*ER* 145).

Preus was surely right to say that the academic study of religion must be naturalistic in this sense, which is no longer a matter for serious debate.

2. More relevant to current controversies is what can be called *epistemic naturalism$_{du}$* (du = "domain uniformitarianism"), which is the insistence that religion is to be explained in terms of the *same causal categories used in other cultural domains* (ER x, xvi). "[T]he religious element in culture," said Preus, is not to be exempted "from the processes that produce all the rest of it" (*ER* 153). Preus illustrated this dimension by pointing out that Giambattista Vico's "explanation [of religion] was naturalistic except for one remaining theological residue—a divinely implanted, universal religious sense," and by referring to Tylor's rejection of "the wish of theologians to be excused from the universal process of evolution by claiming an exemption for religion, or a particular form of religion, in the name of an entirely autonomous supernatural realm of law and causality" (*ER* 206, 153).

In rejecting the assumption that religion has a "privileged status," epistemic naturalism$_{du}$ rejects not only the use of different causal categories to explain it but also the view that religion should be exempted from causal explanation altogether (*ER* xix, 81). For example, in relation to Mircea Eliade's statement that "the 'sacred' is an element in the structure of consciousness, and not a state in the history of consciousness," Preus said: "[I]n an academic setting where other scholars are struggling with the evolutionary emergence of our species . . . one legitimately wants to know how Eliade's remarkable 'element in the structure of consciousness' might have gotten there" (*ER* xix).

Preus was entirely right about all this. The proper approach, as he said, is one that "pushes explanation to the limit" (*ER* 210), and in this effort we should work towards a uniform set of explanatory categories for all features of the world.

Preus's discussion of domain uniformitarianism, however, was problematic. Although he rightly said that we need a "unified science of [humanity]" with "a single web of relationships, none of which is autonomous" (*ER* 203), he confused two possible meanings of "autonomy." It is surely proper to reject *complete* autonomy, according to which religion would be "a law unto itself, entirely self-determined" (*ER* 203).

But in denying the claim that "'transcendence' is an independent variable" (*ER* 203), Preus implied the rejection of even *partial* autonomy to religion. It is now customary to take the political, the economic, the sociological, psychological, and the cultural realms all to involve independent variables, so that none is wholly reducible to any or all of the others. Preus, however, was suggesting that religion, usually taken as central to the cultural realm, is completely reducible to one or more of the other realms. Indeed, his rejection of the claim that "religion is [even partly] a response to transcendence was simply the reverse side of his view that "psychosocial causes" provide a sufficient explanation for religious experience (*ER* 204, 161, 197). This notion reflected Preus's conviction that Freud and Durkheim have provided the most complete theories of religion thus far, and that a fully adequate theory would need somehow to combine their insights (*ER* 158, 161-62, 196, 209).

As Preus's own account showed, however, neither Freud nor Durkheim came close to providing an adequate account of religion, and Preus himself did not even try to show how their radically different views could be combined into an adequate psychosocial theory. His confidence that psychosocial causes will prove sufficient for explaining religious experience, accordingly, seems to be based on what Freud declared to be the basis of religion: wishful thinking.

Preus's wishful thinking here seemed to have two aspects, one of which was simply the wish to have religion understood in some purely reductionistic way. But another aspect seems to be the *wish to belong*, to have the study of religion fully accepted as part of the academy. For example, after saying that theology in all its modes "fails as a unifying paradigm because its peculiar insistence that religions are 'manifestations of the sacred' isolates it from the presuppositions that are otherwise operative in the humanities and social sciences," and that this insistence "excludes fruitful intellectual interaction with people in other disciplines," Preus made this amazing statement: "The issue is not whether 'transcendence' refers to something extramentally real, but whether the study of religion wishes to enter as a full partner in the study of culture" (*ER* 210). It was disappointing at the end of Preus's long book to learn that it may have been motivated less by the concern for truth than by the concern to belong.

We can, nevertheless, assume that Preus really did believe that "transcendence" does *not* refer to something extramentally real, so that a true account of religious experience would be a reductionistic account. We are still left, however, with no good reason for accepting this view. I have argued thus far that this view is not entailed simply by the acceptance of epistemic naturalism$_{nsr}$ combined with epistemic naturalism$_{du}$.

3. A third dimension of Preus's epistemic naturalism was indicated by his statement that the theories of Durkheim and Freud were crucial for the naturalistic paradigm "because their allegation that psychoso-cial causes are at the root of religious experience was subject to testing through scientific methods of observation and correction" (*ER* 161-62). This doctrine, which can be called *epistemic naturalism$_{eg}$* (eg = "empiri-cal groundedness"), is used by Preus to differentiate the scientific from the religious or theological perspective: "The critical difference is that the vitality and fruitfulness of the Freudian-Durkheimian approaches is due to the reciprocal relation that holds between theory and data," which allows these approaches to have "progressive and self-correcting results" (*ER* 195). By contrast, "theology is controlled," Preus claims, "by no reality principle" (*ER* 195).

However, one can agree with Preus that any academic theory of religion should be experientially grounded while doubting that this criterion necessarily rules out theological theories. Various forms of theology, some of which have used the label "empirical theology," have insisted that all talk of a Divine Reality be rooted in immediate experience. Preus paused to acknowledge that some examinations of experience have led to theological revisions, but he dismissed these efforts with, instead of an argument, simply sarcasm, saying: "[O]ne wonders whether that experience is 'religious experience' as much as it is the experience of implausibility and the demand for apologetic projects aimed at legitimating religion itself in the modern world" (*ER* 196).

4. This dismissal, by seeming to rule out a priori the possibility of genuine religious experience, pointed to the fourth and decisive dimension of the epistemic side of Preus's naturalism, which can be called *epistemic naturalism$_S$* (s = "sensationism"). This doctrine further specifies the previous one, insisting that to be naturalistic a theory of religion must be based not simply on empiricism but on *sensate* empiricism, according to which we can have no experience of anything beyond ourselves except through our physical sensory organs. That this was Preus's meaning was suggested by his statement that "naturalistic theories of religion" were implied once revelation and innate ideas were rejected, so that "religion had to be accounted for as a response to experience" (*ER* 54-55)—which seemed to mean that religion had to be accounted for as a response to *sensory* experience.

This assumption seems to be common to all the figures in Preus's historical account of the naturalistic paradigm for interpreting religion. For example, this paradigm was, according to Preus, first fully expressed in Hume (*ER* xiv-xv, 84), and *sensate empiricism* is virtually synonymous with *Humean empiricism*. Also, Durkheim, one of those said to have brought this tradition to its culmination, was cited as saying that the task of the scientific study of religion is "explaining 'the sacred'"— that is, explaining why religious people see the world in terms of the distinction between the "sacred" and the "profane," even though "nothing in sensible experience seems able to suggest the idea of so radical a duality to them" (*ER* 168). The suggestion that the idea of the sacred might arise in "nonsensible" experience was not seriously entertained: Although distinctively human faculties have often been explained the-istically, Durkheim rejected this explanation of such faculties with the comment that it would "attach them to some superexperimental reality . . . whose existence could be established by no observation" (*ER* 165)—a comment that Preus quoted without demurrer.

The centrality of sensationism for Preus's understanding of natural-ism was also suggested by the fact that William James was not included in Preus's canon of major theorists of religion. James, of course, rejected Humean empiricism in favor of a "radical empiricism," which allowed for nonsensory perception. Indeed, one of James's most famous state-ments—that it takes only one white crow to prove that not all crows are black—was aimed against the dogma that there is nothing in the intellect that was not first in the senses.[5] It was this nonsensationist form of empiricism that allowed James to take religious experience seriously, as possibly revelatory of a "larger power."[6]

It is probably precisely because of this fact that James, who is included in most lists of major theorists of religion, was *not* included in Preus's list. This dimension of Preus's epistemic naturalism, in any case, lay behind his conviction that the existence and persistence of religion must be explained on the assumption that "God is not given." This conviction is, however, also supported by the ontological side of Preus's naturalism, to which I now turn (and to which the final four of Preus's meanings of "naturalism" belonged).

5. The most obvious meaning of ontological naturalism, which can be called *ontological naturalism$_{ns}$* ("ns" = "nonsupernaturalism"), is the rejection of the belief in a supernatural being that can interrupt the world's normal causal processes. Naturalism in this sense is the most important aspect of ontological *uniformitarianism*, the insistence that no causes operated in the past other than the kinds of causes operating today.

This doctrine is exemplified in Preus's discussion of Tylor's position. Saying that the uniformity of civilization can largely be ascribed to "the uniform action of uniform causes," Tylor rejected all "considerations of extra-natural interference." Against Archbishop Whately's idea that the emergence of civilization out of "savagery" required a supernatural revelation, Tylor said that such a revelation would be "an impossibility according to the present course of nature" (*ER*132-35). Preus's endorsement of ontological naturalism$_{ns}$ was also exemplified in his statement that Vico's explanation of religion "was naturalistic except for . . . a divinely implanted, universal religious sense" (*ER* 206).

The idea that the academic study of religion should be naturalistic in this sense seems to me entirely correct. But ontological naturalism$_{ns}$ does not necessarily exclude theistic explanations, because many theologians believe that theism should be naturalistic in this sense. Preus did note that the incommensurability of naturalistic with theological paradigms is today "much less clear" than it was in "the days of traditional theology," especially given the existence of "[theological] campaigns against 'supernaturalism.'" But Preus sought to overcome this difficulty for his general thesis by mocking this type of theology, repeating Freud's view of refined concepts of God as "pitiful remnants of the mighty Father of tradition" (*ER* 196).

Preus here simply resorts to one of the standard moves of those who wish to dismiss theism in all its forms: Theologians, to be *real* theologians, are required to hold the supernaturalistic idea of deity, which the critic can then reject as obviously false. It is as if a physicist, to be a *real* physicist, would have to hold all of Newton's ideas. In any case, Preus did believe that naturalism excludes theism of any form, because his ontological naturalism has dimensions other than simply the rejection of supernatural interruptions.

6. The dimension most directly pertinent to the subject at hand can be called *ontological naturalism$_a$* (a = "atheism"). It could also be

called *ontological naturalism*$_{fc}$ (fc = "finite causation"), because it is the doctrine that there are no causal powers beyond the totality of finite causes. This doctrine was already illustrated in our earlier discussion of Preus's naturalism, with its reductionism, its denial that religion is rooted in any "objective, transcendent ground," and its denial of any "mysterious transcendent powers beyond the realm of natural [read 'finite'] causation" (*ER* xvi, xx, 174).

The fact that Preus's atheism was ontological, not simply epistemic and methodological, was shown by the fact that he rejected what he called the "absolutes" not only of confessional theology but also of natural theology (*ER* xiv). It was also reflected in his statement that "Hume produced a thoroughgoing naturalistic critique of all available theological explanations of religion, *whether rationalistic or revelational*," thereby "undercut[ting] all appeals to supernatural or transcendent causes of religion" (*ER* xv; emphasis added).

7. A third dimension of Preus's ontological position can be called *ontological naturalism*$_m$ (m = "materialism"). This doctrine, which denied not only theism but also the idea of a soul or mind distinct from the physical body, was especially relevant to Tylor's equation of religion with "animism," understood as belief in spirits, both creaturely and divine (*ER* 139). This relevance was shown by Preus's summary of Tylor's definition of religion as "*belief in spiritual beings* (that do not exist)" (*ER* 139). "In Tylor's view," Preus staged, "the world is now divided between only two completely opposed doctrines: animism and materialism."

One implication of the materialistic denial of animism was Tylor's rejection of "an animating, separable, surviving entity" (*ER* 144, 143). However, besides making life after death inconceivable, the rejection of an anima also provided support for the sensationist doctrine of perception: If what we call the mind is not distinct from the brain, it would be natural to assume that the mind has no means of perception other than the brain's sensory system. Preus's ontological naturalism$_m$ thereby provided additional support, beyond his epistemic naturalism$_s$ and ontological naturalism$_a$, for his assumption that there is no genuine religious experience.

8. The Tylor-Preus rejection of animism had yet another implication: the rejection of personal causation. In Tylor's view, said Preus: "Science has gradually deanthropomorphized the universe, replacing the idea of personalistic causality, life, and will, with the impersonal notions of natural laws and forces" (*ER* 143). Preus's endorsement of this idea reflected a final dimension of his naturalism, which can be called *ontological naturalism$_{nl}$* (nl = "natural law"), because it holds that everything, from the behavior of subatomic particles to the operation of the human mind and the course of history, is governed by natural laws. Preus described Tylor's uniformitarianism as his belief in "the universal extent of the operation of natural laws," and he quoted Tylor's view that "the history of mankind is part and parcel of the history of nature, that our thoughts, wills, and actions accord with laws as definite as those that govern the motion of waves" (*ER* 152, 133).

The ontological naturalism$_{nl}$ of Preus was shown by his criticism of Tylor for not holding to it consistently. Following the lead of Marvin Harris's "cultural materialism," Preus pointed out that Tylor continued to assume that "mind determines itself," that "[b]elief itself is a 'cause,'" and that "reasons are not merely rationalizations but the actual *causes* of actions and events," so that "causes need not be sought beneath reasons" (*ER* 148, 149). Preus, by contrast, agreed with H.P. Rickman's view that "in the human sphere, as well as the physical," we need explanation in the sense of "the discovery of general laws that govern the connections between events" (*ER* 79). This feature of Preus's materialism added yet another ground, in his view, for religion scholars to reject the idea of divine influence and the idea of a distinct mind (which could conceivably experience such influence), because both ideas would run counter to the assumption that all things are determined by impersonal causes.

TRANSITION

Now that we have before us the various dimensions of what Preus considered a fully developed naturalism, we can ask whether all these dimensions are properly presupposed by the academic study of religion. Because our ultimate question is whether the academic study of religion necessarily excludes all theological interpretations of religion, we can approach this question by asking which dimensions of Preus's naturalism might be compatible with a theological perspective.

The first and fifth doctrines—epistemic naturalism$_{nsr}$ and ontological naturalism$_{ns}$—would, of course, be incompatible with *supernaturalistic* theologies, which affirm the possibility of supernatural interruptions, including supernatural revelations. There are, however, forms of theism that reject ontological supernaturalism and thereby epistemic supernaturalism.

These naturalistic theisms, furthermore, would not necessarily be incompatible with epistemic naturalism$_{du}$ (domain uniformitarianism). Some forms of naturalistic theism, in other words, say that, insofar as the category of divine influence is needed to explain religious experience, it is also needed to explain other types of human experience and, perhaps, all kinds of events whatsoever. A naturalistic theism, furthermore, would also probably agree with epistemic naturalism$_{eg}$, which says that any explanatory theory should be experientially grounded, so that the theory can be tested against observations.

There *would* be a conflict, however, between naturalistic theism and epistemic naturalism$_s$, because the sensationist doctrine of perception rules out the possibility of genuine religious experience of a divine actuality. Accordingly, a naturalistic theism, having rejected supernatural revelation, could—if it accepted naturalism$_s$—have no empirical grounding.

Besides being incompatible with sensationism, a naturalistic theism would also be in conflict with the latter three doctrines of Preus's ontological naturalism: its atheism, its materialism, and its insistence that all things are determined by natural laws. Because the last of these doctrines— ontological naturalism$_{nl}$—can be regarded simply as an aspect of ontological naturalism$_m$ (materialism), we can reduce the problematic doctrines to three: sensationism, atheism, and materialism. This threefold form of naturalism can, therefore, be abbreviated as naturalism$_{sam}$.[10]

The question whether the naturalism proper to the academic study of religion necessarily excludes a theological explanation of religion is, therefore, the question whether the study of religion should presuppose naturalism$_{sam}$. Given the acceptance of epistemic naturalism$_{nsr}$, epistemic naturalism$_{du}$, epistemic naturalism$_{eg}$, and ontological naturalism$_{ns}$, we would have a "minimal naturalism," meaning the naturalistic presuppositions that are arguably necessary for participation in academic, including scientific, conversations. The Preus-Segal proposal, however, is that those wanting to be "full partners" in the academic study of religion should also affirm naturalism$_{sam}$. It is to this issue that I now turn.

SHOULD THE ACADEMIC STUDY OF RELIGION PRESUPPOSE NATURALISM$_{SAM}$?

As to whether the academic study of religion should presuppose naturalism$_{sam}$, one basis for a positive answer would be the assumption that "naturalism" as currently understood is all of a piece, so that the rejection of supernatural interruptions necessarily entails the acceptance of sensationism, atheism, and materialism. We have seen, however, that one could accept the other dimensions of Preus's naturalism without accepting naturalism$_{sam}$. The agreement that we need to have an approach that is minimally naturalistic (as distinct from supernaturalistic) does not settle the question as to whether naturalism$_{sam}$, which rules out *all* theistic explanations of the existence of religion—naturalistic as well as supernaturalistic—should be accepted.

One reason why some thinkers prefer naturalism$_{sam}$ is, of course, precisely the fact that it rules out all theistic explanations. But this is not a valid reason. For example, Preus, complaining about "hidden apologetic intentions," rightly said that answers to the question of the true causes of religious belief cannot be limited to those that support religion, because the goal of the academic study of religion "is not to legitimate religion but to explain it" (*ER* xxi, xx). However, the Preus-Segal program would limit the answers that could count as academic explanations of religion to those that *delegitimate* it. To his credit, Preus pointed out that the field is "still struggling with the question of how to address these problems in a more unified way without creating a new dogmatism that would undermine pluralism" (*ER* 210). Segal, likewise, spoke in favor of "multiple programs," saying that "[c]ompetition is indispensable to staving off dogmatism" (*EIR* 39).

However, the proposals of Preus and Segal, if accepted, *would* involve a dogmatic exclusion of theistic accounts, even if such accounts otherwise exemplified the naturalism presupposed by the academy. In any case, negative apologetic intentions do not, any more than positive ones, provide a valid basis for deciding upon an appropriate conceptual framework for the study of religion.

Another reason for assuming that a nontheistic framework is needed for the academic study of religion, at least in state-supported schools in the United States, is the widespread belief that theistic explanations would violate the First Amendment of the U. S. Constitution. However, such explanations are not excluded if they are based on rational-empirical grounds, rather than on confessional (in the sense of epistemically supernaturalistic) grounds. Furthermore, the Constitution enjoins the state not only from supporting religion but also from showing hostility to it. Therefore, given the fact that antitheistic interpretations are allowed in the academy (as in the advocacy of the neo-Darwinian theory of evolution), it is the *exclusion* of all theistic interpretations that would actually be unconstitutional.[11]

One basis for Preus's advocacy of naturalism$_{sam}$ seems to be his conviction that for the study of religion to overcome its current "identity crisis," it should return to "the path of critical inquiry that characterized the study of religion in its vital formative period—namely, the proposal of alternatives to the explanations that the *religious* offer for religion" (*ER* xviii, xx). However, even if that was heretofore the most vital period in the study of religion, vitality is not necessarily indicative of truth, which should be our goal. Vitality, in any case, is likely to be engendered today by employing a new approach, not by returning to the program of yesteryear.

Preus's acceptance of naturalism$_{sam}$ also seems to be influenced by his view that the Enlightenment's aspiration to explain everything, including religion, is "fully operational" only when "every aspect of religion [is] regarded as amenable to nonreligious explanation" (*ER* xvi). That, however, is mere prejudice. Although Preus rightly advocates an approach that "pushes explanation to the limit" (*ER* 210), many thinkers seeking to do this have found that they have been led to theistic explanations.

Alfred North Whitehead, for example, endorsed "the belief that clarity can only be reached by pushing explanation to its utmost limits."[12] But when he began trying to find the most complete explanation possible (in moving from the "philosophy of nature," understood as a limited enterprise, to "metaphysics," understood as including the knower within the system), he found himself led—minimally in *Science and the Modern World* (1925) and then more fully in *Religion in the*

Making (1926)—to give up his longstanding atheism, or at least agnosticism, for a naturalistic type of theism.[13]

Yet another motive for Preus's endorsement of naturalism$_{sam}$ was his desire for domain uniformity, so that religious studies can be "a full partner in the study of culture" (*ER* 210). Preus, as we have seen, indicts theology because "its peculiar insistence that religions are 'manifestations of the sacred' isolates it from the presuppositions that are otherwise operative in the humanities and human sciences" (*ER* 210).

Preus is right to say that this isolation needs to be overcome, that the study of religion should employ the same explanatory categories that are used elsewhere in the academy. But he evidently simply assumed that the only way to achieve this goal is for the study of religion to accommodate itself to the currently dominant "rough consensus of the academy at large" (*ER* 210), which *would* imply the acceptance of naturalism$_{sam}$. But another way to achieve domain uniformity would be for religious philosophers and theologians to convince the remainder of the academy that a categorial revision is needed in order to achieve more adequate explanatory theories *in all domains*, a revision that might involve the rejection of materialism and the addition of the categories of nonsensory perception and divine influence (as suggested in other parts of the present book, especially Chapters 5 and 7). This program might seem quixotic, but whether it should be attempted rests on a judgment as to which form of naturalism seems the closest approximation to the *truth*, and that is a *philosophical* judgment.

A possible argument against this program might be based on the widespread assumption that naturalism$_{sam}$ simply *is* the "modern scientific worldview," so that it is necessarily presupposed in the social sciences and thereby in the academy in general. As I pointed out in Chapter 1, however, the current entrenchment of science within this worldview is due to highly contingent developments. At the root of these developments was the theologically motivated adoption, in the latter half of the seventeenth century, of the sensationist doctrine of perception and the mechanistic-materialistic doctrine of (physical) nature for the purpose of supporting a dualistic doctrine of human beings and a supernaturalistic doctrine of the universe as a whole. Naturalism$_{sam}$ resulted simply from decapitating that early modern worldview, lopping off its human and divine minds, *not* from looking at all the evidence and rationally deciding that a sensationist, atheistic, materialistic worldview could best do justice to it.

So, although it is indeed *sociologically* the case that the worldview of naturalism$_{sam}$ is currently dominant in scientific circles, the crucial issue, which has not been adequately debated, is the *philosophical* question of whether this worldview *should* continue to remain dominant. We should seek to explain the existence of religion from the perspective of this worldview only if an affirmative answer to this question seems warranted. The only valid reason for advocating naturalism$_{sam}$ for the academic study of religion, in other words, would be the philosophical argument that this form of naturalism is superior to all other forms, providing a more adequate framework for interpreting all the evidence of human experience, including scientific experience. Otherwise, there would be no reason for an a priori rejection of theistic interpretations of religion, at least if they embody naturalism in the minimal sense.

Although both Preus and Segal seemed to realize that the issue is finally philosophical, Segal had evidently so fully accepted the identification of the "scientific worldview" with naturalism$_{sam}$ that he sometimes suggested that the question whether religion is to be understood religiously or nonreligiously is a (social) scientific, as distinct from a philosophical, issue. For example, against the view that the ultimate nature of religion is knowable a priori, Segal said: "The issue must be settled by *research*" (*EIR* 7). Also, after saying that Freud and Karl

Marx denied that *overtly* religious data are *most deeply* religious, Segal said: "[T]hey do so *nondogmatically*: by demonstrating how the subject matter is better categorized psychologically and economically" (*EIR* 46). The terms "research" and "demonstrating" suggested the issue to be primarily empirical.

Elsewhere, however, Segal pointed out that for those classical social scientists who declare religion to be false, such as Tylor, Marx, Freud, and James Frazer, "religion is false on philosophical, not social scientific, grounds." These thinkers, in other words, "do not argue [the falsity of religion] on the basis of their social scientific findings." They instead "argue for the secular origin and function [of religion] on the grounds of the falsity of religion," which, they assumed, had been established philosophically (*EIR* 16). (This judgment, incidentally, fits with Tylor's statement, cited by Preus [*ER* 142], that Hume's *Natural History of Religion* "is perhaps more than any other work the source of modern opinions as to the development of religion.")

It is hard to see, therefore, how Segal could suggest that Marx and Freud *demonstrated* the (entirely) secular or nonreligious origin of religion through social scientific *research*. Segal's alleged conflict between "religionists" and the "social sciences" was really, by his own account, simply a conflict between religious and nonreligious *philosophies*.

The same ambiguity showed up in the different questions he assigned to philosophy and the social sciences. "The assessment of [the truth of] religious belief," said Segal, "is the task of philosophy," whereas the social sciences have the task of assessing the *origin* of religious belief and thereby "the truth of religious *explanations* of religious belief." Segal apparently portrayed, therefore, a division of labor: "Philosophy determines whether the reasons believers provide for believing are sound reasons for believing. The social sciences determine whether the reasons believers provide for *coming* to believe are truly the reasons for which they have come to believe."

It turned out, however, that the assessment of truth was *not* left to philosophy, because "a social scientific explanation of the origin of religious belief has [some] bearing on the truth of the belief" (*RSS* 75). This was because, as we recall, Segal insisted that social scientific explanations are, virtually by definition, nonreligious explanations. Therefore, Segal concluded: "A social scientific explanation, once accepted, renders the truth of religious belief improbable" (*RSS* 79).

Segal was entirely correct on two dimensions of this issue. He rightly criticized those who dismiss, as instances of the "genetic fallacy," all arguments based on the origins of belief. Assuming that a (nontheistic) social science account provided a *sufficient* explanation of that origin, then a theistic account of that origin would be, as Segal said, superfluous (*RSS* 78). And if divine influence were thereby shown not to be even a partial cause of the origin of religious experience, then "the social sciences undermine the genetic justification for the truth of religious belief" (*RSS* 82). Segal was right, furthermore, to consider this genetic justification to be so important that, if it *were* undermined—so that we would have no reason to think that religions originated even partly through divine influence or, otherwise put, through genuine religious experience—then the truth of religious belief in a divine reality would be undermined, because it would be implausible to assume this belief just coincidentally to be true.

We are here at the heart of what Segal considers the "confrontation" between *religionists*, who defend the religiosity of religion, and the *social sciences*. But is there really such a confrontation? In one place, Segal "den[ied] that the social sciences always, let alone *must,* deem religion false" (*EIR* 27). Moreover, as we saw earlier, he indicated that a person can be a social scientist, even if an "unconventional" one, while making a "social scientific affirmation of the truth of religion" (*EIR* 15, 107).

It would seem, therefore, that it is not the social sciences as such that are antithetical to religious interpretations of religion but only *conventional social scientists,* those who are in continuity with the "classical" social scientists, such as Marx, Tylor, Frazer, Comte, Durkheim, and Freud. As Segal himself repeatedly stated (*EIR* 16, 31, 123; *RSS* 80 n.15, 83), these classical figures did *not* come to regard religious beliefs to be philosophically false because of scientific investigations into their origins. Rather, they developed these "scientific" accounts on the basis of their *prior philosophical convictions* as to the falsity of religion.

Segal's view, incidentally, corresponded with the position of E.E. Evans-Pritchard, who wrote:

> [T]he persons whose writings [on primitive religion] have been most influential have been at the time they wrote agnostics or atheists. . . . Religious belief was to these anthropologists absurd. . . . But some explanation of the absurdity seemed to be required, and it was offered in psychological or sociological terms.[14]

Given this Pritchard-Segal view, then, the confrontation is not between *religionists* and the *social sciences,* as if the latter were necessarily anti-religious, but only between religious and antireligious *philosophies.* The issue must, therefore, be adjudicated in terms of philosophical criteria.

It might be argued, to be sure, that although the motivation to look for secular causes of religious beliefs first came from a prior philosophical conviction as to the falsity of religion, these secular explanations, once provided by these social scientists, do show the falsity of religious belief by revealing that it originates in purely secular causes. This would indeed be the case *if* these accounts really showed religion to be rooted in *purely* secular causes. It would not be the case, however, if they only show that any concrete religion is *significantly shaped* by psychological, sociological, and economic factors, so that it might also be partly shaped by a religious cause. Segal's recognition of this point was reflected in his statement that the (conventional) social scientist claims to be offering a *sufficient* cause of religious experience (*RSS* 82), along with his statement that every social scientific explanation involves "a naturalistic *rather than* a divine origin" (*EIR* 19; emphasis added). The recognition of the importance of this point—that his antithesis would be destroyed by the view that religion is shaped partly by religious and partly be secular causes—is also reflected in the fact that, after saying "surely religion can have an origin that is partly sociological and partly religious," Segal quickly dismissed this possibility as "unlikely" (*EIR* 9).

We must ask, however, about the basis for assuming this partly-partly view to be unlikely. What is the basis, in other words, for assuming that the evidence that religious beliefs are always shaped by psycho-social factors also shows that they are not also partly rooted in genuine religious experience? No empirical evidence could provide a sufficient basis for such a sweeping negative claim. The basis, it seems clear, is nothing other than a prior conviction of the truth of naturalism$_{sam}$, which implies that we have no capacity to perceive anything other than material objects and that, even if we did, there is no divine reality to perceive. The basic question, then, is whether naturalism$_{sam}$ is, as widely assumed, the most adequate philosophical position available.

Is Naturalism$_{SAM}$ Philosophically Warranted?

Both Preus and Segal showed that, besides the other reasons they may have for favoring naturalism$_{sam}$, they presupposed that its endorsement by the scientific community is justified, so that theistic interpretations of religion can be excluded as antiscientific and thereby false. Preus said, for example, that "Tylor *rightly* saw religious explanations of the world as relics" (*ER* 209; emphasis added). Preus's justification for this stance, however, was remarkably brief, consisting of a one-sentence argument: Saying that his naturalistic approach did not take religious explanations seriously, Preus added: "for, as Occam held, explanatory entities (such as 'transcendence' . . .) must not be multiplied beyond necessity" (*ER* 211).

This argument, of course, begged the basic question, because it simply assumed that a causal power transcending the totality of finite causes is *not* necessary to explain religion and perhaps much else besides (which Occam himself certainly did not assume). Although simplicity should be a desideratum, adequacy is surely more important.

Segal, besides also appealing to this argument from simplicity, provided some other arguments for the superiority of "a naturalistic, social scientific explanation" to a religious explanation, which he assumed would necessarily be a "supernatural explanation" (*RSS* 78; *EIR* 71).

One of these arguments is that a (nonreligious) social scientific account of religion, "however inadequate, is more adequate than a religious one" (*RSS* 70). Segal's reason for this contention was that social scientists "provide a host of processes and entities like projection, wish fulfillment, complexes, collective representations, and symbols to account for how and why religion originates and functions," whereas religionists, such as Eliade, Rudolf Otto, and Friedrich Schleiermacher "provide nothing"—except "the litany that religion originates as a response to the transcendent" (*EIR* 70).

This argument calls for several comments. First, Segal was correct to say that most philosophers of religion and theologians have failed to give any explanation of how a divine reality might be experienced, especially an explanation that would pass the test of domain uniformitarianism. It is false, however, to suggest that *nothing* by way of explanation has been provided by any "religionists," even if we restrict our view to the three that Segal mentioned. Schleiermacher, for example, certainly took great pains to explain how the (nonsensory) "feeling of absolute dependence" could arise. (Segal's contention that Schleiermacher provided no explanation whatsoever perhaps simply reflected a belief that nonsensory perception is unintelligible.) Other religious philosophers, furthermore, have arguably done better than Schleiermacher.

Second, in saying that a social scientific account, *however inadequate,* is better than a religious one, Segal was evidently forgetting that he has set a far higher standard for a (nonreligious) social scientific account to be adequate: It must provide a *sufficient* explanation for the existence and persistence of religion. The mere fact that a (nonreligious) social scientific account provides *something,* therefore, does not necessarily obviate the need for a religious account. A partly-partly account might be needed for a *sufficient* account.

Third, religious explanations, by contrast, need *not* claim to provide sufficient explanations of religion. Needing only to account for the religious nature of religions, they can rely on various psychosocial explanations to account for most of the concrete details of the various religions. Therefore, unless naturalism_sam is already presupposed, antecedent probability would arguably favor an explanation that combines religious and nonreligious factors.

In another argument, however, Segal claimed antecedent probability for a purely nonreligious account. He argued:

> [A] social scientific explanation of religious belief has a higher prior probability than a supernatural one. For it is linked to natural science, which has provided the most persuasive explanation so far of the physical world. Social science . . . extends to the study of humans the nonsupernatural framework of natural science (*EIR* 79).

This argument, which illustrated especially well the importance of distinguishing between the various meanings of "naturalism," seems to involve the following points:

1. Natural science has provided the best explanations of the physical world.

2. Natural science employs naturalistic rather than supernaturalistic explanations.

3. Social science, studying human beings, also employs naturalistic rather than supernaturalistic explanations.

4. Being naturalistic, social scientific explanations of human religiosity are, therefore, antecedently more probable than religious explanations, which are supernaturalistic.

To assess the soundness of this argument, we would need to unpack ambiguities and other problems in each thesis. For example, the first thesis—that natural science has provided the best explanations of the world—evokes the question, What kind of "explanation" is in view, ultimate or proximate? If Segal is referring to explanations of why the Grand Canyon exists, why the continents have shifted, and why hurricanes occur, then natural science is by definition the enterprise devoted to giving such explanations. The statement that it has provided the *best* explanations of the physical world is, therefore, tautological.

But if one is asking about ultimate explanations—answering questions such as why the physical world even exists and why it embodies natural laws that have allowed life to emerge—then most scientists would say that science prescinds from such ultimate questions, giving no answer whatsoever to them. Insofar as this self-limitation of the scientific enterprise is accepted, the question as to whether some other approach, such as philosophical theology, is needed depends upon whether one thinks we should try to answer those ultimate questions from which science prescinds. Furthermore, insofar as some scientists have sought to give explanations for ultimate, or at least semi-ultimate, questions—such as how our universe began, how matter, when organized into an animal body, can give birth to experience, and why evolution has led to more complex creatures with higher forms of experience—then the important question is *how adequate* the kinds of explanations allowed by naturalism$_{sam}$ are. Insofar as they are inadequate, the need for a better set of explanatory categories is suggested. I will return to this question below.

Segal's second thesis, which asserted that natural science uses naturalistic explanations, is not true of modern natural science from the seventeenth century through most of the nineteenth, which occurred within a supernaturalistic, even if increasingly deistic, framework.[15] So, the scientific successes of this period cannot be credited to a nonsupernaturalistic, let alone fully atheistic, worldview.

Regarding Segal's second, third, and fourth theses: Insofar as the scientific community *has* had a better explanatory framework since the latter part of the nineteenth century by virtue of rejecting supernaturalistic explanations, this fact does not entail that any of the scientific successes of this period have been due to the acceptance of sensationism, materialism, and atheism. That is, the greater success is arguably due entirely to the acceptance of ontological naturalism$_{ns}$ and epistemic naturalism$_{nsr}$, not to the acceptance of naturalism$_{sam}$. The assumption of naturalism$_{sam}$ by some social scientists, accordingly, provides no reason for expecting their explanations of religion to be superior to nonsupernaturalistic explanations that did not endorse sensationism, atheism, and materialism.

Indeed, I suggest, we should expect the opposite: that social scientific explanations will be inadequate precisely insofar as they do presuppose naturalism$_{sam}$, because *scientific explanations in general have been inadequate insofar as they have presupposed naturalism$_{sam}$*. Having explained many reasons for this claim in the previous chapter, I will here simply summarize these points, adding, where appropriate, connections to the views of Preus and Segal. I begin with the epistemological dimension of naturalism$_{sam}$—its *sensate empiricism*.

Those in the naturalistic tradition endorsed by Preus and Segal, as we have seen, rejected the theistic interpretation of religious experience. That is, although it has seemed to countless numbers of people that they have had genuine religious experiences, in the sense of experiencing a divine or holy power distinct from all worldly powers, these naturalists declare that these experiences were not what they seemed to be. The epistemological basis for this a priori dismissal of the experiencers' self-interpretations seems to be the assumption that the sensationist doctrine of perception, which rules out such religious experiences, is perfectly adequate for science and common sense.

But this is not the case. As pointed out in the previous chapter, the sensationist doctrine of perception has led most of the scientific community to an a priori rejection of the evidence for extrasensory perception, even though this evidence, when actually examined, is now arguably incontrovertible.[16] Moreover, it is not only or even primarily in relation to the controversial science of parapsychology that the sensationist doctrine of perception has created problems for science. More serious is the fact that it makes impossible any empirical grounding for many ideas that are inevitably presupposed in all our practice, including our practice of science. As we saw in the previous chapter, these ideas include the external world, the past, time, causation, induction, mathematical objects, logical principles, and moral norms. It is emphatically not the case, therefore, that the sensationism of naturalism$_{sam}$ supports science overagainst religion. It is as threatening to the rationality of science as it is to the rationality of religion.

The fact that sensationism cannot allow for experience of a divine reality says nothing about the possibility of such experience, given the fact that sensationism also cannot allow for experiential knowledge of all these other things. It would seem to be sensationism that is in trouble, not genuine religious experience. Indeed, sensationism's inability to allow for genuine religious experience becomes, from this perspective, simply one more sign of its general inadequacy.

The *materialism* of naturalism_{sam} also creates its share of problems. Some of these follow directly from that feature of materialism that puts it most in conflict with religious beliefs: its doctrine that the mind or soul is identical with the brain. This identism, as we have seen, supports sensationism, so the problems for sensationism are thereby problems for materialism. But this materialistic identism is also used, as we saw in the previous chapter, to make a priori denials of the possibility of out-of-body experiences, even though there is a growing collection of well-documented evidence for experiences of this type that is being provided not only by parapsychologists but also by members of the medical profession. Having an experience of seeming to be out of one's body does not necessarily mean, to be sure, that one really is, and some students of these experiences reject the extrasomatic interpretation of them. The empirical evidence, however, is far more consistent with this interpretation, whereas the only support for the intrasomatic interpretation is the philosophical assumption, based on a materialistic view of human beings, that it *must* be true.[17]

Moreover, the main difficulties created for science by materialism involve more commonplace features of the mind-body relation. The most obvious problem is that of explaining how conscious experience could have emerged in the evolutionary process, a problem that Colin McGinn and a number of other materialist philosophers have declared to be insoluble in principle. Given the fact that the existence of conscious experience is that of which we are most certain, it is hard to imagine a failure more damning to a philosophical position than making the existence of conscious experience seem impossible.

Equally problematic, however, is the twofold problem of accounting for mental causation and freedom. We all inevitably presuppose in practice that we and other people have beliefs, motives, and plans, and that these mental states causally influence our behavior. As illustrated by Preus's criticism of Tylor, however, a fully consistent materialistic theory must deny that they do: Mental states must be regarded always as concomitants or epiphenomena of bodily states, never the cause thereof. This means, in turn, that materialist philosophers, as Hilary Putnam pointed out, cannot account for their own rational activity. As John Searle and many other materialists admit, their position also cannot accommodate our presupposition, which we cannot help pre-supposing in practice, that our mental causation involves a degree of freedom. In light of all these failures, materialism is about as self-stultifying as a position can be.

The *atheism* of naturalism$_{sam}$, with its denial of any cosmic power transcending the totality of finite, local causes, creates a distinctive set of problems for fulfilling the Preus-Whitehead ideal of pushing expla-nation to the limit. Atheism, as we have seen, has trouble explaining the order of the universe, including the apparently "fine-tuned constants" that evidently existed at the outset of our universe; and the evident directionality and progress of the evolutionary process.

Finally, the fact that although the critique of theism is usually car-ried out in the name of truth and—with the problem of evil in view—goodness, atheism makes it difficult to account for the objectivity of cognitive and moral norms that the critics of theism are thereby pre-supposing. This is because, as the following chapter will emphasize, atheism involves the denial that the universe contains a locus *in* which truth and other normative values could subsist and *by* which they could be given causal efficacy to impress themselves on our experience.

In sum, the point I made above with regard to sensationism in particular can be made with regard to naturalism$_{sam}$ as a whole: The fact that it is incompatible with genuine religious experience arguably says less about religion than it says about naturalism$_{sam}$. Given the realization of how inadequate this version of naturalism is to a wide range of indubitable and other well-grounded facts, we can take the incompatibility of religious experience with this version of naturalism as simply one more sign of the latter's inadequacy to serve as the framework for the natural sciences, the social sciences, and the academy in general. At the very least, we can say that, given the fact that naturalism$_{sam}$ has not proven itself adequate in relation to a wide-range of phenomena, including many inevitable presuppositions of scientific activity itself, there is no reason to consider this form of naturalism a standard to which any theory of religion, to be considered academic or even scientific, must conform.

SUMMARY AND CONCLUSION

The sciences in particular and the academy in general should, I agree, presuppose naturalism in the minimal sense—meaning primarily the rejection of ontological and epistemic supernaturalism. This minimal naturalism does, of course, rule out various historic beliefs of various religions. But it does not necessarily rule out all significant religious beliefs, including the belief that religions exist and persist partly because human beings have genuine religious experiences.

This and other significant religious beliefs are, however, ruled out by the sensationistic, atheistic, materialistic version of naturalism that is now widely regarded as the "modern scientific worldview." If this version of naturalism were truly adequate for the natural sciences and the other social sciences, it would make sense, given the desirability of domain uniformity, to say that this version of naturalism should also be presupposed by the study of religion. This version of naturalism, however, is adequate for only a very limited range of purposes. Far from allowing us to push explanation to the limit in all areas, it threatens to leave a wide range of our inevitable presuppositions and other well-grounded facts in the category of permanent mysteries.

The fact that this worldview is currently dominant among the ideological leaders of the scientific community, therefore, does not imply that it should be adopted by those engaged in the study of religion—assuming, of course, that the concern for truth should take priority over the wish to belong.

But we could move toward domain uniformity in another way: A form of naturalism that is truly adequate for scientific explanations might also allow for a nonreductionistic explanation of religion. Insofar as my argument is sound, this would indeed be the case, because such a naturalism would move beyond sensationism, atheism, and materialism—but without returning to dualism, the problems of which led to materialism. I have argued in this book that such a naturalism is available.

The present chapter has focused on the negative point that the kind of naturalism required by the sciences, both natural and social, does not rule out the possibility of genuine religious experience and thereby the appropriateness of theological explanations of religion. Social scientists should not simply assume, accordingly, that accounts of religion are more scientific or academic simply by virtue of rejecting such explanations. Just as advocates of religious accounts should not argue that attempts to explain religion reductionistically are to be excluded a priori, advocates of reductionistic accounts should not argue that attempts to provide religious and even theistic accounts are to be excluded a priori.

NOTES

1. Robert A. Segal, *Religion and the Social Sciences: Essays on the Confrontation* (Atlanta: Scholars Press, 1989); *Explaining and Interpreting Religion: Essays on the Issue* (New York: Peter Lang, 1992).

2. J. Samuel Preus, *Explaining Religion: Criticism and Theory from Bodin*

to Freud (New Haven & London: Yale University Press, 1987).

3. In using the past sense, I mean to be discussing only the positions by Segal and Preus discussed in the writings discussed here, because I am interested in these two scholars only insofar as they advocate a particular type of opposition between "academic" (or "social scientific") and "religious" (or "theological") interpretations of religion. I do not claim that later books by Segal and Preus necessarily maintained all the same views.

4. I am uncertain how much Preus and Segal meant to *limit* the "academic" study of religion to the "social scientific" study of religion, as distinct from simply insisting that the former should *include*—at least in the sense of being *compatible* with—the latter. Insofar as I use the two terms—the "academic study of religion" and the "social scientific study of religion"—interchangeably in discussing the Preus-Segal position, I mean this usage to be open to either understanding.

5. This chapter does *indirectly* address this issue, however, in articulating a framework in which scientific explanations need not be reductionistic and even need not, in fact, exclude the category of divine causation. My position overcomes, therefore, the fundamental assumption behind the widespread conviction that the methods and categories of the *Geisteswissenschaften* in general, and the study of religion in particular, must be different in kind from those of the natural sciences.

6. Some philosophers and theologians would challenge the second claim—that all academically correct explanations of religion must be social scientific explanations—from a supernaturalist standpoint, saying that the origin of religion, or at least *true* religion, can be correctly explained only in terms of supernatural intervention. The second claim could also be challenged, however, by one who (1) affirms a version of naturalistic theism that allows for variable divine influence in the world while (2) accepting the conventional view that scientific explanations by definition methodologically exclude any reference to divine influence. Although I could accept such a position, my preferred

position would be to challenge the *third* claim by arguing that the very nature of science can and should be reconceived so that scientists, *qua* scientists, could refer to divine influence, naturalistically understood, as a causal factor.

7. Some religion scholars speak of religion as based on true beliefs, to be sure, by defining "truth" in a completely relativistic way, so that whatever a community believes is true.

8. William James, *Essays in Psychical Research*, ed. Robert A. McDermott (Cambridge: Harvard University Press, 1986), 131.

9. James, *The Varieties of Religious Experience* (New York: Longmans, Green, 1902), 525.

10. It just happened, incidentally, that I first settled on this term—naturalism$_{sam}$—while analyzing the position of Preus, whose nickname was "Sam."

11. See David Ray Griffin, "Professing Theology in the State University," in David Ray Griffin and Joseph C. Hough, eds., *Theology and the University: Essays in Honor of John B. Cobb, Jr.* (Albany: State University of New York Press, 1991), 3-34.

12. Whitehead, *Process and Reality*, 153.

13. For a discussion of the factors that led Whitehead to this kind of theism, see my *Reenchantment without Supernaturalism*, Ch. 5.

14. E.E. Evans-Pritchard, *Theories of Primitive Religion* (Oxford: Clarendon Press, 1965), 15.

15. This statement refers to developments in England. Leading French intellectuals moved to naturalism$_{sam}$ in the latter part of the 18th century.

16. See "White Crows Abounding: Evidence for the Paranormal," which is Chap. 2 of my *Parapsychology, Philosophy, and Spirituality*, or

"Parapsychology, Science, and Religion," Chap. 7 of my *Religion and Scientific Naturalism*.

17. See "Evidence from Out-of-Body Experiences," which is Chap. 8 of my *Parapsychology, Philosophy, and Spirituality*.

CHAPTER SEVEN

Scientific Naturalism and Human Morality

A book entitled *Prospects for a Common Morality* was motivated—said its editors, Gene Outka and John Reeder—by the paradoxical fact that at the same time that a "remarkable kind of cross-cultural moral agreement about human rights" has emerged in the practical world of international affairs, the *intellectual* world reflected "an apparent loss of confidence in any such consensus [about] any notion of a common morality that applies and can be justified to persons as such.[1] This loss of confidence reflects a growing conviction that late modern moral philosophy has failed to justify any universal moral norms or rights. For example, Alasdair MacIntyre, having asserted with respect to the idea of "rights attaching to human beings simply *qua* human beings" that "there are no such rights, and that belief in them is one with belief in witches and unicorns," said that the best reason for asserting this is "of precisely the same type as the best reason which we possess for asserting that there are no witches and . . . no unicorns: every attempt to give good reasons for believing that there *are* such rights has failed."[2]

Insofar as MacIntyre was right, this failure of late modern philosophy is arguably its most disastrous failure. The modern world, organized in terms of sovereign nation-states, has had little place in its public policies for the idea of human rights—the idea that human beings, simply by virtue of being human, have certain inalienable rights, such as the right not to die of starvation or thirst if sufficient food and water are available, the right not to be arbitrarily killed or imprisoned, and the right to freedom of speech and religion. Within the system of sovereign states, people have only *effectively* had these rights if they have been citizens of states that proclaim and enforce these rights. The situation has been that these rights, rather than effectively being *human* rights, have been merely *citizen* rights (which are not enjoyed by much of the human race).

The creation of the United Nations, however, brought with it the Universal Declaration of Human Rights, the principles of which were then embodied in two covenants, one on Civil and Political Rights, the other on Economic, Social, and Cultural Rights. The enforcement of these rights has been very imperfect—indeed, virtually nonexistent. But at least the idea of human rights has, during the intervening decades, been increasingly recognized as part of international law, and this fact has been the source of normative pressures to improve the international system. It has even led a growing number of thinkers to propose a move toward a global democracy,[3] in which a global bill of rights could be enforced. This development means that the idea that all human beings are equal in some fundamental sense—which is derived from the universal religions, such as Christianity, Islam, and Buddhism, and religiously inspired philosophies, such as Stoicism and Platonism—might finally become recognized in the political organization of our planet, so that the moral implications of our common humanity would not be negated by state boundaries.

If, however, those thinkers who examine the idea of human rights conclude that it is intellectually baseless, the movement toward a universal morality will be undermined. Those global corporations and imperialistic governments operating on the principle that "might makes right" will be implicitly supported, because the complaints that their activities are violating human rights can be dismissed with the retort that our best philosophers say that the idea of "human rights" is a myth, on the level with belief in witches and unicorns. It is very important, therefore, to examine MacIntyre's conclusion that "every attempt to give good reasons for believing that there *are* such rights has failed."

By "every attempt," MacIntyre meant every attempt within what he calls "the Enlightenment project" of providing "an independent rational justification of morality," with "independent" meaning: *independent from religious ideas.*[4] It is this tradition that I am calling "late modern moral philosophy" (which is a more accurate label than MacIntyre's term "Enlightenment morality," because most of the early Enlightenment thinkers did *not* regard morality as wholly independent from religious beliefs).

Agreeing that late modern morality has failed, I respond in terms of five theses: (1) the widespread rejection of universal moral principles by moral philosophers reflects their rejection of moral realism; (2) the Kantian alternative, which seeks to defend universal moral principles without moral realism, does not succeed; (3) the rejection of moral realism is based on naturalism$_{sam}$ (as articulated in previous chapters); (4) naturalism$_{sam}$, while supposedly adopted on the authority of science, is inadequate for science as well as our hard-core commonsense notions, which include moral notions; and (5) Whiteheadian naturalism$_{ppp}$ (as articulated in previous chapters), besides overcoming naturalism$_{sam}$'s inadequacies for science, also supports moral realism.

My conclusion, in other words, is that late modern philosophers have failed to support a common morality, based on the notion of human rights, because they have accepted a form of naturalism that makes such support impossible, but this failure does not mean that the idea of human rights cannot be intellectually supported at all. Unlike most criticisms of the moral failure of modern naturalism, furthermore, my analysis does not require a return to a supernaturalistic worldview in order to have intellectual support for the idea of human rights. A naturalistic theism—a type of theism that can be intellectually justified—can provide all that is necessary.

THE WIDESPREAD DENIAL OF MORAL REALISM

One of our hard-core commonsense assumptions—an assumption that we cannot avoid presupposing in practice—is that some things are better than others. This assumption is exemplified in our moral beliefs, as we cannot help presupposing that some attitudes, intentions, modes of behavior, and consequences are better than others.

We inevitably assume, moreover, the objectivity and hence universal validity of certain moral principles, such as the principle that we should not inflict suffering on other sentient beings simply for fun.[5] This objectivism usually takes the form of "moral realism," the belief that moral values and principles somehow exist in the very nature of things[6]—that they are, in the phrase made famous by Oxford's John Mackie, "part of the fabric of the world."[7]

Insofar as modern moral philosophy accepts naturalism_{sam}, however, it necessarily rejects moral realism, and because of this it has been unable do justice to the objectivity of morality and hence to this portion of our hard-core commonsense.

JOHN MACKIE

Perhaps the most well-known rejection of moral realism was that by Mackie himself, who subtitled his book on ethics *Inventing Right and Wrong*. Having said, "There are no objective values," Mackie made this abstract point concrete, saying that the idea "that actions which are cruel . . . are to be condemned" is not a "hard fact" about the universe. Likewise, social requirements—such as "if someone is writhing in agony before your eyes" you should "do something about it if you can"—are not "objective, intrinsic, requirements of the nature of things." Unlike some philosophers who take this view, Mackie did not try to claim that common sense and ordinary language, properly analyzed, were on his side. He instead frankly affirmed an "error theory" of ordinary moral thought, saying that "although most people in making moral judgments implicitly claim, among other things, to be pointing to something objectively prescriptive, these claims are all false."[8] He was fully conscious, therefore, that he was rejecting the commonsense view.

GILBERT HARMAN

Princeton's Gilbert Harman suggested that he would do more justice to the commonsense than did Mackie, saying that "if a philosophical theory conflicts with ordinary ways of thinking and speaking, ... something has probably gone wrong." Giving a name to the position that Mackie affirmed, Harman rightly called it nihilism—"the doctrine that there are no moral facts, no moral truths, and no moral knowledge." Then, pointing out that, because we "ordinarily do speak of moral judgments as true or false," nihilism "runs counter to much that we ordinarily think and say," Harman initially gave the impression that he would retain "our ordinary views and [avoid] endorsing some form of nihilism."[9] He did this, however, only verbally, as the most that he could affirm was the existence of "relative facts about what is right or wrong"—relative, that is, to some set of conventions adopted by a particular society. "[T]here are," he said, "no absolute facts of right or wrong, apart from one or another set of conventions." But this is precisely what nihilism maintains. Accordingly, in spite of Harman's statement that something has probably gone wrong "if a philosophical theory conflicts with ordinary ways of thinking and speaking," he said: "We cannot have morality as it is ordinarily conceived."[10]

RICHARD RORTY

Richard Rorty's rejection of the objectivity and universality of moral principles was even more forthright. Affirming *nominalism*, according to which there are no Platonic forms and hence no "order beyond time and change which . . . establishes a hierarchy of responsibilities," Rorty held that moral truths are made, not discovered.[11] In a fully enlightened culture, Rorty held, the distinction between morality and expediency would seem obsolete, so that questions about "objective moral values" would seem "merely quaint." Although Rorty personally was *against* cruelty and *for* liberal democracy, he could not, he said, provide any answer to the question "Why not be cruel?" or any defense of the superiority of liberal democracy to Nazi tyranny. And although he was in favor of the rhetoric of "human solidarity," there was no basis in the nature of things, he said, for the idea that we should feel obligations to all human beings.[12]

BERNARD WILLIAMS

The implications of this denial of moral realism, illustrated by Mackie, Harman, and Rorty, were brought out in Arthur Allen Leff's essay "Unspeakable Ethics, Unnatural Law," which concludes:

Napalming babies is bad.

Starving the poor is wicked. . . .

There is in the world such a thing as evil.

[All together now:] Sez who?

God help us.[13]

The inability of the currently dominant philosophy to provide a moral theory that "sez" these things was reflected in the title of Bernard Williams' *Ethics and the Limits of Philosophy*. Saying that moral philosophy, unlike the natural sciences, cannot produce objective truth, Williams argued that philosophers should simply admit that they cannot provide an "ethical theory" in the sense of an account of "how we should think in ethics." This point reflected the overall thesis of Williams' book, which was his denial that morality "can be justified by philosophy."[14]

The Failure of the Kantian Approach

Although I have been speaking as if the denial of moral realism entailed the denial of objective moral norms, the Kantian approach to moral philosophy explicitly disconnects these two points. Kantian philosophers such as Alan Gewirth and Jürgen Habermas, while denying that universal moral norms can be derived from the nature of the universe,[15] have argued that they can be generated out of human reason.

It is widely held, however, that this approach has not succeeded. For example, J.D. Goldsworthy not only argues that "moral philosophers have conspicuously failed to find any plausible foundation for the supposed authority of moral precepts." He also says specifically of the attempt "to show that egoism is inherently self-contradictory or irrational," as carried out by philosophers such as John Finnis, Alan Gewirth, and Thomas Nagel: "All of these attempts have failed."[16]

Alan Gewirth

Of these Kantian attempts, Alan Gewirth's was the most extensive.[17] But it also has been the most examined, and this examination largely supports Goldsworthy's opinion. MacIntyre singles out Gewirth's position to illustrate the failure of analytical moral philosophy to carry out the project of providing a "secular, rational justification for [the autonomous moral agent's] moral allegiances."[18]

That MacIntyre's conclusion that Gewirth's project, with its attempt to generate the moral point of view out of the need for self-consistency, has failed is also supported in careful critiques by R.M. Hare, W.D. Hudson, Kai Nielsen, and D.D. Raphael.[19]

Bernard Williams' Critique

Bernard Williams, who also shared the view that Gewirth's project has failed,[20] sums up the problem with the Kantian approach in general by saying, simply: "[T]here is no route to the impartial standpoint from rational deliberation alone."[21] Spelling out the problem more fully, Williams wrote:

> The *I* that stands back in rational reflection from my desires is still the *I* that has those desires and will, empirically and concretely, act; and it is not, simply by standing in reflection, converted into a being whose fundamental interest lies in the harmony of all interests. It cannot, just by taking this step, acquire the motivations of justice.[22]

Williams' thesis—that philosophy cannot provide a justification for the moral point of view, was, in fact, directed primarily against the Kantian attempt to do this.

Jürgen Habermas

Jürgen Habermas believes that it is unfair to judge the Kantian approach primarily on the basis of Gewirth's position, which Habermas calls "an untypical and rather easily criticizable example of a universalistic position.[23] Habermas' own position, however, is also widely considered a failure.[24] More important, Habermas himself concedes that because his "postmetaphysical," nontheistic position cannot speak of something "incomparably important," it can provide no answer to the question "Why be moral?"—that is, Why take an impartial point of view?

This concession by Habermas means that his philosophy can provide no "ultimate justification" for morality and hence no motivation to be moral.[25] For motivation, Habermas says, we must rely on socialization, especially from religion.[26] By his own admission, therefore, Habermas's position provides no exception to what Williams sees as the main failure of the Kantian position: its inability to provide "the motivations of justice" out of reason alone.

Paul Taylor

Some Kantians, rather than trying to generate the impartiality of the moral point of view out of practical reason, simply define practical reason so that it includes this impartiality. Paul Taylor, for example, has argued that an inclusive way of life, which takes everyone's interests into account, is the only one that could be rationally chosen.[27] But his argument is circular, because he stipulates that a choice is rational only insofar as it is "free, enlightened, and *impartial*."[28]

Conclusion

The view of Williams—that "there is no route to the impartial stand-point from rational deliberation alone"—seems to stand. I will continue to assume, therefore, that the denial of moral realism implies the rejection of any objective, universally true, moral principles. I turn now to the primary basis for this denial.

Naturalism_{SAM} as the Basis for the Denial of Moral Realism

The main reason for the denial of moral realism by modern philosophers is their acceptance of naturalism$_{sam}$. Although older histories of science and philosophy portrayed this naturalistic worldview as inaugurated by the scientific revolution of the 17th century, most of the early Enlightenment thinkers were moral realists. The reason for the gulf between the dominant moral philosophy of that era and that of today is a series of transmutations in the generally accepted "scientific worldview."

Having told the story of these transmutations in Chapter 1, I will briefly recap it here in terms of its implications for moral theory. What is often referred to as the "mechanical worldview," shared by Descartes, Boyle, and Newton, was really a supernaturalistic worldview with a sensationist doctrine of perception, a mechanistic doctrine of nature, and a dualistic doctrine of human beings. Although the sensationist doctrine of perception meant that there could be no direct perception of moral norms, these norms could still be known. For Locke, they were found in the Bible, which was supernaturally inspired.

The first transmutation in the "scientific worldview" was to a deistic position, which rejected supernatural inspiration. But deists such as Adam Ferguson and Thomas Jefferson could explain our knowledge of moral principles—while continuing to affirm the sensationist doctrine of perception—in terms of moral knowledge deistically implanted in the human mind at creation.[29] This first transmutation of the scientific worldview, therefore, created no crisis in moral philosophy.

But the next transmutation, which retained the sensationism of the early modern view while replacing its supernaturalism with atheism and its dualism with materialism, resulted in a disenchanted naturalism with no room for moral knowledge, or even for moral truths. Because this form of naturalism is widely thought to be authorized by science—as shown by the fact that it is often simply called "scientific naturalism"[30]—it is widely accepted as *the* standard of acceptable belief. It is this acceptance, I will now illustrate, that lies behind the denial of objective moral principles by our representative philosophers.

Sensationism

At the heart of Mackie's argument against the objectivity of moral values was his "argument from queerness," which has both an epistemological and a metaphysical part. The epistemological part says that if we were aware of objective moral values, "it would have to be by some special faculty of moral perception or intuition, utterly different from our ordinary ways of knowing everything else," which are "sensory perception or introspection."[31] Mackie's point was that, aside from what we know about our own experience from introspection, everything we know about the world originates in sensory perception. Therefore, the idea that moral principles alone are known by some special faculty should be, as a purely *ad hoc* hypothesis, rejected.

Sensationism has been even more central to Harman's denial of objectivity. Ethics differs fundamentally from science, he has argued, in having no observational evidence.[32]

> Facts about protons can affect what you observe, since a proton passing through the cloud chamber can cause a vapor trail that reflects light to your eye. . . . But there does not seem to be any way in which the actual rightness or wrongness of a given situation can have any effect on your perceptual apparatus.[33]

Accordingly, if there were such a thing as moral knowledge, Harman says, it "would have to be a kind of knowledge that can be acquired other than by observation."[34]

At this point, Harman faces the embarrassing fact that ethics in this respect is in the same boat as mathematics. "We do not and cannot perceive numbers," says Harman. "Relations among numbers cannot have any more of an effect on our perceptual apparatus than moral facts can."[35] This fact is embarrassing because Harman, believing his naturalism to be vouchsafed by natural science, would be loath to admit that his epistemology is inadequate for mathematical physics, generally regarded as the preeminent natural science. Harman can handle this problem only through a resort to special pleading, concluding that we can speak of mathematical knowledge because mathematics has "indirect observational evidence."[36]

Harman's position is thereby similar to that of Willard Quine, who used his "tribunal of sense experience" to exclude moral judgments from the realm of cognitive assertions,[37] even though he (inconsistently) allowed admission to assertions about "the abstract objects of mathematics.[38] Although Quine and Harman had to cheat to do so, they both used sensationism to contrast ethical judgments unfavorably with scientific ones.

A similar contrast between science and ethics was central to Williams' denial of an objectivist view of ethics. In scientific inquiry, he said, we expect convergence of opinion, with the convergence explained by the fact that the thinking of the scientists is guided by the way the world really is. But in ethical thinking, Williams claimed, there is no basis for expecting convergence: We cannot perceive moral norms, so there is no way for the world to guide the thinking of moral philosophers.[39]

We cannot, therefore, speak of "knowledge" in ethics, Williams said, because knowledge requires not only that a proposition believed by a person be true but also that this truth and the belief be "nonaccidentally linked." In science, this link is provided by perception of the physical world, but ethical beliefs, Williams held, are not based on perception.[40] Although he recognized that some philosophers have claimed that "something like perception," sometimes called moral intuition, accounts for our ethical concepts, Williams believed that "the appeal to intuition as a faculty . . . seemed to say that these truths were known, but there was no way in which they were known."[41] Williams evidently found inconceivable the idea that we could know things through nonsensory perception.

Although Richard Rorty's sensationism was less explicit, many of his statements made clear that he rejected the idea that we have any capacity to intuit eternal, universal principles existing beyond the contingencies of history. Overagainst the idea that there is some "deepest level of the self" that is connected to something outside of history, Rorty endorsed the historicist insistence "that socialization, and thus historical circumstance, goes all the way down." Rejecting Kant's view that the moral self is "not a product of time and chance, not an effect of natural, spatiotemporal causes," Rorty praised Freud for helping "de-divinize the self by tracking conscience home to its origin in the contingencies of our upbringing," a tracking through which Freud "de-universalizes the moral sense." We are to think of morality, Rorty said, not "as the voice of the divine part of ourselves" but "as the voice of ourselves as members of a community."[42]

This rejection of the idea that the moral conscience arises partly out of nonsensory intuitions was part and parcel of Rorty's acceptance of the program that not only "naturalizes mind," by "making all questions about the relation of [it] to the rest of [the] universe *causal* questions," but also understands all causal forces as "material, spatio-temporal causes," so that Saint Paul's and Isaac Newton's ideas might have been "the results of cosmic rays scrambling the fine structure of some crucial neurons in their respective brains."[43]

ATHEISM

Theistic belief in the existence of a divine agent provided traditional thought with an answer to the two questions about the existence of "Platonic forms" mentioned above: Where do they exist? and How can they, as ideal rather than actual entities, exert influence in the world? Philosophers who accept naturalism$_{sam}$, with its atheism, cannot accept this answer.

Mackie, having said that values are *not* "part of the fabric of the world," added: "The difficulty of seeing how values could be objective is a fairly strong reason for thinking that they are not." The basic difficulty involves the *metaphysical* part of Mackie's argument from queerness: Objective values, he said, "would be entities or qualities or relations of a very strange sort, utterly different from anything else in the universe."[44] They would be so different because they would have *prescriptivity* built into them, as do some Platonic Forms. The Form of the Good, for example, "has to-be-pursuedness somehow built into it."[45]

Mackie's difficulty in understanding how objective values could exist was due to his presumption of atheism. Describing his book as "a discussion of what we can make of morality without recourse to God," he "conceded that if the requisite theological doctrine could be defended, a kind of objective ethical prescriptivity could be defended.[46]

Harman explicitly makes naturalism the reason for denying ethical objectivity; he even has a chapter entitled "Nihilism and Naturalism."[47] Showing that naturalism as he understands it entails the rejection of any divine actuality, he defines naturalism as "the sensible thesis that *all* facts are facts of nature."[48] "Our scientific conception of the world," he added, "has no place for gods."[49] The implication is that because "nature" neither includes, nor is included in, nor is the product of, a divine being, there is no "place" for normative values.

This can be called the "Platonic problem," because one of the main criticisms of Plato's philosophy from the outset was that his "forms" or "ideas" seemed to exist on their own—floating in the void, as it were. The Middle Platonists solved this problem, which was raised already by Aristotle, by placing the ideas in the divine creator, a solution that was largely presupposed throughout most of the Middle Ages. But Harman, holding that scientific naturalism "has no place for gods," concluded that the universe has no place for moral norms.

Although Harman, who continues to accept mathematical principles, fails to acknowledge the Platonic problem as to where *these* forms exist, he does refer to the second problem, which can be called the "Benacerraf problem." Paul Benacerraf, in an influential article titled "Mathematical Truth," rightly argued that true beliefs can be considered knowledge only if that which makes the belief true is somehow *causally* responsible for the belief (so that the belief and the truth of its propositional content are, in Williams' words, "nonaccidentally linked"). As philosophers of mathematics have seen, this view of knowledge, combined with the Platonic view of numbers as ideal entities, implies that there can be no mathematical knowledge. Penelope Maddy puts the problem thus: "[H]ow can entities that don't even inhabit the physical universe take part in any causal interaction whatsoever? Surely to be abstract is to be causally inert. Thus if Platonism is true, we can have no mathematical knowledge."[50]

This conclusion only follows, of course, given one other presupposition: that ideal entities do not exist in an actual entity that gives them causal agency. The importance of this atheistic presupposition is brought out by Reuben Hersh, who says: "For Leibniz and Berkeley, abstractions like numbers are thoughts in the mind of God . . . [But] Heaven and the Mind of God are no longer heard of in academic discourse."[51] As Hersh sees, the Benacerraf problem was created by the rejection of theism.

Although this problem was originally formulated in terms of mathematical knowledge, Harman uses it to deny only the possibility of *moral* knowledge. Harman's discussion of mathematics, however, reveals his awareness of Benacerraf's point that causation and perception are two sides of the same relation. That is, for us to perceive X is for X to exert causal influence on us. The problem involved in mathematical knowledge has, therefore, two sides: On the one hand, if all our perception is *sensory* perception, we cannot perceive numbers. On the other hand, even if we had a nonsensory mode of perception, numbers on their own could not exert causal efficacy on us. We would still, therefore, not be able to perceive (or "intuit") them. Harman, with reference to Benacerraf's article, says:

> We do not and cannot perceive numbers . . . , since we cannot be in causal contact with them. . . . Relations among numbers cannot have any more of an effect on our perceptual apparatus than moral facts can.

It is at this point that Harman, having acknowledged that numbers and moral facts are in the same boat, lets numbers climb out through special pleading, so that he can conclude that "ethics is cut off from observation in a way that science is not."[52] In any case, whether even-handedly or not, Harman uses the Benacerraf problem as well as the Platonic problem, both of which are created by atheism, to reject the possibility of moral knowledge.

The assumption that atheism is true was also central to Williams' ethical thought, as shown by his puzzling over the meaning of our inescapable sense that some things are important not merely for some people but "important *überhaupt.*" Asking what this means, Williams declared: "It does not mean that it is important to the universe; in that sense, nothing is important." It is no surprise, therefore, to see that Williams, like Mackie and Harman, held that "our values are not 'in the world.'" He considered this the basic idea—which he considers a *discovery*—behind the notion that it is a fallacy (the so-called natural-istic fallacy) to think that value can somehow be derived from fact, so that *ought* could be derived from *is.*

This "discovery" followed, he pointed out, on the collapse of the-ism's teleological worldview, which Williams saw as the crucial event for contemporary moral thinking, saying of the assumptions provided by that worldview: "No one has yet found a good way of doing without those assumptions."[53] Accordingly, what Williams in his *Ethics and the Limits of Philosophy* meant by these limits—which refer to philosophy's inability to justify morality—presuppose the falsity of any form of theism. He should, therefore, have entitled his book, more modestly, "Ethics and the Limits of Atheistic Philosophy."

The importance of the shift from theism to atheism was especially emphasized by Rorty, whose various writings can be read as an ongoing hermeneutic of the death of God. "To say, with Nietzsche, that God is dead," said Rorty, "is to say that we serve no higher purposes." Rorty also, like Nietzsche and Heidegger, connected atheism with the rejec-tion of Platonic forms in favor of a fully nominalistic vision, accord-ing to which there are "no eternal relations between eternal objects."[54]

This nominalism entails, Rorty said, that *everything* is historical and thereby contingent, so that none of our beliefs "refer back to something beyond the reach of time and chance." Anyone who believes "in an order beyond time and chance which both determines the point of human existence and establishes a hierarchy of responsibilities," Rorty asserted, "is still, in his heart, a theologian," and thereby not fully in step with the "process of de-divinization" that Rorty hoped to accelerate.[55]

The reason why purely secular philosophies, working without a notion of a Holy Reality, can see no basis for a move from *is* to *ought*, and thereby no motivation or even ultimate justification for morality, has been pointed out, in effect, by the anthropologist Clifford Geertz's account of "the religious perspective." This perspective, said Geertz, is "the conviction that the values one holds are grounded in the inherent structure of reality, that between the way one ought to live and the way things really are there is an unbreakable inner connection." It is this connection, Geertz said, that accounts for religion's moral vitality: "The powerfully coercive 'ought' is felt to grow out of a comprehensive factual 'is.'"[56]

To reject the idea of a Holy Reality is to reject this idea of a comprehensive factual "is" in which normative values are rooted—values that indicate how we ought to live if we want to be in harmony with this Holy Reality. And we naturally *do* want to be in harmony with the Holy as we understand it, I would add, because the Holy by definition is that which is intrinsically good in an ultimate, nonderivative way. If we understand the Holy to be a Holy Actuality that grounds moral values, therefore, our religious drive to be in harmony with the Holy will provide motivation for the moral life: moral "oughts" will be dictated by the desire to be in harmony with the Holy "is."

To the extent that the decline of traditional theism has meant a decline of *any* conception of a Holy Reality, which is clearly the case for those who accept naturalism_{sam}, the fact that the rejection of tradi-tional theism has led to a crisis in moral theory is no surprise. It follows inevitably, as Williams acknowledged, from the fact that there is no longer any factual statement from which one can infer an ought-state-ment, and certainly not one that would provide motivation to obey this ought-statement when doing so seems to threaten one's self-interest.

MATERIALISM

The materialism of naturalism_{sam}, besides reinforcing the two other dimensions, adds two more denials hostile to a moral worldview.

Denial of Freedom: One of these is the *denial of freedom*. Although I have discussed this issue in prior chapters, it is especially important for moral theory, given the fact that virtually all philosophers admit that moral responsibility implies genuine freedom, in the sense of the capacity to have acted otherwise than one did. Freedom in this sense is one of our hard-core commonsense presuppositions. As Whitehead—against the claim that our feeling of freedom is an illusion—said: "This element in experience is too large to be put aside merely as miscon-struction. It governs the whole tone of human life." Whitehead was also explicit about the importance of freedom for morality, saying that, apart from the notion of partial self-determination, "there can be no moral responsibility."[57]

The philosophers we have examined, however, have failed to address this issue. Rorty—who at one time explicitly affirmed elimi-native materialism, according to which words such as "conscious-ness" and "freedom," which cannot correspond to anything within a materialistic world, should simply be eliminated from our vocabu-lary[58]—came the closest. But he discussed the issue only in the sense of arguing that we should *not* discuss it. That is, although Rorty affirmed that everything, including the human mind and its activities, can in principle be explained in terms of "material, spatio-temporal causes," he said that we should not ask questions such as, "What is the place of consciousness in a world of molecules?" and "What is the place of intentionality in a world of causation?"[59] Rorty thereby admitted, in effect, that his materialism allowed for no intelligible account of consciousness and freedom.

Denial of Platonic Forms: Materialism's other denial hostile to materialism involves *Platonic forms.* Whereas atheism denies the existence of a nonlocal agent, which could give such forms residence and agency, and sensationism denies that we could perceive any such forms even if they exist, materialism adds the flat-out denial that any such forms exist.

Although it was Rorty who most explicitly endorsed a nominalistic vision, insisting that there are "no eternal relations between eternal objects,"[60] this anti-Platonic view is shared by all the philosophers we have examined. It is expressed, for example, in Harman's definition of naturalism as the thesis that "*all* facts are facts of nature."

This nominalistic rejection of eternal forms in the name of naturalism—which if carried out consistently requires the denial of mathematical as well as moral forms[61]—has been challenged by a modern philosopher not yet discussed, Charles E. Larmore.

The Contrary Vision of Charles Larmore: Defining "naturalism" as the view that the world is exhausted by the objects of the natural sciences, Larmore argues that we cannot do justice to human experience unless we say, with Plato, that the world also contains value, in the sense of a normative dimension. The affirmation of a normative realm, argues Larmore, is necessary to do justice to our moral experience, which assumes that moral judgments presuppose moral truths that exist independently of our preferences.[62]

More generally, the affirmation of a normative realm is necessary to do justice to *any* of our normative beliefs about values, including cognitive values about "the way we ought to think." That is, the reasons for doubting that there are moral values, such as Mackie's charge that they would be epistemically and metaphysically "queer," apply equally to *cognitive* values. But to deny that there are any objective cognitive values would mean that the idea that we *ought* to avoid self-contradiction is merely a preference, with no inherent authority. Stating that this Nietzschean outlook "boggles the mind," Larmore explains:

> Imagine thinking that even so basic a rule of reasoning as the avoidance of contradiction has no more authority than what we choose to give it. Imagine thinking that we could just as well have willed the opposite, seeking out contradictions and believing each and every one. Has anyone the slightest idea of what it would be like really to believe this?[63]

Larmore's conclusion is that, because we cannot without self-contradiction deny the existence of *cognitive* facts with in-built prescriptivity, there is no reason to deny the existence of inherently prescriptive *moral* facts.

This case against Mackie's metaphysical queerness argument had previously been made by Hilary Putnam, who said: "There are 'ought-implying facts' in the realm of belief fixation; and that is an excellent reason not to accept the view that there cannot be 'ought-implying facts' anywhere."[64] Although anti-Platonic naturalism is widely thought to be based on the authority of science, Larmore says, "the belief that the achievements of modern science ought to command our assent . . . puts us beyond [anti-Platonic] naturalism. For this belief makes reference to a truth about what we ought to believe."[65]

This side of Larmore's position makes it extremely different from that of Harman, Mackie, Rorty, and Williams. But although Larmore rejects the materialism of naturalism$_{sam}$, he does not reject its sensationism and atheism. Because of Larmore's retention of sensationism, he cannot explain how we can perceive Platonic values. And because of his retention of atheism, he has no answer to either the Platonic problem or the Benacerraf problem of how, even if Platonic forms could somehow exist on their own, they could influence our experience.[66]

Despite these problems, however, Larmore has cogently argued that the currently dominant form of scientific naturalism is inadequate for science itself, so it should not be used to veto moral realism. I will now expand on this point.

THE INADEQUACY OF NATURALISM$_{SAM}$ FOR SCIENCE AND COMMON SENSE

A widely held intellectual ideal, introduced in Chapter 6 under the name *domain uniformitarianism*, is that we should try to interpret the objects in every domain of thought in terms of one and the same set of basic principles. This ideal, which lies behind Mackie's "queerness" arguments, is a good one. Given the assumption that naturalism$_{sam}$ had already proven itself adequate for virtually everything except moral experience, it would certainly make sense to try to bring our interpretation of morality into line with it.

As we have seen in previous chapters, however, the assumption that this adequacy has been demonstration is groundless. Each of the dimensions of this form of naturalism—its sensationism, its materialism, its atheism—prevents it from being able to accommodate various ideas that are presupposed by science, including the external world, the past, time, causation, induction, consciousness, mental causation, rational activity, mathematical objects, and logical principles. Because naturalism$_{sam}$ is not even close to providing a worldview adequate for scientific experience, there is no reason to try to bring our understanding of morality into harmony with it.

Furthermore, although our age widely assumes that it is primarily science to which a philosophical worldview must be adequate, morality, with its inevitable presuppositions, is an equally important standard.

"It is the primary aim of philosophy," wrote the great English moral philosopher Henry Sidgwick, "to unify completely, bring into clear coherence, all departments of rational thought, and this aim cannot be realised by any philosophy that leaves out of its view the important body of judgments and reasonings which form the subject matter of ethics." Whitehead, besides quoting this statement by Sidgwick with approval,[67] indicated that he understood certain basic moral notions to belong to our hard-core commonsense presuppositions, saying that "the impact of aesthetic, religious and moral notions is inescapable," and that "our moral and aesthetic judgments . . . involve the ultimate notions of 'better' and 'worse.'"[68]

In light of the fact that those who endorse naturalism$_{sam}$ cannot account for many of the inevitable presuppositions of both our scientific and our moral practice, there is no justification for the fact that this version of naturalism is, as Larmore points out, "used as a standard for acceptable belief."[69]

This conclusion does not mean, however, that we can do without *some* standard for acceptable belief. It also does not mean that this standard need not be naturalistic in the generic sense. For one thing, the best arguments against theism, such as the problem of evil, are actually only arguments against the supernaturalist version of theism. Also, naturalism in the generic sense—naturalism$_{ns}$—is far more widely presupposed by the scientific community as a whole (as distinct from its ideological leadership) than is its embodiment in naturalism$_{sam}$. Finally, naturalism$_{ns}$, unlike naturalism$_{sam}$, does not contradict any of our inevitable presuppositions or any well-documented phenomena.

WHITEHEAD'S MORAL-SCIENTIFIC NATURALISM

If we need a worldview that is broadly naturalistic, and yet naturalism$_{sam}$ is inadequate, we need a more adequate version of naturalism$_{ns}$. Such a version, I have been arguing, is provided by Whitehead's naturalism$_{ppp}$. In this final section, I briefly point how this version of naturalism can—by virtue of accounting for the inevitable presuppositions of practice to which naturalism$_{sam}$ cannot do justice—support our moral as well as our scientific activities. It can do this justice by reason of all three of its dimensions: its panexperientialism, its panentheism, and its prehensive doctrine of perception.

PANEXPERIENTIALISM

According to the panexperientialism of this position, experience and spontaneity, which we know to be features of what we call our minds or souls, are also possessed (by hypothesis), to a lesser degree, by the individual components of the brain, namely, its cells and *their* components (organelles, macromolecules, and so on).

This position, by allowing for *nondualistic interactionism*, can do justice to our presuppositions about freedom and rational activity. Like dualism, this view says that the mind and brain are numerically distinct entities, a fact that provides a necessary condition for their interaction. But unlike dualism, panexperientialism denies that the mind and the brain's components are ontologically different in kind—which was the Cartesian assumption that led to the conclusion that they could *not* interact. The primary reason why philosophers turned from interaction to materialistic identism is, therefore, overcome, and the mind's capacity to exercise rational self-determination, then to direct its body's activities, can be conceptualized.

PANENTHEISM

The panentheism of naturalism$_{ppp}$ allows us to reaffirm the old idea that mathematical, logical, moral, aesthetic, and cognitive ideals can exist, and also have causal efficacy in the world, because they exist in God. In Whitehead's language, they exist in the "primordial nature" of God, having influence in the world by virtue of being envisaged by God with appetition for their actualization in the world.

Solving both the Platonic and the Benacerraf problems, Whitehead says that we experience ideals by virtue of their presence in the divine, nonlocal agent: "There are experiences of ideals—of ideals entertained, of ideals aimed at, of ideals achieved, of ideals defaced. This is the experience of the deity of the universe."[70]

PREHENSIVE DOCTRINE OF PERCEPTION

Finally, this naturalism$_{ppp}$'s prehensive doctrine of perception enables us to understand why we have many of our hard-core commonsense presuppositions. We inevitably presuppose the reality of the external world, the past, time, and causation, because *we constantly have a direct, presensory experience of them.* Also the apparent reality of moral intuitions—along with our mathematical, logical, aesthetic, and cognitive intuitions—can be understood as real perceptions of normative principles belonging to the fabric of the world. The idea that we perceive these ideal forms through the same mode of perception as we perceive the external world and its causation means that moral experience does not require the *ad hoc* assumption of a special moral "sense" or "faculty." Domain uniformitarianism is, therefore, not violated. These ideal forms can exist and influence our experience, according to this panentheistic worldview, because they exist in "the mind of God."

Whitehead's prehensive doctrine of perception, combined with his doctrine of God, can also explain why we experience such ideals with the feeling that we *ought* to actualize them, why they come to us with prescriptivity, or ("to-be-pursuedness") built in. Every prehension, as we saw in Chapter 5, has not only an objective datum, which is *what* is prehended, but also a subjective form, which is *how* that datum is prehended. This idea applies not only to our prehensions but also to God's, including God's primordial prehension of the possibilities, including those possibilities that constitute moral ideals. The subjective form with which God prehends these ideals is *appetition that they be realized in the finite world*. Accordingly, because all creatures prehend God, there is, in Whitehead's words, a "prehension by every creature of the . . . appetitions constituting the primordial nature of God."[71] This idea constitutes the first step in Whitehead's explanation of why we experience moral ideals with the feeling that we ought to actualize them.

The second step involves his doctrine that is best called "the initial conformation of subjective form." The basic idea is that, when we feel (or prehend) the feelings of another occasion of experience, our feeling conforms, at least initially, to the subjective form of that prior feeling. For example, if the cells in my leg are suffering from an injury, I—as the dominant member of the bodily organism—tend to suffer with them. Likewise, when I feel my own past occasions of experience, I tend to take over their subjective forms. If my experience a half-second ago had an appetite for food or drink, my present occasion of experience begins with that same appetite.

For this reason, Whitehead calls our prehension or feeling of another occasion of experience a "conformal feeling," because its subjective form conforms to that of the prior feeling. This point is so important that Whitehead gives it a name, "the Doctrine of Conformation of Feeling."[72] He also uses the language of "sympathy," saying:

> The primitive form of physical experience is emotional—blind emotion—received as felt elsewhere in another occasion and conformally appropriated as a subjective passion. In the language appropriate to the higher stages of experience, the primitive element is *sympathy,* that is, feeling the feeling *in another* and feeling conformally *with* another.[73]

If this were the totality of Whitehead's view, the result would be determinism, because the subjective forms of our experiences, and hence our desires and purposes, would be fully determined by our prehensions of prior experiences, divine and creaturely. But this doctrine of necessary conformation applies only to the first phase of an occasion of experience, which is its *physical* pole. Each occasion's physical pole is followed by a *mental* pole, which involves self-determination. In this pole, the subjective forms of the inherited feelings can be modified. As Whitehead puts it, "[a feeling's] subjective form, though it must always have reproductive reference to the data, is not wholly determined by them."[74] Rather than total conformation, there is only "initial conformation."

Whitehead's doctrine with regard to an actual occasion as a whole, therefore, should be called "the doctrine of the *initial* conformation of subjective form," as indicated by his statement that "the continuity of subjective form is the initial sympathy of B for A."[75] Following this initial conformation, the occasion, in its mental or conceptual pole, determines the final subjective forms of its various feelings in the process of determining its overall aim, called the "subjective aim." This subjective aim may diverge drastically from the ideal presented to it by God, which Whitehead calls the "initial subjective aim," or simply the "initial aim."[76]

In feeling the divine feeling of an ideal, a creature feels it, at least initially, with a conformal subjective form—that is, with appetition to realize it.[77] This divinely derived feeling is only the *initial* subjective aim, rather than the subjective aim as such, because the causality from God, like the causality from other actual entities, is not all-determining. The finite subject, once constituted by its prehension of God and the past world, is then "autonomous master" of its own becoming, deciding precisely what to make of its endowments. The subject, therefore, "is conditioned, though not determined, by [the] initial subjective aim."[78] It is our freedom to depart from the divine ideal (as well as past finite causation) that explains why we have the experience not only of "ideals aimed at" and "ideals achieved," as Whitehead put it, but also of "ideals defaced."[79] In this way, Whitehead's prehensive doctrine of perception, with its category of the initial conformation of subjective form, can explain human conscience.

To say that moral norms are derived from God is to say that they are rooted in the Holy Reality, with which we naturally want to be in harmony (because "the Holy" by definition is that which is intrinsically good in an ultimate sense). The prehensive doctrine of perception also provides a basis for the perception of God *as* Holy Actuality. The idea that, in Whitehead's words, our experience of ideals is "the experience of the deity of the universe" does not, therefore, need to rest purely on an intellectual inference, but can be supported by direct experience.

CONCLUSION

The apparent conflict between scientific naturalism and our hard-core commonsense moral presuppositions, I have argued, is due to the fact that in the currently dominant "scientific worldview," naturalism in the generic sense (naturalism$_{ns}$) has been embodied in naturalism$_{sam}$; that although this version of naturalism has been adopted in the name of science, it is inadequate for science as well as for morality; and that the lack of any *necessary* conflict between naturalism$_{ns}$ and our moral presuppositions is shown by the fact that Whitehead's philosophy provides a moral-scientific naturalism (naturalism$_{ppp}$), which is supportive of the presuppositions of our moral as well as our scientific activities.

NOTES

1. Gene Outka and John P. Reeder, Jr., eds., *Prospects for a Common Morality* (Princeton: Princeton University Press, 1993), 3.

2. Alasdair MacIntyre, *After Virtue: A Study in Moral Theory* (Notre Dame: University of Notre Dame, 1981), 67.

3. See, for example, B.S. Chimni, "Global Capitalism and Global Democracy: Subverting the Other?" in Daniele Archibugi, Mathias Koenig-Archibugi, and Raffaele Marchetti, *Global Democracy: Normative and Empirical Perspectives* (Cambridge: Cambridge University Press, 2012), 233-53; Jürgen Habermas, "Kant's Idea of Perpetual Peace, With the Benefit of Two Hundred Years' Hindsight," in James Bohman and Matthias Lutz-Bachmann, *Perpetual Peace: Essays on Kant's Cosmopolitan Ideal* (Massachusetts: MIT, 1997), 113-53; David Held, *Democracy and the Global Order: From the Modern State to Cosmopolitan Governance* (Stanford: Stanford University Press, 1995); Mathias Koenig-Archibugi, "Is Global Democracy Possible?" *European Journal of International Relations*, June 16, 2010; Raffaele Marchetti, *Global Democracy: For and Against. Ethical Theory, Institutional Design, and Social Struggles* (New York: Routledge, 2008); Tim Murithi, "Towards the Metamorphosis of the United Nations: A Proposal for Establishing Global Democracy," in Archibugi, Koenig-Archibugi, and Marchetti, *Global Democracy* (132-49).

4. MacIntyre, *After Virtue*, 38, 48. The idea that human rights cannot justified within "the Enlightenment project" as characterized by MacIntyre has also been articulated in works arguing that morality *can* be justified on a *theistic* basis—books such as Basil Mitchell's *Morality: Religious and Secular: The Dilemma of the Traditional Conscience* (Oxford University Press, 1980), and Franklin I. Gamwell's *The Divine Good: Modern Moral Theory and the Necessity of God* (Dallas: Southern Methodist University, 1996).

5. I should perhaps explain the distinction between the claim made in this sentence and that of the preceding ones. The first claim is simply that people in every culture think in terms of a distinction between "better and worse," which is applied to attitudes, intentions, and modes of behavior. An extreme cultural relativist might grant this point but then state that it does little to qualify relativism, because each culture's ideas of *which* attitudes, intentions, and modes of behavior are good, and which bad, are entirely culture-specific ideas. My second claim, introduced by "moreover," is that people commonly assume that at least

some of their concrete moral norms reflect universally valid principles.

6. It might be thought that theists hold that moral principles are not inherent in "the nature of things" or (to use the following phrase) "the fabric of the world." But with regard to the issue at hand, no antithesis exists: For theists, nothing is more inherent in "the nature of things" or "the fabric of the world" than God.

7. John Mackie, *Ethics: Inventing Right and Wrong* (New York: Penguin, 1977), 24. The extent to which the falsity of moral realism is simply presupposed by recent philosophers is illustrated by R.M. Hare's nonchalant remark, "It was John Mackie's great contribution to ethics to display clearly the absurdity of realism" ("Ontology in Ethics," in *Morality and Objectivity: A Tribute to J.L. Mackie*, ed. Ted Honderich [London: Routledge & Kegan Paul, 1985], 39-53, at 53). Hare, from whom Mackie evidently got the phrase about the fabric of the world, even purported not to understand what it, employed with respect to moral values, might mean (42).

8. Mackie, *Ethics*, 15, 17, 79-80, 35.

9. Gilbert Harman, *The Nature of Morality: An Introduction to Ethics* (New York: Oxford University Press, 1977), 34, 11, 12-13.

10. Ibid., 131-32, 90. Maddy suggested that the problem could be solved by simply thinking of mathematical objects as part of the physical world, so that they can be perceived by sensory perception (Maddy 1990, 44, 59, 178). Likewise, a type of thought has arisen called "moral naturalism," according to which the gulf between facts and values can be overcome by "reveal[ing] value to us as straightforwardly part of the domain of natural fact." Some advocates of this approach have challenged Harman's statement that, whereas the physical sciences are based on observations, ethics is not based on observations in an analogous way. For an example, if you see some kids setting a cat on fire just for fun, you will likely see that this is wrong. But making this judgment is not based on observing facts, similar to the way that scientists have concluded that the universe is many billions of years old. In response, moral

naturalist James Lenman has argued that there can be moral explanations of natural facts. For example, he says, "we believe Hitler was morally depraved . . . because he was" (James Lenman, "Moral Naturalism," The Stanford Encyclopedia of Philosophy [Spring 2014 Edition], ed. Edward N. Zalta). As Maddy and Lenman illustrate, the belief that we must perceive both mathematical and moral truths by means of our physical senses has led many philosophers to desperate lengths.

11. Richard R. Rorty, *Contingency, Irony, and Solidarity* (Cambridge: Cambridge University Press, 1989), xv, 3-5, 77.

12. Ibid., 44-45, 53-54, 197, 191-92.

13. Allen Leff, "Unspeakable Ethics, Unnatural Law" (*Duke Law Journal*, 1979), 1229-49, at 1249.

14. Bernard Williams, *Ethics and the Limits of Philosophy* (Cambridge: Harvard University Press, 1985), 17, 22, 74, 148-52.

15. Habermas has said, for example; "What ought to be is [not] an entity," and moral commands "do not relate to anything in the objective world," so that moral truths are not true by virtue of corresponding to "moral facts" in the sense of "an antecedent realm of value objects" (*Justification and Application: Remarks on Discourse Ethics,* trans. Ciaran Cronin [Cambridge: Polity Press, 1993], 26; cf. 29).

16. J.D. Goldsworthy, "God or Mackie? The Dilemma of Secular Moral Philosophy," *American Journal of Jurisprudence* 30 (1985), 43-78 45, 75. For the attempt by John Finnis, see *Natural Law and Natural Rights* (New York: Oxford University Press, 1980); for Thomas Nagel's attempt, see *The Possibility of Altruism* (Princeton: Princeton University Press, 1970).

17. See Alan Gewirth, *Reason and Morality* (Chicago: University of Chicago Press, 1978), and his reply to critics in Edward Regis, ed. *Gewirth's Ethical Rationalism* (Chicago: University of Chicago Press, 1984).

18. MacIntyre, *After Virtue*, 64-65.

19. All these critiques are in Regis, ed., *Gewirth's Ethical Rationalism*.

20. Williams, *Ethics and the Limits of Philosophy*, 210 n. 2.

21. Ibid., 70.

22. Ibid., 69.

23. Habermas, *Justification*, 150.

24. See, for example, Charles E. Larmore, *The Morals of Modernity* (Cambridge: Cambridge University Press, 1996), 205.

25. Habermas, *Justification*, 71, 74, 75, 79, 146.

26. Habermas, *Justification*, 79; *Postmetaphysical Thinking: Philosophical Essays,* trans. William Mark Hohengarten (Cambridge: MIT Press, 1992), 51; "Transcendence from Within, Transcendence in this World," in Don Browning and Francis Schüssler Fiorenza, eds., *Habermas, Modernity, and Public Theology* (New York: Crossroad, 1992), 226-50, at 239.

27. Paul Taylor, *Normative Discourse* (Westport, Conn.: Greenwood, 1961), 147-48.

28. Ibid., 164-65; emphasis added. On the way a similar circularity vitiates the argument of John Finnis in *Natural Law and Natural Rights*, see Goldsworthy, "God or Mackie?" 74.

29. See Garry Wills, *Inventing America: Jefferson's Declaration of Independence* (New York: Vintage Books, 1978).

30. For example, the terms "scientific naturalism" and "scientific materialism" are used interchangeably by Edward O. Wilson, an advocate (*On Human Nature* [New York: Bantam Books, 1979], 200-01), and by Phillip E. Johnson, a critic (*Darwin on Trial,* 2nd ed. [Downers Grove, Ill.: Intervarsity Press, 1993], 116n). For more examples of this

equation, see my *Religion and Scientific Naturalism: Overcoming the Conflicts* (Albany: State University of New York, 2000), 35-37.

31. Mackie, *Ethics*, 38-39.

32. Harman, *The Nature of Morality,* vii, viii, 6-9.

33. Ibid., 9.

34. Ibid., 66.

35. Ibid., 9-10.

36. Ibid., 10.

37. Willard V. O. Quine, *From A Logical Point of View* (Cambridge: Harvard University Press, 1953), 41; "Reply to Morton Smith," in *The Philosophy of W.V. Quine*, ed. Lewis Edwin Hahn and Paul Arthur Schilpp (LaSalle, Ill.: Open Court: 1986), 663-65.

38. Willard V.O. Quine, *From Stimulus to Science* (Cambridge: Harvard University Press, 1995), 14.

39. Williams, *Ethics and the Limits of Philosophy*, 136, 149, 151-52.

40. Ibid., 142, 149.

41. Ibid., 149, 94.

42. Rorty, *Contingency, Irony, and Solidarity*, xiii, 30, 59, 60.

43. Ibid., 15-17.

44. Mackie, *Ethics*, 24, 38.

45. Ibid., 40.

46. Ibid., 48. In an essay on Mackie's position entitled "Ethics and the Fabric of the World" (in Ted Honderich, ed., *Morality and Objectivity: A Tribute to J.L. Mackie* [London: Routledge & Kegan Paul, 1985], 203-14), Williams brought out the atheistic presupposition behind Mackie's

denial of a divine reality. He did this by pointing out, in response to the question "what it could mean to say that a requirement or demand was 'part of the fabric of the world,'" that it "might possibly mean that some agency which made the demand or imposed the requirement was part of the fabric" (205). Williams, of course, believed in such an agency no more than did Mackie.

47. Harman, *The Nature of Morality*, Ch. 2.

48. Ibid., 17. This definition by Harman is an example of what I have called naturalism$_{nati}$, with "nati" standing for "nature is all there is" (and with "nature" here understood as "the totality of finite existents"). This definition lies behind Phillip Johnson's complete rejection of naturalism. Having said that naturalism is similar to materialism, Johnson adds: "The essential point is that nature is understood by both naturalists and materialists to be 'all there is'" (*Reason in the Balance: The Case Against Naturalism in Science, Law, and Education* [Downers Grove, Ill.: Intervarsity Press, 1993], 38n). What Johnson and many others have not seen is that naturalism in this sense, which is implied by naturalism$_{sam}$, is *not* implied by *generic* naturalism.

49. Harman, "Is There a Single True Morality?" in Michael Krausz, ed., *Relativism: Interpretation and Confrontation* (Notre Dame: University of Notre Dame Press, 1989), 363-386, at 381.

50. Penelope Maddy, *Realism in Mathematics* (Oxford: Clarendon Press, 1990), 37.

51. Reuben Hersh, *What is Mathematics, Really?* New York: Oxford University Press, 1997), 12.

52. Harman, *The Nature of Morality*, 9-10.

53. Williams, *Ethics and the Limits of Philosophy*, 182, 128-29, 53.

54. Rorty, *Contingency, Irony, and Solidarity*, 20, xv, 107-08. (On Heidegger and Nietzsche, see "Nietzsche's Word: 'God is Dead,'" in Martin Heidegger, *The Question Concerning Technology: Heidegger's*

Critique of the Modern Age, trans. William Lovett [New York: Harper and Row, 1977], 53-112).

55. Rorty, *Contingency, Irony, and Solidarity*, xv, 45.

56. Clifford Geertz, *Islam Observed: Religious Development in Morocco and Indonesia* (New Haven: Yale University Press, 1968), 97; *Interpretation of Cultures: Selected Essays* (New York: Basic Books, 1973), 126-27.

57. Whitehead, *Process and Reality*, 47; *Symbolism: Its Meaning and Effect* (orig. 1927) (New York: Capricorn, 1959), 8.

58. See Rorty's 1970 essay, "Mind-Body Identity, Privacy and Categories" (in C.V. Borst, *The Mind-Brain Identity Theory* [London: Macmillan, 1970], 187-212), which expresses a position that he continues to presuppose, even though he later tried not to make any ontological assertions. As Peter Dews commented: "Rorty—for all his hermeneutic gestures—regards [the indifferent universe of physicalism] as the ontological bottom line" (*The Limits of Disenchantment: Essays on Contemporary European Philosophy* [London: Verso, 1995], 2).

59. Rorty, *Contingency, Irony, and Solidarity*, 16-17, 11.

60. Ibid., xv, 107-08.

61. The idea that naturalism requires the denial of both mathematical and moral forms is illustrated in Simon Blackburn's article "Naturalism" (*Oxford Dictionary of Philosophy* [Oxford and New York: Oxford University Press, 1996], 255), in which he states that "a naturalist will be opposed . . . to acceptance of numbers or concepts as real . . . and opposed to accepting real moral duties and rights as absolute and self-standing facets of the natural order" (255).

62. Charles E. Larmore, *The Morals of Modernity* (Cambridge: Cambridge University Press, 1996), 8, 86, 87, 89, 116, 91-96.

63. Ibid., 86, 87, 99.

64. Hilary Putnam (in *Words and Life*, ed. James Conant [Cambridge: Harvard University Press, 1994], 170), had earlier made this case against Mackie's metaphysical queerness argument, writing: "There are 'ought-implying facts' in the realm of belief fixation; and that is an excellent reason not to accept the view that there cannot be 'ought-implying facts' anywhere."

65. Larmore, *The Morals of Modernity*, 90.

66. On Larmore's sensationist rejection of a direct intuition of moral norms, along with his failed attempt to explain our knowledge of them through "reason", see ibid., 8, 51, 53, 62, 96-98, 110-17. On his acceptance of a godless, disenchanted universe, see 42-44, 55.

67. Whitehead, *Science and the Modern World* (New York: Free Press, 1967), 142, quoting *Henry Sidgwick: A Memoir*, Appendix I (London: Macmillan, 1906).

68. Whitehead, *Modes of Thought* (orig. 1938) (New York: Free Press 1968), 19; *Essays in Science and Philosophy*, 80.

69. Larmore, *The Morals of Modernity*, 89. Harman substantiates Larmore's point, admitting that "the naturalist's only argument" for the view "that a belief that something is right cannot be explained by that thing's being actually right . . . depends on accepting the general applicability of naturalism" ("Is There a Single True Morality?" 383).

70. Whitehead, *Modes of Thought*, 103.

71. *Process and Reality*, 32, 207.

72. Ibid., 237-38; *Adventures of Ideas*, 183.

73. *Process and Reality*, 162.

74. Ibid., 232; see also 85: "the *how* of feeling, though it is germane to the data, is not fully determined by the data."

75. *Adventures of Ideas*, 253, 183.

76. *Process and Reality*, 27, 108, 235, 244-46.

77. Ibid., 225.

78. Ibid., 245, 108.

79. *Modes of Thought*, 103. Whitehead's inclusion of both freedom and evil among our inevitable presuppositions provides the basis for his rejection of Leibniz's doctrine that this is the "best of possible worlds," which Whitehead called "an audacious fudge produced in order to save the face of a Creator constructed by contemporary, and antecedent, theologians" (*Process and Reality*, 47).

CHAPTER EIGHT

Panentheism and Religious Pluralism

Religious pluralism, besides being one of the central issues in contemporary religious thought, is an issue to which Whiteheadian
process theology, with its panentheism, has made an especially important contribution. Although the Whiteheadian approach to religious
pluralism was originally developed within the Christian tradition, this
approach has proved itself to be helpful to theologians and religious
thinkers of other religious traditions.[1] Nevertheless, most of the discussion of religious pluralism thus far occurred within the Christian tradition, so in this chapter, I will, partly for this reason and partly for the sake
of simplicity, deal with religious pluralism as it has been discussed by
Christian theologians and by process Christian theologians in particular.

I will explain first what religious pluralism in the generic sense is
and why it has arisen, giving special attention to the rise of scientific
naturalism. I then discuss widespread criticisms of religious pluralism,
pointing out that most of them are based on an equation of religious
pluralism as such with one particular version of it—a version that is
very different from process theology's version. In the final section, I
discuss this process version as pioneered by John B. Cobb, Jr., showing
how it avoids the problems associated with the other version.

WHAT RELIGIOUS PLURALISM IS

"Religious pluralism" is not simply the sociological fact that there are
many different religions. That fact is usually called "religious diversity."

To be a religious pluralist is to make two assertions. First, religious pluralists reject any a priori claim that their own religion is the only valid one. For example, John Hick says that pluralism rejects the view that "there can be at most one true religion, in the sense of a religion teaching saving truth." Pluralists are open in principle, in other words, to the possibility that other religions may be valid. The second assertion goes beyond this mere statement of possibility to affirm that other religions are actually valid, as when Christians, in Hick's words, assume that their "Jewish or Muslim or Hindu or Sikh or Buddhist friends and acquaintances are as fully entitled in the sight of God to live by their own religious traditions as we are to live by ours."[2]

To be a religious pluralist, therefore, is to reject absolutism, according to which one's own religion is considered the One True Way. The most severe form of Christian absolutism is "exclusivism," according to which no one can be saved except through Christian faith. A less severe form of absolutism is "inclusivism," which says that, although people in other religious traditions may be saved, they are saved only by virtue of God's saving act in Jesus Christ. The inclusivist, like the exclusivist, denies that other religions can be authentic paths to salvation. The pluralist says that other religions can be this, and that at least some of them are.[3]

What I have discussed in this section can be called *generic* religious pluralism, because it is what all varieties of religious pluralists have in common.

NATURALISM AND THE RISE OF RELIGIOUS PLURALISM

This generic religious pluralism, which has become an increasingly important factor since it began to emerge in the 17th and 18th centuries,[4] has had at least five bases: theological, ethical, sociological, scientific, and dialogical.

THEOLOGICAL BASIS

The major theological basis has been the doctrine of divine love. John Hick said that he became a pluralist because he could not reconcile the idea that God is "infinite love" with the idea that "only by responding in faith to God in Christ can we be saved," because this would mean that "infinite love has ordained that human beings can be saved only in a way that in fact excludes the large majority of them."[5] Catholic theologian Paul Knitter, having felt a tension "between two fundamental beliefs: God's universal love and desire to save, and the necessity of the church for salvation," decided that the doctrine of God's universal salvific will implies that the revelation given to others must be a potentially *saving* revelation, so that "Christians not only can but must look on other religions as possible *ways of salvation*."[6]

ETHICAL BASIS

The ethical motivation behind religious pluralism begins, Mark Heim observes, "with revulsion at the crimes of religious pride."[7] Illustrating this point, Hick devotes several pages to the "destructive effects of the assumption of Christian superiority," pointing out, for example, that "there is a clear connection between fifteen or so centuries of the 'absoluteness' of Christianity, with its corollary of the radical inferiority and perverseness of the Judaism it 'superseded,' and the consequent endemic anti-Semitism of Christian civilization," which led to the Holocaust. If each religion could overcome its absoluteness "by the realization that one's own religion is one among several valid human responses to the Divine," Hick argues, "religion could become a healing instead of a divisive force in the world."[9]

SOCIOLOGICAL BASIS

The theological and ethical bases for pluralism have been supported by a sociological fact about the modern world—that many people, through increased familiarity, are overcoming old stereotypes about other religions. Modernity, partly by means of its capitalist economy, which has promoted global trade, has brought people of diverse religions into regular contact with each other. Today, besides learning about other religions from books and mass media, people increasingly have neighbors belonging to other religious traditions. When they compare the lives of these people with those of fellow Christians, it becomes increasingly difficult to maintain the old view that the spiritual and moral fruits produced by Christianity prove it to be in a class by itself.[10]

NATURALISTIC BASIS

The major stimulus for the rise of religious pluralism, however, has been the emergence of a naturalistic worldview. Evidence for the centrality of this factor is provided by the fact that the theological and ethical motivations had existed for a long time and, at least in many parts of the world, the sociological factor of religious diversity has long existed. This combination of the theological, ethical, and sociological factors did not, by itself, result in the rise and wide spread of religious pluralism, which has occurred only recently. Some other factor must have arisen in recent times to account for the great pluralistic turn.

This factor is what can be called the presumption of naturalism, which has been promoted by the growth and spread of the modern scientific tradition. By "naturalism" here, I do not mean naturalism$_{sam}$, but simply the more general position that I have called naturalism$_{ns}$, with its denial of supernatural interruptions of the world's normal causal processes.[11] Also, in saying that this presumption of naturalism has been promoted by modern science, I am not referring solely to the natural sciences, but also to the historical sciences, including the science of biblical criticism, which undermined the earlier reasons for supposing the Bible to have been written through supernatural, infallible inspiration.

Much modern theology—that broad movement often called "liberal theology"—has accepted scientific naturalism in this sense. Hick, for example, says that the form of Christianity that "believed in miracles which arbitrarily disrupt the order of nature" is "incompatible with the scientific project."[12] This rejection of supernaturalism has not necessarily meant a rejection of theism. Process theology, as we have seen in previous chapters, has developed a version of "theistic naturalism," or "naturalistic theism." But process theology is simply one version of a more general acceptance of theistic naturalism (or naturalistic theism).

This denial by liberal theologians in general of supernatural interventions does not even necessarily entail that they reject ongoing divine activity in the world, a fact illustrated especially by process theology. But it does mean that they no longer assume that the founding events of Christian history involved a divine incursion into the world that was different in kind from the way that God works always and everywhere. For example, Ernst Troeltsch, the first major pluralist of the 20th century, rejected, in Knitter's words, "concepts of revelation that had God swooping down from heaven and intervening into history at particular spots."[13] In a similar vein, Wilfred Cantwell Smith rejected the idea "that God has constructed Christianity" in favor of the idea that God "has inspired us to construct it, as He/She/It has inspired Muslims to construct what the world knows as Islam."[14]

The doctrinal revisions undertaken by pluralistic theologians have especially focused on traditional Christian theology's supernaturalistic christology. According to that christology, points out Hick, Jesus "was God—more precisely, God the Son, the second person of the Holy Trinity—incarnate." This doctrine implied "that Christianity, alone among the religions, was founded by God in person" so that it was "God's own religion in a sense in which no other can be."[15] John Cobb's first major statement of his pluralistic position—which was

entitled, significantly, *Christ in a Pluralistic Age*—rejected the traditional "supernaturalist and exclusivist" interpretation of the incarnation
of the divine Logos in Jesus, according to which Jesus was "a supernatural being," namely, "the transcendent, omnipotent, omniscient ruler of
the world . . . walking about on earth in human form."[16]

The rejection of supernaturalism applies also to the traditional idea
of salvation, according to which it involves a divine decision, based
on arbitrary standards, that saves some people from eternal damna-
tion. Recognizing that Christian exclusivism and inclusivism both
depend on some such definition of salvation, such as "being forgiven
and accepted by God because of the atoning death of Jesus," Hick suggests that "we define salvation . . . as an actual change in human beings"
that involves "a long process," not a sudden, supernaturally effected
transformation.[17] Cobb, likewise, speaks of "salvation as something we
participate in here and now rather than, or in addition to, life beyond."[18]

DIALOGICAL BASIS

This rejection of a religious exclusivism based on supernaturalistic
assumptions has contributed, finally, to a fifth basis behind the development of pluralistic forms of Christian theology, which is what some
have called the "dialogical imperative."[19] The conviction that dialogue
is now imperative is based partly on the recognition that many of our
planet's problems are so great that they can be overcome, if at all, only
through the cooperation of the world's various religions. For example,
Knitter argues that all the religions today are facing the human demand
for "some form of this-worldly, earthly (as opposed to purely spiritual)
liberation," so that "*liberation*—what it is and how to achieve it—constitutes a new arena for the encounter of religions."[20]

But the idea that dialogue is now imperative is also based on the
realization that, if our own religion is not the one and only true religion, other traditions may have truths and values that are not provided,

at least as clearly, in our own religion. The conclusion that Christianity, like every other religion, is limited, says Knitter, leads to the dialogical imperative, because it is through dialogue with members of other religious traditions that "we can expand or correct the truth that we have," thereby overcoming the "limitations of our own viewpoint."[21] This motive, as we will see, is central to Cobb's pluralistic theology.

However, before turning to process theology's pluralism as developed by Cobb, we will look at criticisms that have been directed at religious pluralism.

CRITICISMS OF RELIGIOUS PLURALISM

For many theologians, the need for Christianity to embrace pluralism is now beyond question, but not all theologians agree. From the perspective of many Christian thinkers, "Christian pluralism" is a self-contradiction. One cannot hold Christian faith in an authentic form, they believe, and be a pluralist. Much of this rejection of Christian pluralism arises from an absolutist, supernaturalist notion of Christian faith, which simply presupposes that the only authentic form of Christian faith is one that assumes, a priori, that it is the only religion sanctioned by God. This kind of criticism can be largely ignored by pluralists, because the controversy is not about pluralism as such but about the proper Christian response to modern thought—whether the liberal rejection of the supernaturalist framework is a necessary adjustment by Christian faith or a betrayal of that faith. For most pluralists, that issue has long been settled. But there are some criticisms that must be taken more seriously.

DOES DEBILITATING RELATIVISM NECESSARILY RESULT?

One criticism is that pluralism inevitably leads to a kind of relativism that is antithetical to Christian faith. The centrality of this issue was pointed out in a landmark book by Alan Race, who said: "The pertinent question mark which hovers over all theories of pluralism is how far they succeed in overcoming the sense of 'debilitating relativism' which is their apparent danger." By "debilitating relativism," Race meant the view that all religions are equally true in a way that makes them equally false.[22] At least one pluralist theologian, Langdon Gilkey, believed that this danger cannot be avoided. Seeing "no consistent theological way to relativize and yet to assert our own symbols," Gilkey concluded that giving up our absolute starting point leads to an "unavoidable relativism."[23]

The reason this concern looms so large is not only the fact that the way to affirm pluralism without relativism is not immediately obvious, but also the fact that some of the most prominent pluralists have been led to relativism. For example, Ernst Troeltsch has been called not only the first great Christian pluralist but also "the first great Christian relativist."[24] And the position of John Hick has been widely criticized as leading to a complete relativism.

Does Hick's position lead to relativism?

This fact is of great significance, because Hick's version of pluralism, besides being the version that has been discussed far more than any other,[25] has been widely taken as representative of pluralism as such. For example, Kevin Meeker and Philip Quinn have said that they reserve the term *religious pluralism* "to refer to the position John Hick adopts in response to the fact of religious diversity."[26] They thereby simply equated religious pluralism as such with Hick's version of it. Mark Heim came close to doing the same: Seeing Hick as having made "the philosophical case for a pluralistic outlook," Heim treated Hick's position as the paradigmatic pluralistic theology.[27] Any weaknesses in Hick's position have, therefore, widely been taken to be weaknesses of pluralism as such. It is important, accordingly, to see that the weaknesses in Hick's position, which have led to such widespread criticism, follow from his particular version of pluralism, rather than from pluralism as such.

Although Hick's move to (generic) pluralism began, as we saw, with his conviction about what the divine love would not do, the particular way Hick worked out his pluralistic position led him to the conclusion that personalistic words, such as "love," could not be applied to the Divine Reality in itself. What led Hick to this conclusion was a fact combined with an assumption.

The fact is that the reports of profound religious (mystical) experience can be divided into at least two major types: those that describe communion with a good, loving, personal deity, distinct from the experiencer, and those that describe a realization of identity with ultimate reality experienced as formless, impersonal, ineffable, and "beyond good and evil." The existence of these two types of religious experience creates a problem partly because they are both reported, as Caroline Franks Davis has pointed out, as apprehensions of "the nature of *ultimate* reality."[28]

But this fact would not have created a problem except for a crucial assumption on Hick's part, which is that, as Cobb critically puts it, "what is approached as 'ultimate reality' must be one and the same."[29] As Hick himself puts it, "there cannot be a plurality of ultimates."[30] Given that assumption, Hick faces a serious question, which is, in Davis's words:

> How can "ultimate reality" be both a personal being and an impersonal principle, identical to our inmost self and forever "other," loving and utterly indifferent, good and amoral, knowable and unknowable, a plenitude and "emptiness"?[31]

Hick, in seeking to answer this question, decided that as a pluralist he could not play favorites by saying that the one kind of religious experience was more authentic—more revelatory of ultimate reality—than the other. He decided, accordingly, that ultimate reality in itself—which he often calls simply the "Real in itself"—must be considered completely unknowable (like Immanuel Kant's "noumenal reality"), and must, therefore, be distinguished from all human ideas about ultimate reality. These human ideas are then divided into two types: divine *personae*, such as the biblical God and Advaita Vedanta's saguna Brahman (Brahman with qualities), and the divine *impersonae*, such as Advaita Vedanta's nirguna Brahman (Brahman without qualities) and Buddhism's "Sunyata" (usually translated "emptiness"). But none of these human ideas correspond to the Real in itself, says Hick, because it "cannot be said to be one or many, person or thing, substance or process, good or evil, purposive or non-purposive." We cannot, Hick emphasizes, apply to ultimate reality in itself any substantive predicates, such as "being good," "being powerful," and "having knowledge."[32]

Hick's position thereby does lead to the "debilitating relativism" of which Alan Race spoke. In his eagerness to show all religions to be equally true, Hick has in effect declared them to be equally false, thereby undercutting their support for moral and spiritual attitudes. Hick does, to be sure, claim that "the major world religions constitute varying human responses to the transcendent Reality, and are thus at least to some extent *in alignment with that Reality*," so that they can provide criteria for valuing various human attitudes.[33] For example, pointing out that saints in all religious traditions manifest "compassion/love towards other human beings or towards all life,"[34] Hick implies that this attitude is in alignment with "transcendent Reality." But given Hick's assertion that this "transcendent Reality" is entirely devoid of purpose, goodness, compassion, and love, he cannot really say that the saint's "compassion/love" is any more in alignment with it than Hitler's hate and indifference. Because its complete relativism undermines Christian faith and ethics, Hick's version of religious pluralism is widely rejected.[35]

Another widespread criticism is that Hick's so-called pluralistic position is not really pluralistic. This criticism is based on the fact that Hick,
besides holding that all religions are oriented toward the same ultimate
reality, also contends that they all aim at essentially the same "salvation," which Hick describes as a "transformation of human existence
from self-centredness to Reality-centredness."[36] Mark Heim, whose
book *Salvations* argues, as the title suggests, that different religions offer
different kinds of salvation, is especially critical of Hick's account, which
"grounds the cognitive and experiential cores of the great religious
traditions in one common object and one common salvific process."[37]

For this twofold reason, Hick's position can be called *identist* pluralism. It *is* a version of pluralism, because it affirms all of the characteristics of generic pluralism described earlier. But the criticism of it
as "not really pluralistic" is right in the sense that it sees all religions
as essentially identical—as oriented to one and the same ultimate and
aiming at one and the same salvation. A problem created by this lack
of genuine pluralism, Heim points out, is that by implying that "the
specific and special aspects of another faith tell us [nothing] that is of
significant importance," it provides no motivation for dialogue.[38]

But the fact that Hick developed an identist version of pluralism
would not have created a bad name for religious pluralism as such if
Heim and others had not equated Hick's version of religious pluralism
with religious pluralism as such. The fact that Heim makes this equation is shown by his comment that "the pluralistic hypothesis" rests
on two dubious assumptions: "a metaphysical dogma that there can
be but one religious object, and a soteriological dogma that there can
be but one religious end."[39] By virtue of this conflation of the genus
(generic religious pluralism) with one of its species, Heim ends up
with the paradoxical claim that, "Despite their appropriation of the

title, ['pluralistic'] theologies are not religiously pluralistic at all." On that basis, Heim argues that we need a "truly pluralistic hypothesis."[40] Repeatedly referring negatively to "pluralism" and "pluralistic theology,"[41] he calls for a "post-pluralistic" theology.[42]

However, although this call to go "beyond pluralism" for the sake of having a truly pluralistic position is self-contradictory, it still contains a positive reference to pluralism. Unfortunately, however, what often seems to comes through as the dominant message of Heim's book is that pluralism should be left behind altogether, as illustrated by a rave review simply titled "Beyond Pluralism."[43] Heim's book has hence reinforced a wider tendency by defenders of Christian absolutism to use problems in Hick's version of pluralism to call for the rejection of pluralistic theologies as such.[44]

PROCESS THEOLOGY'S COMPLEMENTARY RELIGIOUS PLURALISM

The main point of the previous section is that religious pluralism has gotten a bad name, even among many who should support it, because religious pluralism in the generic sense has been virtually equated with the Hickian version of religious pluralism. Whitehead's process philosophy provides the basis for a very different version of religious pluralism. Two features of Whitehead's philosophy are especially relevant.

One of these is his concern, in dealing with different systems of thought, to show how assertions that at first sight appear to be contradictory may actually express complementary truths. He suggested this approach with regard to science and religion, saying that a clash between their teachings is "a sign that there are wider truths . . . within which a reconciliation of a deeper religion and a more subtle science will be found."[45] He also suggested it with regard to Buddhism and Christianity, saying that instead of sheltering themselves from each other, they should be "looking to each other for deeper meanings."[46]

In each case, the task is to overcome formulations that, while express-ing a measure of truth, have done so in "over-assertive" ways, "thereby implying an exclusion of complementary truths."[47]

The other feature that is especially germane is Whitehead's panentheism, with its view of the relation between God and creativity. Explaining this view, along with its importance for religious pluralism, will take some time.

TWO ULTIMATES: GOD AND CREATIVITY

"Creativity," which involves a generalization of the physicist's "energy," refers to the power embodied in all actual things—both God and finite actualities. According to Whitehead's view of actual entities, as we have seen, they are momentary events, which he calls "actual occasions" or "occasions of experience." Each occasion comes into existence out of the causal influence of the past, exercises a degree of self-determi-nation, and then comes to completion, after which it exerts causal influence on future occasions. Your experience during a few seconds is composed of several dozen occasions of experience. Whitehead's term "creativity" points to the twofold power of each such occasion to exert a degree of self-determination in forming itself and then to exert causal influence on future occasions. Whitehead's "creativity" thus provides a new understanding of what previous philosophers have simply called "being" or "being itself," and which theologian Paul Tillich called "the power of being."

The distinctive feature of Whitehead's position is that God and creativity are equally primordial. Although traditional theologians regarded the power to create as eternal, this power belonged to God alone, so the fact that a world with its own power exists was due to a voluntary divine decision. This idea, as we have seen in prior chapters, was enshrined in the doctrine of *creatio ex nihilo*, according to which our world was created out of a complete absence of finite actual entities.

By contrast, Whitehead suggested that our world was created—as the Bible itself suggests[48]—out of a primeval chaos. Although our particular world is a contingent divine creation, there has always been *a* world, in the sense of a multiplicity of finite actualities embodying creativity. To say that God has always co-existed with creativity, therefore, means that creativity has always been embodied in a world as well as in God - that there has always been worldly creativity as well as divine creativity.

This doctrine is doubly important for the issue of religious pluralism. In the first place, this doctrine, according to which worldly creativity is equally primordial with divine creativity, entails that supernatural interruptions in the world are impossible. From this perspective, there is no basis for claiming that God had overridden the normal fallibility of human beings so that they could produce infallible scriptures, which could be used to prove that Christianity is the only true religion.[49]

Equally important for religious pluralism is the fact that the distinction between God and creativity provides a basis for speaking of *two* ultimates. This idea has been most fully worked out by John Cobb, whose position, in contrast with Hick's identist pluralism, can be called *complementary* pluralism.[50] Different religions, Cobb holds, have seen different truths and have offered different paths to salvation.

In developing the idea that there are two ultimates, Cobb suggests that one of these, corresponding with Whitehead's "creativity," has been called "Emptiness" ("*Sunyata*") or "Dharmakaya" by Buddhists, "nirguna Brahman" by Advaita Vedantists, "the Godhead" by Meister Eckhart, and "Being Itself" by Heidegger and Tillich. It is the *formless* ultimate. The other ultimate, corresponding with what Whitehead calls "God," is not Being Itself but the *Supreme* Being. Far from being formless, it is the world's source of all forms, such as truth, beauty, and justice. It has been called "Amida Buddha" or "Sambhogakaya," "saguna Brahman," "Ishvara," "Yahweh," "Christ," and "Allah."[51]

Cobb has several reasons for preferring this hypothesis to Hick's. One is that he simply does not find it illuminating to say that God, who is *worshipped*, and Emptiness, which is *realized*, are "two names for the same noumenal reality."[52] Cobb's hypothesis also allows Christian theologians to avoid the "relativization and even negation of basic Christian commitments" implicit in Hick's hypothesis.[53] "[T]hose who assume that all traditions must be focusing on the same aspects of reality," Cobb says, are led to believe that what Zen Buddhists call Emptying "must be the same as God," which can in turn lead the Christian thinker to "employ the negative theology on the Christian heritage so radically as to dissolve God into Emptying. In that process everything distinctive of the biblical heritage is lost."[54]

This problem is illustrated in the thought of David Tracy, who, although he has been influenced by process philosophy, has retained the traditional equation of God and ultimate reality. Tracy thereby affirms that what Buddhists call "Emptiness" is the same reality that Christians call "God."[55] He confesses, however, that trying to think of ultimate reality as emptiness is "a deeply disorienting matter, for any Christian who holds her/his profound trust in and loyalty to the one God."[56] The Buddhist idea of ultimate reality as emptiness has led Tracy to explore the apophatic or negative theology of Meister Eckhart, but he doubts that "the Christian understanding of God can receive as radically an apophatic character as Eckhart sometimes insists upon."[57] Given his commitment to liberation theology and his faith in God as the one by whom "hope is granted" for "acts of resistance to the status quo," Tracy realizes that he must pull back from a *completely* negative theology, with its negation of all positive and thereby morality-supporting divine attributes.[58] But the fact that he has felt impelled to go even part way in that direction is due to the fact that he, like Hick, cannot relinquish the metaphysical assumption that there must be only one ultimate reality.

By contrast, Whiteheadian pluralists, Cobb points out, can affirm the existence of a Divine Actuality with many characteristics in common with the biblical God, including those that support the concern for a just social order, without rejecting the description, provided by nontheistic Hindus and Buddhists, of ultimate reality as formless.[59] The idea that there are two ultimates allows us to recognize the truth of both descriptions. Finally, Cobb says: "When we understand global religious experience and thought in this way, it is easier to view the contributions of diverse traditions as complementary."[60]

This last point is crucial, given Cobb's view that the challenge of interreligious dialogue is "to transform contradictory statements into different but not contradictory ones," thereby moving "toward a more comprehensive vision in which the deepest insights of both sides are reconciled."[61] One basis for such reconciliation is to recognize that claims that may at first glance seem contradictory are really answers to different questions. "[T]here is no contradiction in the claim of one that problem A is solved by X and the claim of the other that problem B is solved by Y. . . . The claims are complementary rather than contradictory."[62] For example:

> Consider the Buddhist claim that Gautama is the Buddha. That is a very different statement from the assertion that God was incarnate in Jesus. The Buddha is the one who is enlightened. To be enlightened is to realize the fundamental nature of reality, its insubstantiality, its relativity, its emptiness. . . . That Jesus was the incarnation of God does not deny that Gautama was the Enlightened One.[63]

Three ultimates

Thus far, this account of Cobb's complementary pluralism has been based on the distinction between God and creativity, as two ultimates. Not all religions, however, can be regarded as being oriented around one or the other of these ultimates. Some religions, such as Taoism and many primal religions, including Native American religions, regard the cosmos as such as sacred. Whitehead's philosophy, with its panentheism, provides the basis, as Cobb points out, for speaking of a *third* ultimate, this being the cosmos, "the totality of [finite] things." Whitehead's philosophy thereby provides a basis for validating the basic idea between three fundamentally different types of religion, which John Hutchison had called theistic, acosmic, and cosmic. All three types can thereby be seen as responding to something truly ultimate in the nature of things.[65]

Although traditional Christian theology, with its doctrine of *creatio ex nihilo*, could not regard the cosmos as in any sense ultimate, Whitehead's philosophy does. Although our particular cosmos—our "cosmic epoch"—is contingent, being originally rooted in a divine volition, the fact that there is *a* world—some world or other consisting of a multiplicity of finite actual entities—is not contingent. What exists necessarily is not simply God, as in traditional Christian theism, and not simply the world understood as the totality of finite things, as in atheistic naturalism, but God-and-a-world, with both God and worldly actualities being embodiments of creativity. Although these three ultimates within the totality are distinct, they are, Cobb emphasizes, "not in fact separable from one another." He adds: "I would propose that without a cosmic reality there can be no acosmic one, and that without God there can be neither. Similarly, without both the cosmic and acosmic features of reality there can be no God."[66]

Those who have been conditioned, especially through the doctrine of *creatio ex nihilo*, to believe that there can be only one ultimate, tend to hear any talk of multiple ultimates as polytheism. But this characterization would not, Cobb points out, be appropriate for his Whiteheadian worldview, as the three ultimates do not exist on the same level. They differ as the one Supreme Being, the many finite beings, and Being Itself, which is embodied by both God and finite beings. Creativity, as Being Itself, is in no way a second god alongside the Supreme Being, because it is not a being and has no reality apart from its embodiments in the divine and finite actualities.

It makes no sense to say, as some have, that Whitehead's God is subordinate to creativity, because, as Cobb argues, "between reality as such and actual things there can be no ranking of superior and inferior. Such ranking makes sense only among actualities. Among actualities [God] is ultimate."[67] This statement also makes clear that Whitehead's position does not make the world of finite being equal with God. Although Tillich said that a Supreme Being would be merely "one being alongside other beings," this pejorative description would not fit the Whiteheadian idea of God, who "must be so different from the others that the term 'alongside' does not fit," because God must be "inclusive of all things."[68]

This pluralistic ontology allows us to understand the possibility that a wide variety of religious experiences could be authentic. Although these three ultimates are inseparable, individuals and religious traditions can concentrate on one or two features alone. Insofar as there is concentration solely on God, on the universe in distinction from God, or on creativity as such, there would be the pure case of theistic, cosmic, or acosmic religious experience.

However, Cobb adds, "much religious language blurs the distinctions and relates to more than one of the three ultimates." For example, the fact that "[t]he universe reverenced as ultimate is the embodiment of Being Itself or [nirguna] Brahman and is pervaded by God . . . is often attested unintentionally in the rhetoric of those who find meaning in appreciating their part in this whole."[69] Likewise, "Language about God often draws on what is strictly true only of Being Itself."[70] This mixing occurs especially in Western theism, Cobb points out, because "it has incorporated acosmic elements from its Neo-Platonic sources" with the result that "the religious experience of Western mystics seems to be at once of theistic and acosmic reality—one might say that it is of the theistic as embodying the acosmic reality, or of the acosmic as qualified by the theistic reality."[71]

As a final example, the truth that "Being Itself does not exist at all except in God and the creatures" is reflected in a twofold fact. On the one hand, "Very little is said of Being Itself or [nirguna] Brahman that does not hint at characteristics that actually belong to God."[72] On the other hand, "Being Itself, being the being of all things, is also closely associated with the thought of the whole."[73]

Cobb's view that the totality of reality contains three ultimates, along with the recognition that a particular tradition could concentrate on one, two, or even all three of them, gives us a basis for understanding a wide variety of religious experiences as genuine responses to something that is really there to be experienced. "When we understand global religious experience and thought in this way," Cobb emphasizes, "it is easier to view the contributions of diverse traditions as complementary."[74]

Complementary Truths within Religions of the Same Type

Cobb's view of complementary religious truths does not, however, depend entirely on the notion of different ultimates. There can also be complementary truths between two religions of the same type. One example involves the tension between the Christian assertion "that Jesus is the Christ" and the Jewish insistence "that the Messiah has not come." Jews and Christians, Cobb suggests, should "work together repeatedly to clarify the difference between what Jews mean by 'Messiah' and what Christians legitimately mean by 'Christ.'"[75]

Conclusion

In his landmark book on religious pluralism, Alan Race, after warning of the danger of "debilitating relativism," pointed to Cobb's version as an exception. "The virtue of Cobb's contribution," said Race, "is that he combines fidelity to Christ with unqualified openness to other faiths."[76] Cobb illustrates this assessment by saying that, to enter into interreligious dialogue, "we do not need to relativize our beliefs. . . . We can affirm our insights as universally valid! What we cannot do, without lapsing back into unjustified arrogance, is to deny that the insights of other traditions are also universally valid."[77]

Cobb has presented a form of (generic) religious pluralism that is truly pluralistic without being relativistic, thereby overcoming the two major complaints that have been leveled against pluralistic theologies. Heim, incidentally, recognizes that Cobb's theology has the ingredients he sees to be necessary to a truly pluralistic position, namely, multiple ultimates and multiple forms of salvation. However, because of Heim's tendency to equate pluralism as such with Hick's type of identist pluralism, he has regarded Cobb as a critic of pluralism rather as an advocate of a distinctive form of it. Once this fallacious equation of the genus (religious pluralism) with one of its species is overcome, it becomes evident that Cobb has provided a version of religious pluralism that meets the criteria for a genuine religious pluralism implicit in Heim's critique.

Discussions of religious pluralism and discussions of the relation between science and religion are usually carried on in different contexts, by different authors. The two issues are, however, closely related, as suggested by Whitehead's contention that Christianity's relation to Buddhism should be seen as analogous to its relation to modern science. Although there are many factors behind the rise and spread of religious pluralism, the most important of them is the development of scientific naturalism, with its prohibition of any interruptions of the world's normal causal processes, even in human experience.

By ruling out infallible revelation and inerrant inspiration, this rejection of supernatural interventions removed the traditional a priori basis for assuming the absoluteness of Christianity. If Christian apologists were to continue arguing for the absolute superiority of Christianity to other religious traditions, they would henceforth have to do so on an empirical, *a posteriori* basis. Once the case had to be argued on this basis, an increasing number of thinkers found the case impossible to make. When judged simply in terms of its effects on its devotees, the idea that Christianity was the only religion that mediated divine values and saving effects was added to the list of dogmas that the rejection of supernaturalism undermined. The rise of scientific naturalism was, hence, crucial for the pluralistic turn of modern thought in general and modern theology in particular.

This pluralistic turn by itself, however, created new problems as well as overcoming old ones. One major problem proved to be whether pluralism could be formulated in such a way as to avoid complete relativism. Another problem, closely related, is whether theologians of one tradition, such as Christianity, could formulate a theology that embodied religious pluralism without implying that their own tradition had no distinctive truths and values of universal import. Cobb has shown that Whitehead's version of naturalism, especially its panentheistic rejection of creation *ex nihilo*, provides the basis for a form of religious pluralism that can overcome these problems.

Notes

1. For examples of Jewish process pluralism, see Sandra Lubarsky, "Deep Religious Pluralism and Contemporary Jewish Thought," in David Ray Griffin, ed., *Deep Religious Pluralism* (Louisville: Westminster John Knox, 2005), and her book *Tolerance and Transformation: Jewish Approaches to Religious Pluralism* (Cincinnati: Hebrew Union College Press, 1990).

For examples of Muslim process pluralism, Mohammad Iqbal, *The Reconstruction of Religious Thought in Islam* (London: Oxford University Press, 1934), and Mustafa Ruzgar, "Islam and Deep Religious Pluralism," in Griffin, ed., *Deep Religious Pluralism*, 158-76.

For examples of Buddhist process pluralism, see Ryusei Takeda, "Mutual Transformation of Pure Land Buddhism and Christianity: Methodology and Possibilities in the Light of Shinran's Doctrine," *Bulletin of the Nanzan Institute for Religion and Culture* 22 (Spring 1998), 6-40; John Shunji Yokota, "Where Beyond Dialog? Reconsiderations of a Buddhist Pluralist," in Griffin, ed., *Deep Religious Pluralism* (2005), 91-108; Christopher Ives, "Liberating Truth: A Buddhist Approach to Religious Pluralism," in Griffin, ed., *Deep Religious Pluralism* (2005), 178-92.

For examples of Hindu process pluralism, see Jeffery D. Long, "Anekanta Vedanta: Toward a Deep Hindu Religious Pluralism," in Griffin, ed., *Deep Religious Pluralism* (2005), 130-57; and Nicholas F. Gier, "Gandhi, Deep Religious Pluralism, and Multiculturalism," *Philosophy East and West,* April 2014: 319-39.

For Chinese process pluralism, see Chung-ying Cheng, "Toward an Integrative Religious Pluralism: Embodying Whitehead, Cobb, and the Yijing," in Griffin, ed., *Deep Religious Pluralism* (2005), 210-25; and Zhihe Wang, *Process and Pluralism: Chinese Thought on the Harmony of Diversity* (Heusenstamm, Germany: Ontos Verlag, 2012).

A 2013 book entitled *Panentheism across the World* (see note 2 of Ch. 1, above) has shown how panentheism of various types—not only Whiteheadian panentheism—has been exemplified in a number of religious traditions.

2. John Hick, *A Christian Theology of Religions: The Rainbow of Faiths* (Louisville: Westminster John Knox, 1995), 24, 125.

3. This typology of exclusivism, inclusivism, and pluralism was introduced by Alan Race in *Christians and Religious Pluralism: Patterns in Christian Theology of Religions* (Maryknoll: Orbis, 1983).

4. The beginning of religious pluralism is often dated as early as 1624, with the publication of *De Veritate* by Lord Herbert of Cherbury (1583-1648). Pluralistic convictions were expressed by many 18th-century deists, such as Matthew Tindal in *Christianity as Old as Creation* (1730) and G.E. Lessing in *Nathan the Wise* (1779). Many developments in

19th-century theology, especially in Germany, promoted pluralistic convictions, which broke forth most fully and famously in Ernst Troeltsch's 1923 essay, "The Place of Christianity Among the World Religions," in Troeltsch, *Christian Thought: Its History and Application* (Meridian Books, 1947).

5. John Hick, *Philosophy of Religion*, 3d edition (Englewood Cliffs, N. J.: Prentice-Hall, 1983), 117-18.

6. Knitter, *No Other Name? A Critical Survey of Christian Attitudes Toward the World Religions* (Maryknoll: Orbis, 1985), 121, 125, 116-17, 140.

7. Mark S. Heim, *Salvations: Truth and Difference in Religion* (Maryknoll: Orbis, 1995), 72.

8. John Hick, "The Non-Absoluteness of Christianity," in John Hick and Paul F. Knitter, eds., *The Myth of Christian Uniqueness: Toward a Pluralistic Theology of Religions* (Maryknoll: Orbis, 1987),16-36 at 18.

9. Hick, *A Christian Theology of Religions*, 123.

10. Ibid., 13.

11. There is, however, one difference between my definition here and the one that I have used in prior chapters. I there defined naturalism$_{ns}$ to mean the denial of the existence of a supernatural being that *could* interrupt the world's normal causal processes. Here I am defining it more liberally, to mean simply the denial that any such interruptions actually occur. This more liberal definition allows the inclusion of those, such as John Hick, who have affirmed, or at least not ruled out, a deistic position, according to which, even if the deity has the power to interrupt the normal processes, the deity never in fact does this.

12. Hick, *A Christian Theology of Religions*, 53.

13. Knitter, *No Other Name?* 25.

14. Wilfred Cantwell Smith, "Idolatry in Comparative Perspective," in John Hick and Paul F. Knitter, eds., *The Myth of Christian Uniqueness*, 53-68, at 59.

15. Hick, *A Christian Theology of Religions*, 15.

16. John B. Cobb, Jr., *Christ in a Pluralistic Age* (Philadelphia: Westminster, 1975), 27, 163.

17. Hick, *A Christian Theology of Religions*, 16-18.

18. John B. Cobb, Jr., "Dialogue," in Leonard Swidler, John B. Cobb, Jr., Paul F. Knitter, and Monica K. Hellwig, *Death or Dialogue? From the Age of Monologue to the Age of Dialogue* (Philadelphia: Trinity Press; London: SCM Press, 1990), 1-18, at 13.

19. David Lochhead, *The Dialogical Imperative: A Christian Reflection on Interfaith Encounter* (Maryknoll: Orbis, 1988).

20. Paul F. Knitter, "Interreligious Dialogue: What? Why? How?" in Swidler, Cobb, Knitter, and Hellwig, *Death or Dialogue?* 19-44, at 27.

21. Knitter, *No Other Name?* 36; *Jesus and the Other Names: Christian Mission and Global Responsibility* (Maryknoll: Orbis, 1996), 29, 31.

22. Race, *Christians and Religious Pluralism*, 90, 78.

23. Langdon Gilkey, "Plurality and Its Theological Implications," in Hick and Knitter, eds., *The Myth of Christian Uniqueness* (1986), 37-53, 44-46.

24. John B. Cobb, Jr., *Beyond Dialogue: Toward a Mutual Transformation of Christianity and Buddhism* (Philadelphia: Fortress, 1982), 13.

25. When Hick's *Christian Theology of Religions* was published in 1995, a list of critiques of his position alone filled almost five pages.

26. Kevin Meeker, and Philip L. Quinn, "Introduction: The Philosophical Challenge of Religious Diversity," in Quinn and Meeker,

eds., *The Philosophical Challenge of Religious Diversity*, 1-28, 3.

27. Heim, *Salvations*, 8, 42. Hick himself was partly responsible for this identification of his own position with pluralism as such, as he referred to his own position simply as "The Pluralistic Hypothesis" (the title of Chapter 14 of his *An Interpretation of Religion*), which he in turn seemed simply to equate with "Religious Pluralism" (the title of Part Four).

28. Davis, *The Evidential Force of Religious Experience*, 167.

29. Cobb, *Beyond Dialogue*, 96.

30. Hick, *An Interpretation of Religion* (New Haven: Yale University Press, 1989), 249.

31. Caroline Franks Davis, *The Evidential Force of Religious Experience* (Oxford: Clarendon Press, 1989), 172-73.

32. Hick, *An Interpretation of Religion*, 245, 239.

33. Ibid., 300; emphasis added.

34. Ibid., 301.

35. For negative critiques of Hick's position, see Heim, *Salvations*; Quinn and Meeker, *The Philosophical Challenge of Religious Diversity*; and Gavin D'Costa, ed., *Christian Uniqueness Reconsidered: The Myth of a Pluralistic Theology of Religions* (Maryknoll, N.Y.: Orbis, 1990).

36. Hick, *An Interpretation of Religion*, 300.

37. Heim, *Salvations*, 16.

38. Ibid., 125. Gavin D'Costa likewise says that "'pluralistic theology' ironically often seems to hinder rather than aid a proper recognition of religious plurality" (*Christian Uniqueness Reconsidered*, xi). Another critic who makes this point in D'Costa's edited volume is Christoph Schwöbel, who says that Hick's version of pluralistic theology "seems in

danger of undermining what it sets out to preserve, that is, the plurality of religions" ("Particularity, Universality, and the Religions: Toward a Christian Theology of Religions," in D'Costa, ed., *Christian Uniqueness Reconsidered*, 30-46, at 32). Joseph A. DiNoia, who also has an essay in the D'Costa volume, elsewhere says that its thesis is that pluralist accounts "turn out upon examination to be markedly nonpluralistic" (*The Diversity of Religions: A Christian Perspective* [Washington, D. C.: Catholic University Press, 1992], 194).

39. Heim, *Salvations*, 23.

40. Ibid., 129-30.

41. Ibid., 16, 87, 88, 89, 90, 101, 103, 109, 125, 129, 130, 228.

42. Ibid., 226.

43. Paul J. Griffiths, "Beyond Pluralism," *First Things*, January 1996: 50-52.

44. For example, Gavin D'Costa, having criticized the pluralist project as defined in Hick and Knitter's *Myth of Christian Uniqueness*, questions "whether 'pluralistic theology' is an appropriate or even adequate interpretation of religious plurality" (*Christian Uniqueness Reconsidered*, x-xi).

45. Whitehead, *Science and the Modern World*, 185.

46. Whitehead, *Religion in the Making*, 146.

47. Ibid., 145, 149.

48. Although it has widely been assumed, including by Whitehead himself, that the Bible teaches creation out of nothing, this doctrine, as shown in Chapter 4, did not arise until near the end of the second century of Christian thought. This means that for most of the first two centuries of Christian thought, it held a Hebrew-Platonic view of creation out of chaos.

49. See Edward Farley, and Peter C. Hodgson, "Scripture & Tradition," in Hodgson & Robert H. King, eds., *Christian Theology: An Introduction to Its Traditions and Tasks*, 2nd ed. (Philadelphia: Fortress, 1985: 61-87).

50. I developed this notion in "The Whiteheadian Complementary Pluralism of John Cobb," in Griffin, ed., *Deep Religious Pluralism*, 39-66.

51. Cobb, "Response II," in Swidler, Cobb, Knitter, and Hellwig, *Death or Dialogue?* 115-23; *Beyond Dialogue*, 124-28; *Transforming Christianity and the World: A Way beyond Absolutism and Relativism*, ed. Paul F. Knitter (Maryknoll: Orbis, 1999), 184-85.

52. Cobb, *Beyond Dialogue*, 43.

53. Cobb, *Transforming Christianity and the World*, 79.

54. Cobb, "Dialogue," 6.

55. Tracy, *Plurality and Ambiguity: Hermeneutics, Religion, Hope* (University of Chicago Press, 1987), 85.

56. Tracy, *Dialogue with the Other: The Inter-Religious Dialogue* (Louvain: Peeters Press, 1990), 74.

57. Ibid., 91, 103.

58. *Plurality and Ambiguity*, 85.

59. Having described God as the ultimate in the line of efficient, formal, and final causes, Cobb describes the "other ultimate" as "that which, without possessing any form, is subject to taking on any form. It is the formless" (*Transforming Christianity and the World*, 184).

60. Cobb, *Transforming Christianity and the World*, 186.

61. Ibid., 74; "Response II," 120.

62. "Dialogue," 14.

63. *Transforming Christianity and the World*, 140.

64. Ibid., 185.

65. Ibid., 120-23, 136-37, 140, 185. See John A. Hutchison, *Paths of Faith* (New York: McGraw Hill, 1969).

66. *Transforming Christianity and the World*, 121. Cobb is here reflecting the position of Whitehead himself, who said "there is no meaning to 'creativity' apart from its 'creatures,' and no meaning to 'God' apart from the 'creativity' and the 'temporal creatures,' and no meaning to the 'temporal creatures' apart from 'creativity' and 'God'" (*Process and Reality*, 225).

67. Cobb, "Being Itself and the Existence of God," in John R. Jacobson and Robert Lloyd Mitchell, eds., *The Existence of God* (Lewiston, N.Y.: Edwin Mellen, 1988), 5-19, at 19.

68. Ibid., 16.

69. *Transforming Christianity and the World*, 121. Sri Aurobindo, Cobb mentions, reports having had all three types of experience. Aurobindo's experiences and his attempt to understand them are discussed in Ernest Lee Simmons, Jr., "Process Pluralism and Integral Nondualism: A Comparative Study of the Nature of the Divine in the Thought of Alfred North Whitehead and Sri Aurobindo Ghose," Ph.D. dissertation, Claremont Graduate School, 1981, a dissertation written under Cobb's guidance. See also Simmons, "Mystical Consciousness in a Process Perspective," *Process Studies* 14 (Spring 1984), 1-10, in which some of the material from the dissertation is summarized.

70. *Transforming Christianity and the World*, 185-186.

71. Ibid., 124.

72. Ibid., 186. Cobb's point can be illustrated by the fact that although Shankara's Advaita Vedanta holds that nirguna Brahman is devoid of qualities, it is also said to be *sat-chit-ananda* (consciousness-existence-bliss). Another illustration, given by Cobb himself, is that although many Buddhists would say that Emptiness or *Dharmakaya* can be

realized "as such apart from all forms," it is always expected that those who fully realize ultimate reality thus understood will be characterized by wisdom and compassion (*Beyond Dialogue*, 127).

73. *Transforming Christianity and the World*, 186.

74. Ibid., 186.

75. Ibid., 86-87.

76. *Race, Christians and Religious Pluralism*, 98.

77. *Transforming Christianity and the World*, 137.

Epilogue

I f there is to be a reconciliation between the worldview of the scientific tradition and that of the theistic religious traditions, I have argued, there needs to be a growing acceptance in our culture, within both scientific and religious circles, of a naturalistic form of theism as part of a nondualistic but nonmaterialistic view of reality as a whole. This type of vision[1]—theistic but naturalistic, not materialistic but also not dualistic—is equally needed, I have suggested, if we are to have, even apart from science-religion reconciliation, a scientific philosophy that approaches adequacy, or at least avoids absurdity.

Although it is rarely acknowledged, at least in public, that our current "scientific worldview" implies all sorts of absurdities, it would be hard to find ideas more absurd than the following six: (1) that we do not really know that there is a past, that time occurs, or that a there is a real world beyond our own experience; (2) that our own conscious experience—which, as Descartes emphasized, is the thing we know most immediately and indubitably—is not really real; (3) that our freedom to choose between alternatives is illusory, because our actions, including our conscious choices, are in reality as fully determined as the behavior of billiard balls; (4) that logical principles, including the law of noncontradiction, have no authority beyond our decisions to obey them ("decisions" that were, of course, fully determined by antecedent conditions); (5) that mathematical "discoveries" are really only *inventions*, because mathematics is merely a game, with no reference to any pre-existent patterns in the nature of things; (6) and that moral norms, likewise, are purely human inventions, so that rape and genocide violate no norms inherent in the fabric of the universe.

All past systems of thought have, of course, had their absurdities. But it would be difficult to argue that they were greater than the absurdities to which our modern "enlightenment" has led. Of course, most of those who live within absurd systems, perceiving the world through their lenses, cannot recognize the absurdities, and the few who do are generally too polite, or perhaps too timid, to point them out.

There are, however, some exceptions. One of these in our own time is Richard Lewontin, among our most brilliant biologists. In a review of a book by Carl Sagan, a fellow materialist, Lewontin stated that many of the explanations required by a materialistic standpoint involve "patent absurdity." The context shows, furthermore, that by "materialism," Lewontin primarily meant atheism. He was saying, in effect, that the late modern stipulation that science cannot refer to divine causation—which is usually interpreted to mean that science must presuppose atheism—often leads to explanations that are obviously absurd.

This admission, however, did not lead Lewontin to suggest that the scientific community should rethink this issue, with the hope that, by incorporating some form of theism, more adequate explanations might be given. He said, instead, that scientists must retain the materialist standpoint, with its atheism, because "we cannot allow a Divine Foot in the door." His explanation for why that door must remain closed is most revealing: "To appeal to an omnipotent deity," said Lewontin, "is to allow that at any moment the regularities of nature may be ruptured, that miracles may happen."[2] This statement is revealing because, even though Lewontin is philosophically sophisticated, he simply accepted the identification of theism with its supernatural version, which equates divinity with a being that is "omnipotent" in the sense of being able to interrupt the "regularities of nature."

If we can increase the scientific community's awareness of the existence of naturalistic forms of theism, while at the same time helping theistic religious communities to see that there are forms of naturalism that are not necessarily hostile to a theistic worldview that is robustly religious, we might indeed fulfill Whitehead's hope of moving toward a reconciliation involving "a deeper religion and a more subtle science."[3]

Insofar as such a new reconciliation of science and religion comes about, furthermore, it would have far-reaching implications for public education, which have been increasingly based on a dualism between those beliefs that are called "scientific" and those that are called "religious," as if the former were based entirely on experience and reason and the latter were totally devoid of those supports and hence not publicly defensible. This dualism has supported, and been supported by, the "disenchantment of the world," meaning the disappearance in our consensual worldview of a basis for moral values.

This dualism and disenchantment have been especially promoted by the acceptance of naturalism$_{sam}$ as essential to "the scientific worldview." The recognition that naturalism$_{ppp}$ provides a far more adequate form of naturalism for the scientific community would provide the basis for a different public education. Although religion in the sectarian sense would still be proscribed, recognition that the cosmos provides support for normative values might not be. This new attitude might provide the basis for a mediating position that could be accepted by erstwhile representatives of both sides of this cultural war about education—those who have advocated a purely secular education and those who have wanted the Ten Commandments posted in the classroom.

Crucial for a reconciliation between science and religion, and hence a "scientific worldview" that promotes religious pluralism, will be the acceptance – within both "religious" and "scientific" circles, of the type of naturalism and panentheism advocated in this book.

NOTES

1. Richard Lewontin, "Billions and Billions of Demons" (review of Carl Sagan's *The Demon-Haunted World: Science as a Candle in the Dark*), *New York Review of Books*, January 9, 1997: 28-32, at 31.

2. Whitehead, *Science and the Modern World*, 185.

References

Anderson, John N. "Why I Am Not a Panentheist." *Analogical Thoughts*, January 24, 2012 (online).

Aukerman, Dale. *Darkening Valley: A Biblical Perspective on Nuclear War*. New York: Seabury, 1981.

Ayer, A.J. *Language, Truth, and Logic*. New York: Dover, 1952.

Benacerraf, Paul. "Mathematical Truth." *Journal of Philosophy* 70 (1973); reprinted in *Philosophy of Mathematics,* ed. Paul Benacerraf and Hilary Putnam, 2nd edition. Cambridge: Cambridge University Press, 1983: 403-20.

Bailey, David H. "Bacteria Are More Capable of Complex Decision-Making Than Thought." ScienceDaily, 14 January 2010 <http://www.sciencedaily.com/releases/2010/01/100114143310.htm>.

___. "What Is the Cosmological Constant Paradox, and What Is Its Significance?" Sciencemeetsreligion.org, 1 January 2014.

Barnes, Luke A. "The Fine-Tuning of the Universe for Intelligent Life." Cornell University Library, 11 June 2012.

Berdyaev, Nicholas. *The Destiny of Man*. New York: Harper & Row, 1960.

___. *Truth and Revelation*. New York: Collier Books, 1962.

Biernacki, Loriliai, and Philip Clayton, eds. *Panentheism across the World's Traditions*. Oxford: Oxford University Press, 2013.

Blacher, Richard S. "Near-Death Experiences." *Journal of the American Medical Association* 244 (1980).

Blackburn, Simon. "Naturalism." In *Oxford Dictionary of Philosophy*. Oxford and New York: Oxford University Press, 1996: 255.

Blackmore, Susan J. *Dying to Live: Near-Death Experiences*. Buffalo: Prometheus Books, 1993.

Bohm, David, and B.J. Hiley. *The Undivided Universe: An Ontological Interpretation of Quantum Theory*. London & New York: Routledge, 1993.

Bohman, James, and Matthias Lutz-Bachmann. *Perpetual Peace: Essays on Kant's Cosmopolitan Ideal* (Massachusetts: MIT, 1997).

Brooke, John Hedley. *Science and Religion: Some Historical Perspectives*. Cambridge: Cambridge University Press, 1991.

Brown, Delwin.. "Academic Theology and Religious Studies." *Bulletin of the Council of Societies for the Study of Religion* 26/3 (September 1997): 64-66.

Bultmann, Rudolf. *Jesus Christ and Mythology*. New York: Charles Scribner's Sons, 1958.

____. *Kerygma and Myth: A Theological Debate*, ed. Has Werner Bartsch, trans. Reginald H. Fuller. New York: Harper & Row, 1961.

Case-Winters, Anna. *God's Power: Traditional Understandings and Contemporary Challenges*. Louisville: Westminster/John Knox, 1990.

Chihara, Charles. "A Gödelian Thesis Regarding Mathematical Objects: Do They Exist? And Can We Perceive Them?" *Philosophical Review* 91 (1982): 211-17.

Chimni, B.S. "Global Capitalism and Global Democracy: Subverting the Other?" In Daniele Archibugi, Mathias Koenig-Archibugi, and Raffaele Marchetti, *Global Democracy: Normative and Empirical Perspectives*, eds. Cambridge: Cambridge University Press, 2012: 233-53

Christ, Carol P. *Rebirth of the Goddess: Finding Meaning in Feminist Spirituality.* New York: Addison Wesley, 1997.

___. *She Who Changes: Re-imagining the Divine in the World.* Palgrave Macmillan, 2003.

Clayton, Philip. *In Whom We Live, Move, and Have Our Being: Panentheistic Reflections on God's Presence in a scientific World.* Grand Rapids: Eerdmans Publ. Co., 2004.

Cobb, John B., Jr. *Living Options in Protestant Theology.* Philadelphia: Westminster, 1962.

___. "From Crisis Theology to the Post-Modern World." *Centennial Review* 8 (Spring 1964), 209-20 (reprinted in *Toward a New Christianity: Readings in the Death of God Theology,* ed. Thomas J.J. Altizer [New York: Harcourt, Brace and World, 1967]).

___. *A Christian Natural Theology: Based on the Thought of Alfred North Whitehead.* Philadelphia: Westminster, 1965.

___. *Christ in a Pluralistic Age.* Philadelphia: Westminster, 1975.

___. *Beyond Dialogue: Toward a Mutual Transformation of Christianity and Buddhism.* Philadelphia: Fortress, 1982.

___. "Being Itself and the Existence of God." In *The Existence of God,* ed. John R. Jacobson and Robert Lloyd Mitchell. Lewiston, N.Y.: Edwin Mellen, 1988: 5-19.

___. "Dialogue." in Swidler, Cobb, Knitter, and Hellwig, *Death or Dialogue?* 1-18.

___. "Response II." In Swidler, Cobb, Knitter, and Hellwig, *Death or Dialogue?*, 115-23.

___. "Alfred North Whitehead." In David Ray Griffin et al., *Founders of Constructive Postmodern Philosophy.* Albany: State University of New York Press, 1993: 165-96.

___. *Transforming Christianity and the World: A Way beyond Absolutism and Relativism*, ed. Paul F. Knitter. Maryknoll: Orbis, 1999.

___. *Postmodernism and Public Policy: Reframing Religion, Culture, Education, Sexuality, Class, Race, Politics, and the Economy.* Albany: State University of New York Press, 2002.

Cobb, John B., Jr., and David Ray Griffin. *Process Theology: An Introductory Exposition.* Philadelphia: Westminster Press, 1976.

Cooper, John W. *Panentheism: The Other God of the Philosophers – From Plato to the Present.* Grand Rapids: Baker Academic, 2006.

Darwin, Francis, ed. *The Life and Letters of Charles Darwin,* 2 vols. New York: D. Appleton, 1896.

Davis, Caroline Franks. *The Evidential Force of Religious Experience.* Oxford: Clarendon Press, 1989.

Davis, Stephen T., ed. *Encountering Evil: Live Options in Theodicy,* 2nd edition. Philadelphia: Westminster/John Knox, 2001.

Dawkins, Richard. *The Blind Watchmaker: Why the Evidence of Evolution Reveals a Universe without Design.* New York & London: Norton, 1987.

D'Costa, Gavin, ed. *Christian Uniqueness Reconsidered: The Myth of a Pluralistic Theology of Religions.* Maryknoll, N.Y.: Orbis, 1990.

"Decisions Made by Communities of Bacteria Trump Game Theory," October 12, 2010 <http://www.sciencedaily.com/releases/2010/10/101012121439.htm>.

Dennett, Daniel E. *Consciousness Explained.* Boston: Little, Brown & Co., 1991.

Denton, Michael. *Evolution: A Theory in Crisis.* London: Burnett Books, 1991.

Dews, Peter. *The Limits of Disenchantment: Essays on Contemporary European Philosophy*. London: Verso, 1995.

DiNoia, Joseph A. *The Diversity of Religions: A Christian Perspective*. Washington, D. C.: Catholic University Press, 1992.

Durkheim, Emile. *The Elementary Forms of the Religious Life*, trans. Joseph Ward Swain. New York: Free Press, 1963.

Einstein, Albert. "Maxwell's Influence on the Development of the Conception of Physical Reality." In J.J. Thomson et al., *James Clerk Maxwell: A Commemorative Volume*. Cambridge: Cambridge University Press, 1931: 66-73.

Eliade, Mircea. *History of Religious Ideas*, 2 vols., trans. W.R. Trask. Chicago: University of Chicago Press, 1978.

Erickson, Millard J. *Christian Theology*. Grand Rapids: Baker Book House, 1985.

Evans-Pritchard, E.E. *Theories of Primitive Religion*. Oxford: Clarendon Press, 1965.

Farley, Edward, and Peter Hodgson. "Scripture & Tradition." In Peter C. Hodgson & Robert H. King, eds., *Christian Theology: An Introduction to Its Traditions and Tasks*, 2nd ed. Philadelphia: Fortress, 1985: 61-87.

Ferré, Frederick. *Shaping the Future: Resources for the Post-Modern World*. New York: Harper & Row, 1976.

Finnis, John. *Natural Law and Natural Rights*. New York: Oxford University Press, 1980.

Ford, Marcus P. *William James's Philosophy: A New Perspective*. Amherst: University of Massachusetts Press, 1982.

___. "William James." In David Ray Griffin et al., *Founders of Constructive Postmodern Philosophy: Peirce, James, Bergson,*

Whitehead, and Hartshorne. Albany: State University of New York Press, 1993: 89-132.

___. "James's Psychical Research and Its Philosophical Implications." *Transactions of the Charles S. Peirce Society* 34/3 (Summer, 1998): 605-26.

Forrest, Peter. *God without the Supernatural: A Defense of Scientific Theism*. Ithaca: Cornell University Press, 1966.

Gamwell, Franklin I. *The Divine Good: Modern Moral Theory and the Necessity of God*. Dallas: Southern Methodist University, 1996.

Geertz, Clifford. *Islam Observed: Religious Development in Morocco and Indonesia*. New Haven: Yale University Press, 1968.

___. *Interpretation of Cultures: Selected Essays*. New York: Basic Books, 1973.

"Genius of Bacteria, The." *US News Science*, 25 January 2011.

Gewirth, Alan. *Reason and Morality*. Chicago: University of Chicago Press, 1978.

___. *Creationism on Trial: Evolution and God at Little Rock*. San Francisco: Harper & Row, 1988.

Gier, Nicholas F. "Gandhi, Deep Religious Pluralism, and Multiculturalism." *Philosophy East and West*, April 2014: 319-39.

Gilkey, Langdon. "Plurality and Its Theological Implications." In Hick and Knitter, eds.,*The Myth of Christian Uniqueness*, 37-53.

Gillespie, Neal C. *Charles Darwin and the Problem of Creation*. Chicago: University of Chicago Press, 1979.

Golding, Ido. "Decision Making in Living Cells: Lessons from a Simple System." *Annual Review of Biophysics* 40 (June 2011): 63-80.

Goldsworthy, J. D. "God or Mackie? The Dilemma of Secular Moral

Philosophy." *American Journal of Jurisprudence* 30 (1985): 43-78.

Gomelsky, M. "C-di-GMP-mediated Decisions in the Surface-grown Vibrio Parahaemolyticus: A Different Kind of Motile-to-Sessile Transition." *Journal of Bacteriology*, 22 December 2011.

Gomelsky, M., and W.E. Hoff. "Light Helps Bacteria Make Important Lifestyle Decisions." *Trends in Microbiology*, 19 September 2011.

Gribbin, John, and Martin Rees. *Cosmic Coincidences: Dark Matter, Mankind, and Anthropic Cosmology.* Bantam, 1989.

Griffin, David Ray. *A Process Christology.* Philadelphia: Westminster, 1967; second edition (reprint with new preface), Lanham, Md.: University Press of America, 1990.

___. "Is Revelation Coherent?" *Theology Today* 28 (October 1971): 278-94.

___. "Relativism, Divine Causation, and Biblical Theology." *Encounter* (Indianapolis) 36/4 (Autumn, 1975), 342-60; reprinted in *God's Activity in the World: The Contemporary Problem*, ed. Owen C. Thomas (AAR Studies in Religion No. 31, Scholars Press, 1983): 117-36.

___. *God, Power, and Evil: A Process Theodicy.* Philadelphia: Westminster Press, 1976; reprinted with a new preface, Lanham, Md.: University Press of America, 1991.

___. "Time and the Fallacy of Misplaced Concreteness." In *Physics and the Ultimate Significance of Time: Bohm, Prigogine, and Process Philosophy*, ed. David Ray Griffin. Albany: State University of New York Press, 1986: 1-48.

___. "Introduction to SUNY Series in Constructive Postmodern Thought." Contained in each volume of the series, beginning with *The Reenchantment of Science* (1988). A revised version appears in each volume from 2000 on.

___. "Postmodern Theology and A/theology: A Response to Mark C. Taylor." In David Ray Griffin, William A. Beardslee, and Joe Holland, *Varieties of Postmodern Theology*. Albany: State University of New York Press, 1989: 29-62.

___. *Evil Revisited: Responses and Reconsiderations*. Albany: State University of New York Press, 1991.

___. "Parapsychology and Philosophy: A Whiteheadian Postmodern Perspective." *Journal of the American Society for Psychical Research* 87/3 (July 1993): 217-88. <http://www.anthonyflood.com/griffinparapsychology.htm>.

___. "Constructive Postmodern Philosophy," introduction to David Ray Griffin et al., *Founders of Constructive Postmodern Philosophy: Peirce, James, Bergson, Whitehead, and Hartshorne*. Albany: State University of New York, 1993: 1-42.

___. "Whitehead's Deeply Ecological Worldview." In *Worldviews and Ecology: Religion, Philosophy, and the Environment*, ed. Mary Evelyn Tucker and John Grim. Maryknoll: Orbis Books, 1994: 190-206. A slightly revised version of this essay has been reprinted in my 2007 book, *Whitehead's Radically Different Postmodern Philosophy*.

___. *Parapsychology, Philosophy, and Spirituality: A Postmodern Exploration*. Albany: State University of New York Press, 1996.

___. "Christian Faith and Scientific Naturalism: An Appreciative Critique of Phillip Johnson's Proposal." *Christian Scholar's Review* 28/2 (Winter 1998): 308-28.

___. "Materialist and Panexperientialist Physicalism: A Critique of Jaegwon Kim's *Supervenience and Mind*." *Process Studies* 28 (Spring-Summer 1999): 4-27.

____. *Religion and Scientific Naturalism: Overcoming the Conflicts.* Albany: State University of New York, 2000.

____. "Process Theology and the Christian Good News: A Response to Classical Free Will Theism." In *Searching for an Adequate God: A Dialogue between Process and Free Will Theists*, ed. John B. Cobb, Jr., and Clark H. Pinnock. Grand Rapids: Eerdmans, 2000: 1-38.

____. *Reenchantment without Supernaturalism: A Process Philosophy of Religion.* Ithaca: Cornell University Press, 2001.

____. "Creation out of Nothing, Creation Out of Chaos, and the Problem of Evil." In *Encountering Evil: Live Options in Theodicy*, ed. Stephen T. Davis, 2nd edition. Philadelphia: Westminster/John Knox, 2001: 108-25.

____. "Process Philosophy of Religion." *International Journal for the Philosophy of Religion* 50/1-3 (December 2001): 131-51.

____. "Time in Process Philosophy." *KronoScope: Journal for the Study of Time* 1/1-2 (2001): 75-99.

____, "Reconstructive Theology." In *The Cambridge Companion to Postmodern Theology*, ed. Kevin J. Vanhoozer. Cambridge: Cambridge University Press, 2003.

____. *Unsnarling the World-Knot: Consciousness, Freedom, and the Mind-Body Problem.* Berkeley: University of California Press, 1998; reprint, Eugene: Wipf and Stock, 2008.

____. "The Whiteheadian Complementary Pluralism of John Cobb." In Griffin, ed., *Deep Religious Pluralism*, 39-66.

____. *Whitehead's Radically Different Postmodern Philosophy: An Argument for Its Contemporary Relevance.* Albany: SUNY Press, 2007.

____, ed. *Deep Religious Pluralism.* Louisville: Westminster John Knox, 2005.

____. "Process Thought and Natural Theology." In the *Oxford Handbook of Natural Theology,* ed. Russell Manning. Oxford: Oxford University Press, 2013: 276-94.

Griffiths, Paul J. "Beyond Pluralism." *First Things,* January 1996: 50-52.

Habermas, Jürgen. *Postmetaphysical Thinking: Philosophical Essays,* trans. William Mark Hohengarten. Cambridge: MIT Press, 1992.

____. "Transcendence from Within, Transcendence in this World." In *Habermas, Modernity, and Public Theology,* ed. Don Browning and Francis Schüssler Fiorenza. New York: Crossroad, 1992: 226-50.

____. *Justification and Application: Remarks on Discourse Ethics,* trans. Ciaran Cronin. Cambridge: Polity Press, 1993.

____. "Kant's Idea of Perpetual Peace, With the Benefit of Two Hundred Years' Hindsight" (113-53). In Bohman and Lutz-Bachmann, eds., *Perpetual Peace,* 1997.

Hare, R.M. "Ontology in Ethics." In *Morality and Objectivity: A Tribute to J.L. Mackie,* ed. Ted Honderich. London: Routledge & Kegan Paul, 1985: 39-53.

Harman, Gilbert. *The Nature of Morality: An Introduction to Ethics.* New York: Oxford University Press, 1977.

____. "Is There a Single True Morality?" In *Relativism: Interpretation and Confrontation,* ed. Michael Krausz. Notre Dame: University of Notre Dame Press, 1989: 363-386.

Hartshorne, Charles. "The Compound Individual." In *Philosophical Essays for Alfred North Whitehead,* ed. Otis H. Lee. New York: Longmans Green, 1936: 193-220. Reprinted in Hartshorne, *Whitehead's Philosophy: Selected Essays 1935-1970.* Lincoln: University of Nebraska Press, 1972: 41-61.

___. "Whitehead's Idea of God." In *The Philosophy of Alfred North Whitehead*, ed. Paul Arthur Schilpp, 2nd edition. New York: Tudor, 1951: 513-59.

___. *The Divine Relativity: A Social Conception of God*, 2nd edition. New Haven: Yale University Press, 1964.

___. *Omnipotence and Other Theological Mistakes*. Albany: State University of New York Press, 1984.

___. *The Zero Fallacy and Other Essays in Neoclassical Philosophy*, ed. Mohammed Valady. Peru, Ill.: Open Court, 1997.

Hartshorne, Charles and William L. Reese, eds. *Philosophers Speak of God*. Chicago: University of Chicago Press, 1953.

Hasker, William. "Mr. Johnson for the Prosecution." *Christian Scholar's Review* 22/2 (December 1992): 177-86.

___. "*Darwin on Trial* Revisited: A Review Essay." *Christian Scholar's Review* 24:4 (May 1995): 479-488.

Hawking, Stephen. *A Brief History of Time: From the Big Bang to Black Holes*. New York: Bantam, 1988.

Heidegger, Martin. "Nietzsche's Word: 'God is Dead.'" In Martin Heidegger, *The Question Concerning Technology: Heidegger's Critique of the Modern Age*, trans. William Lovett. New York: Harper and Row, 1977: 53-112.

Heil, John, and Alfred Mele, eds. *Mental Causation*. Oxford: Clarendon, 1995.

Heim, Mark S. *Salvations: Truth and Difference in Religion*. Maryknoll: Orbis, 1995.

Held, David. *Democracy and the Global Order: From the Modern State to Cosmopolitan Governance*. Stanford: Stanford University Press, 1995.

Hersh, Reuben. *What is Mathematics, Really?* New York: Oxford University Press, 1997.

Hick, John. *Philosophy of Religion*, 3d edition. Englewood Cliffs, N. J.: Prentice-Hall, 1983.

___. "The Non-Absoluteness of Christianity," in John Hick and Paul F. Knitter, eds., *The Myth of Christian Uniqueness: Toward a Pluralistic Theology of Religions*. Orbis, 1987.

___. *An Interpretation of Religion.* New Haven: Yale University Press, 1989.

___. *A Christian Theology of Religions: The Rainbow of Faiths.* Louisville: Westminster John Knox, 1995.

___, and Paul F. Knitter, eds. *The Myth of Christian Uniqueness: Toward a Pluralistic Theology of Religions.* Orbis, 1987.

Hintikka, Jaakko. "Cogito, Ergo Sum: Inference or Performance." *Philosophical Review* 71 (1962), 3-32.

Hodge, Charles. *Systematic Theology*, 3 vols. Grand Rapids: Eerdmans, 1982.

Hooykaas, R. *Natural Law and Divine Miracle: A Historical-Critical Study of the Principle of Uniformity in Geology, Biology, and Theology.* Leiden: E.J. Brill, 1959.

Howell, Nancy. *A Feminist Cosmology: Ecology, Solidarity, and Metaphysics.* Amherst: Humanity Books, 2002.

Hutchison, John A. *Paths of Faith.* New York: McGraw Hill, 1969.

Iqbal, Sir Mohammad. *The Reconstruction of Religious Thought in Islam.* London: Oxford University Press, 1934.

Ives, Christopher. "Liberating Truth: A Buddhist Approach to Religious Pluralism." In Griffin, ed., *Deep Religious Pluralism*, 178-92.

James, William. *The Varieties of Religious Experience*. New York: Longmans, Green, 1902.

___. *Some Problems of Philosophy*. London: Longman, Green, 1911.

___. *The Principles of Psychology*. New York: Dover, 1950.

___. *William James on Psychical Research*, ed. Gardner Murphy and Robert O. Ballou. New York: Viking Press, 1960.

___. *Essays in Psychical Research*, ed. Robert A. McDermott. Cambridge: Harvard University Press, 1986.

Jay, Martin. "The Debate over Performative Contradiction: Habermas versus the Poststructuralists." In Martin Jay, *Force Fields: Between Intellectual History and Cultural Critique*. New York & London: Routledge, 1993: 25-37.

Johnson, A.H. "Whitehead as Teacher and Philosopher." *Philosophy and Phenomenological Research* 29 (1969): 351-76.

Johnson, Phillip E. *Darwin on Trial*, 2nd edition. Downers Grove, Ill.: Intervarsity Press, 1993.

___. *Reason in the Balance: The Case Against Naturalism in Science, Law, and Education*. Downers Grove, Ill.: Intervarsity Press, 1993.

Jones, William R. *Is God a White Racist? A Preamble to Black Theology*. Garden City: Anchor Press, 1973.

Kant, Immanuel. *The Critique of Pure Reason*, trans. Norman Kemp Smith. New York: Humanities Press, 1950.

___. *Religion within the Limits of Reason Alone*, trans. Theodore M. Greene and Hoyt H. Hudson. New York: Harper & Row, 1960.

Kaufman, Gordon D. *In Face of Mystery: A Constructive Theology*. Cambridge: Harvard University Press, 1993.

Keller, Catherine. *From a Broken Web: Separation, Sexism and Self.* Boston: Beacon Press, 1986.

____. *The Face of the Deep: A Theology of Becoming.* New York: Routledge, 2003.

____. *On the Mystery: Discerning Divinity in Process.* Fortress, 2008.

Keller, Catherine, and Anne Daniell, ed. *Process and Difference: Between Cosmological and Poststructuralist Postmodernisms.* Albany: State University of New York Press, 2002.

Kim, Jaegwon. *Supervenience and Mind: Selected Philosophical Essays.* Cambridge: Cambridge University Press, 1993.

Knitter, Paul F. *No Other Name? A Critical Survey of Christian Attitudes Toward the World Religions.* Maryknoll: Orbis, 1985.

____. "Interreligious Dialogue: What? Why? How?" in Swidler, Cobb, Knitter, and Hellwig, *Death or Dialogue?*, 19-44.

____. *Jesus and the Other Names: Christian Mission and Global Responsibility.* Orbis, 1996.

Kuchment, Anna. "The Smartest Bacteria on Earth." *Scientific American*, June 2011 <http://www.scientificamerican.com/article.cfm?id=the-smartest-bacteria-on-earth>.

Larmore, Charles E. *The Morals of Modernity.* Cambridge: Cambridge University Press, 1996.

Leff, Allen. "Unspeakable Ethics, Unnatural Law." *Duke Law Journal* 1979: 1229-49.

Lenman, James. "Moral Naturalism." In *The Stanford Encyclopedia of Philosophy,* ed. Edward N. Zalta, Spring 2014.

Levenson, Jon D. *Creation and the Persistence of Evil: The Jewish Drama of Divine Omnipotence.* San Francisco: Harper & Row, 1988.

Lewontin, Richard. "Billions and Billions of Demons" (review of Carl Sagan's *The Demon-Haunted World: Science as a Candle in the Dark*). *New York Review of Books*, January 9, 1997: 28-32.

Lindberg, David C. *The Beginnings of Western Science: The European Scientific Tradition in Philosophical, Religious, and Institutional Context, 600 B.C. to A.D. 1450*. Chicago: University of Chicago Press, 1992.

Lochhead, David. *The Dialogical Imperative: A Christian Reflection on Interfaith Encounter*. Maryknoll: Orbis, 1988.

Lubarsky, Sandra B. *Tolerance and Transformation: Jewish Approaches to Religious Pluralism*. Cincinnati: Hebrew Union College Press, 1990.

___. "Deep Religious Pluralism and Contemporary Jewish Thought," in David Ray Griffin, ed., *Deep Religious Pluralism* (Louisville: Westminster John Knox, 2005), 111-28.

Lycan, William G. *Consciousness*. Cambridge: MIT Press, 1987.

Mackie, John, *Ethics: Inventing Right and Wrong*. New York: Penguin, 1977.

___. *The Miracle of Theism: Arguments for and against the Existence of God*. Oxford: Clarendon, 1982.

MacIntyre, Alasdair. *After Virtue: A Study in Moral Theory*. Notre Dame: University of Notre Dame, 1981.

Maddy, Penelope. *Realism in Mathematics*. Oxford: Clarendon Press, 1990.

Margulis, Lynn. "Gaia Is a Tough Bitch." In John Brockman, *The Third Culture: Beyond the Scientific Revolution*. New York: Simon & Schuster, 1995: 129-51. Also online: <http://www.edge.org/documents/ThirdCulture/n-Ch.7.html>.

___. "Serial Endosymbiotic Theory (SET) and Composite Individuality: Transition from Bacterial To Eukaryotic Genomes." *Microbiology Today* 31 (2004): 172-74 <http://www.sgm.ac.uk/pubs/micro_today/pdf/110406.pdf>.

___. *Symbiotic Planet: A New Look at Evolution.* New York: Basic Books, 1998.

Matson, Floyd W. *The Broken Image: Man, Science and Society.* Garden City: Doubleday, 1966 (originally published in 1964 by George Braziller).

May, Gerhard. *Creatio Ex Nihilo: The Doctrine of "Creation out of Nothing" in Early Christian Thought,* trans. A. S. Worrall. Edinburgh: T. & T. Clark, 1994.

McGinn, Colin. *The Problem of Consciousness: Essays Toward a Resolution.* Oxford: Basil Blackwell, 1991.

McMullin, Ernan. "Natural Science and Belief in a Creator: Historical Notes." *Physics, Philosophy, and Theology: A Common Quest for Understanding,* ed. R.J. Russell, W.R. Stoeger, and G.V. Coyne. Vatican City State: Vatican Observatory, 1988: 49-79.

___. "Plantinga's Defense of Special Creation." *Christian Scholar's Review* 21/1 (1991): 55-79.

Meckenstock, Günter. "Some Remarks on Pantheism and Panentheism." *Traditional Theism and its Modern Alternatives,* ed. Svend Andersen. Aarhus: Aarhus University Press, 1994, 117-29.

Meeker, Kevin, and Philip L. Quinn. "Introduction: The Philosophical Challenge of Religious Diversity." In Quinn and Meeker, eds., *The Philosophical Challenge of Religious Diversity* (Oxford: Oxford University Press, 1999), 1-28.

Mitchell, Basil. *Morality: Religious and Secular: The Dilemma of the Traditional Conscience.* Oxford University Press, 1980.

Murphy, Nancey. "Phillip Johnson on Trial: A Critique of His Critique of Darwin." *Perspectives on Science & Christian Faith* 45:1 (March 1993): 26-36.

Nagel, Thomas. *The Possibility of Altruism*. Princeton: Princeton University Press, 1970.

___. *Mortal Questions*. London: Cambridge University Press, 1979.

___. *The View from Nowhere*. New York: Oxford University Press, 1986.

Nelson, Susan L. *Healing the Broken Heart: Sin, Alienation, and the Gift of Grace*. St. Louis: Chalice, 1977.

Neville, Robert. "Religious Studies and Theological Studies." *Journal of the American Academy of Religion* 61/2 (Summer): 185-200.

Nitecki, Matthew H. *Evolutionary Progress*. Chicago & London: University of Chicago Press, 1988.

Nord, Warren A. *Religion and American Education: Rethinking a National Dilemma*. Chapel Hill & London: University of North Carolina Press, 1995.

Ochs, Peter. "Charles Sanders Peirce." In David Ray Griffin et al., *Founders of Constructive Postmodern Philosophy: Peirce, James, Bergson, Whitehead, and Hartshorne*. Albany: State University of New York Press, 1993: 43-87.Otto, Rudolf. *The Idea of the Holy*, trans. John H. Harvey. New York: Oxford University Press, 1958.

___. *Naturalism and Religion*. London: Williams & Norgate; New York: G. P. Putnam's, 1907.

___. "Darwinism and Religion." In Otto, *Religious Essays: A Supplement to "The Idea of the Holy,'* trans. Brian Lunn. Oxford: Oxford University Press; London: Humphrey Milford, 1931: 121-39.

Outka, Gene, and John P. Reeder, Jr., eds. *Prospects for a Common Morality*. Princeton: Princeton University Press, 1993.

Pederson, Ann. *Where in the World is God? Variations on a Theme.* St. Louis: Chalice, 1998.

___. *God, Creation, and All That Jazz: A Process of Composition and Improvisation.* St. Louis: Chalice, 2001.

Passmore, John. *Philosophical Reasoning.* New York: Basic Books, 1961.

Perry, Michael C. *The Easter Enigma: An Essay on the Resurrection with Special Reference to the Data of Psychical Research.* London: Faber & Faber, l959.

Plantinga, Alvin. "Reply to the Basingers on Divine Omnipotence." *Process Studies* 11/1 (Spring, 1981): 25-29.

___. "When Faith and Reason Clash: Evolution and the Bible." *Christian Scholar's Review* 21/1 (1991): 8-32.

___. "Evolution, Neutrality, and Antecedent Probability: A Reply to McMullin and Van Till." *Christian Scholar's Review* 21/1 (1991): 80-109.

Preus, J. Samuel. *Explaining Religion: Criticism and Theory from Bodin to Freud.* New Haven & London: Yale University Press, 1987.

Proudfoot, Wayne. *Religious Experience.* Berkeley & Los Angeles: University of California Press, 1985.

Provine, William. "Progress in Evolution and Meaning in Life." In *Evolutionary Progress*, ed. Matthew H. Nitecki. Chicago & London: University of Chicago Press, 1988: 49-74.

Putnam, Hilary. *Reason, Truth, and History.* Cambridge: Cambridge University Press, 1981.

___. *Realism and Reason.* New York: Cambridge University Press, 1983.

___. *Words and Life*, ed. James Conant. Cambridge: Harvard University Press, 1994.

Quine, Willard V.O. *From A Logical Point of View*. Cambridge: Harvard University Press, 1953.

___. *Ontological Relativity and Other Essays*. New York: Columbia University Press, 1969.

___. *Theories and Things*. Cambridge: Harvard University Press, 1981.

___. *From Stimulus to Science*. Cambridge: Harvard University Press, 1995.

___. "Autobiography of W.V. Quine." In *The Philosophy of W.V. Quine*, ed. Lewis Edwin Hahn and Paul Arthur Schilpp. Library of Living Philosophers 18. LaSalle, Ill.: Open Court: 1986.

___. "Reply to Morton Smith." In *The Philosophy of W.V. Quine*, ed. Lewis Edwin Hahn and Paul Arthur Schilpp. Library of Living Philosophers 18. LaSalle, Ill.: Open Court: 1986: 663-65.

Quinn, Philip L., and Kevin Meeker, eds. *The Philosophical Challenge of Religious Diversity*. New York: Oxford University Press, 2000.

Race, Alan. *Christians and Religious Pluralism: Patterns in Christian Theology of Religions*. Maryknoll: Orbis, 1983.

Randall, John Herman, Jr. "The Nature of Naturalism." In *Naturalism and the Human Spirit*, ed. Yervant Krikorian. Morningside Heights: Columbia University Press, 1944: 354-82.

Regis, Edward, ed. *Gewirth's Ethical Rationalism*. Chicago: University of Chicago Press, 1984.

Reichenbach, Hans. *Experience and Prediction*. Chicago: University of Chicago Press, 1938.

Robinson, William S. *Brains and People: An Essay on Mentality and Its Causal Conditions*. Philadelphia: Temple University Press, 1988.

Rorty, Richard R. "Mind-Body Identity, Privacy and Categories."

In *The Mind-Brain Identity Theory*, ed. C.V. Borst. London: Macmillan, 1970: 187-212.

___. *Contingency, Irony, and Solidarity*. Cambridge: Cambridge University Press, 1989.

Rubenstein, Richard L. *After Auschwitz: Radical Theology and Contemporary Judaism*. Indianapolis: Bobbs-Merrill, 1966.

Russell, Jeffrey Burton. *Lucifer: The Devil in the Middle Ages*. Ithaca: Cornell University Press, 1984.

Ruzgar, Mustafa. "Islam and Deep Religious Pluralism." In David Ray Griffin, ed., *Deep Religious Pluralism*. Louisville: Westminster John Knox, 2005: 158-76.

Santayana, George. *Scepticism and Animal Faith*. New York: Dover, 1955.

Schilling, Harold K. *The New Consciousness in Science and Religion*. Philadelphia: United Church Press, 1973.

Schleiermacher, Friedrich. *The Christian Faith*, ed. H.R. Mackintosh and J.S. Stewart. New York: Harper, 1963.

Schwöbel, Christoph. "Particularity, Universality, and the Religions: Toward a Christian Theology of Religions." In D'Costa, ed., *Christian Uniqueness Reconsidered*, 30-46.

Seager, William. *Metaphysics of Consciousness*. London & New York: Routledge, 1991.

Searle, John R., *Minds, Brains, and Science: The 1984 Reith Lectures*. London: British Broadcasting Corporation, 1984.

___. *The Rediscovery of the Mind*. Cambridge: MIT Press, 1992.

Segal, Robert A. *Religion and the Social Sciences: Essays on the Confrontation*. Atlanta: Scholars Press, 1989.

___. *Explaining and Interpreting Religion: Essays on the Issue*. New York: Peter Lang, 1992.

Sheldrake, Rupert. "The Laws of Nature as Habits: Postmodern Basis for Science." In *The Reenchantment of Science: Postmodern Proposals*, ed. David Ray Griffin. Albany: State University of New York Press, 1988: 79-86.

___. *The Presence of the Past: Morphic Resonance and the Habits of Nature*. New York: Times Books, 1988.

___. *Seven Experiments That Could Change the World: A Do-It-Yourself Guide to Revolutionary Science*. London, Fourth Estate, 1994.

Sheldrake, Rupert. *The Science Delusion: Freeing the Spirit of Enquiry*. Philadelphia: Coronet Books, 2012. (Also published in the United States as *Science Set Free: 10 Paths to New Discovery*. Deepak Chopra, 2012.)

Sidgwick, Henry, *Henry Sidgwick: A Memoir*. London: Macmillan, 1906.

Simmons, Jr., Ernest Lee. "Process Pluralism and Integral Nondualism: A Comparative Study of the Nature of the Divine in the Thought of Alfred North Whitehead and Sri Aurobindo Ghose." Ph.D. dissertation, Claremont Graduate School, 1981.

___. "Mystical Consciousness in a Process Perspective." *Process Studies* 14 (Spring 1984): 1-10.

Smart, J.J.C. "Religion and Science." In *Philosophy of Religion: A Global Approach*, ed. Stephen H. Phillips. Fort Worth: Harcourt Brace, 1996: 217-24. (Reprinted from Paul Edwards, ed., *Encyclopedia of Philosophy* [New York: Macmillan Press, 1967], Vol. 7.)

Smart, Ninian. "Religious Studies and Theology." *Bulletin of the Council of Societies for the Study of Religion* 26/3 (September): 66-68.

Smith, Wilfred Cantwell. "Idolatry in Comparative Perspective." In Hick and Knitter, eds., *The Myth of Christian Uniqueness*, 53-68.

Strauss, David Friedrich. *The Life of Jesus Critically Examined*, transl. George Eliot, ed. Peter C. Hodgson. Philadelphia: Fortress Press, 1972.

Strawson, Galen. *Mental Reality*. Cambridge: MIT Press, 1994.

Suchocki, Marjorie. *God-Christ-Church: A Practical Guide to Process Theology*, new revised edition. New York: Crossroad, 1989.

____. *The Fall to Violence: Original Sin in Relational Theology*. New York: Continuum, 1994.

Swidler, Leonard, John B. Cobb, Jr., Paul F. Knitter, and Monica K. Hellwig. *Death or Dialogue? From the Age of Monologue to the Age of Dialogue*. Philadelphia: Trinity Press; London: SCM Press, 1990.

Swinburne, Richard. *The Existence of God*. New York: Oxford University Press, 1979.

____. *The Evolution of the Soul*. Oxford: Clarendon, 1986.

____. "Argument from the Fine-Tuning of the Universe." In *Physical Cosmology and Philosophy*, ed. John Leslie. Collier Macmillan, 154–73.

Takeda, Ryusei. "Mutual Transformation of Pure Land Buddhism and Christianity: Methodology and Possibilities in the Light of Shinran's Doctrine." *Bulletin of the Nanzan Institute for Religion and Culture* 22 (Spring 1998): 6-40.

Taylor, Paul. *Normative Discourse*. Westport, Conn.: Greenwood, 1961.

Teresi, Dick. "Lynn Margulis Says She's Not Controversial, She's Right." *Discover Magazine*, April 2011 <http://discovermagazine.

com/2011/apr/16-interview-lynn-margulis-not-controversial-right/article_view?b_start:int=0&-C>.

Tracy, David. *Plurality and Ambiguity: Hermeneutics, Religion, Hope.* University of Chicago Press, 1987.

___. *Dialogue with the Other: The Inter-Religious Dialogue.* Louvain: Peeters Press, 1990.

Troeltsch, Ernst. "The Place of Christianity Among the World Religions." In Troeltsch, *Christian Thought: Its History and Application.* Meridian Books, 1947.

Uttal, William R. *The Psychobiology of Mind.* Hillsdale, N.J.: Lawrence Erlbaum, 1978.

Van Till, Howard J. "Special Creationism in Designer Clothing: A Response to *The Creation Hypothesis*." *Perspectives on Science and Christian Faith* 47/2 (June 1995): 123-31.

___. "Basil, Augustine, and the Doctrine of Creation's Functional Integrity." *Science and Christian Belief* 8/2 (1996): 21-38.

Wang, Zhihe. *Process and Pluralism: Chinese Thought on the Harmony of Diversity.* Heusenstamm, Germany: Ontos Verlag, 2012.

Weinberg, Steven. *Dreams of a Final Theory.* New York: Vintage Books, 1994.

Weinreb, Lloyd. *Natural Law and Justice.* Harvard University Press, 1987.

___. "The Moral Point of View." In *Natural Law, Liberalism, and Morality: Contemporary Essays*, ed. Robert P. George. Oxford: Clarendon, 1996: 195-212.

Whitehead, Alfred North. *Essays in Science and Philosophy.* New York: Philosophical Library, 1947.

___. *Symbolism: Its Meaning and Effect.* 1927. New York: Capricorn, 1959.

____. *Adventures of Ideas.* 1933. New York: Free Press, 1967.

____. *Science and the Modern World.* 1925. New York: Free Press 1967.

____. *The Function of Reason.* 1929. Boston: Beacon Press, 1968.

____. *Modes of Thought.* 1938. New York: Free Press 1968.

____. *Process and Reality.* 1929. Corrected edition, ed. David Ray Griffin and Donald W. Sherburne. New York: Free Press, 1978.

____. *Religion in the Making.* 1926. New York: Fordham University Press, 1996.

Williams, Bernard. *Ethics and the Limits of Philosophy.* Cambridge: Harvard University Press, 1985.

____. "Ethics and the Fabric of the World." In *Morality and Objectivity: A Tribute to J. L. Mackie,* ed. Ted Honderich. London: Routledge & Kegan Paul, 1985: 203-14.

Wills, Garry, *Inventing America: Jefferson's Declaration of Independence.* New York: Vintage Books, 1978.

Wilson, Edward O. *On Human Nature.* New York: Bantam Books, 1979.

Yokota, John Shunji. "Where Beyond Dialog? Reconsiderations of a Buddhist Pluralist." In Griffin, ed., *Deep Religious Pluralism.* 9-1-08.

Acknowledgments

The chapters in this book are more-or-less extensive revisions of published essays, some of which originated as invited lectures. I hereby give my thanks to the respective editors, publishers, and conference organizers for their permission to use the materials in this book.

Chapter 1 is a significantly revised version of "Panentheism: A Postmodern Revelation," which was a chapter of *In Whom We Live and Move and Have Our Being: Reflections on Panentheism for a Scientific Age*, edited by Philip Clayton and Arthur Peacocke (Grand Rapids: Eerdmans, 2003). That paper in turn involved an extensive revision of a paper presented at a conference on "Panentheism," which was organized by Clayton and Peacocke, sponsored by the John Templeton Foundation, and held at St. George's House, Windsor Castle, in December 2001.

Chapter 2 is a moderately revised version of "Divine Activity and Scientific Naturalism," which appeared in *Religion and Its Relevance in Post-Modernism: Essays in Honor of Jack C. Verheyden*, edited by John S. Park and Gayle D. Beebe (Lewiston, N.Y.: Edwin Mellen Press, 2001), 33-51. This essay was in turn based on a lecture, "Divine Causality and Scientific Naturalism," given at Point Loma Nazarene University, in Point Loma, California, in April of 1999, for a lecture series supported by the John Templeton Foundation.

Chapter 3 is a slightly revised version of "Is the Universe Designed? Yes and No," which was included in *Cosmic Questions*, Annals of the

New York Academy of Sciences, Vol. 950, edited by James B. Miller (New York: New York Academy of Sciences, 2001), 191-205. This essay, like the others in that volume, was originally a lecture presented at a conference in Washington, D.C., in April 1999, sponsored by the American Association for the Advancement of Science Program of Dialogue between Science and Religion. I had been asked to address the question: "Is the Universe Designed."

Chapter 4 is a slight revision of "Creation out of Nothing, Creation Out of Chaos, and the Problem of Evil," which appeared in *Encountering Evil: Live Options in Theodicy*, edited by Stephen T. Davis, 2nd edition (Louisville: Westminster John Knox, 2001), 108-25.

Chapter 5 is based on both "Scientific Naturalism, the Mind-Body Relation, and Religious Experience," *Zygon: Journal of Religion and Science* 37/2 (June 2002): 361-80, and on the John Calvin McNair Lecture for 2002 at the University of North Carolina at Chapel Hill, entitled "Is Religious Experience Compatible with Scientific Naturalism?"

Chapter 6 is a moderately revised version of "Religious Experience, Naturalism, and the Social Scientific Study of Religion," which appeared in the *Journal of the American Academy of Religion* 68/1 (March 2000): 99-125. That issue of the journal also contains replies by both Samuel Preus and Robert Segal, followed by a response from me.

Chapter 7 is a significantly revised version of "Morality and Scientific Naturalism: Overcoming the Conflicts," contained in *Philosophy of Religion for a New Century: Essays in Honor of Eugene Thomas Long*, edited by Jeremiah Hackett and Jerald Wallulis (Dordrecht & Boston: Kluwer, 2004), 81-105.

Chapter 8 is a revised and enlarged version of "Religious Pluralism," which appeared in *The Chalice Handbook of Process Theology*, edited by Jay McDaniel and Donna Bowman (St. Louis: Chalice Press, 2006).

49679117R00190

Made in the USA
San Bernardino, CA
24 August 2019